SPITFIRE
PILOTS' STORIES

Press Day at Duxford, 4 May 1939, and a chance for No. 19 Squadron to show off its new equipment. By then the squadron number on the fin had given way to the unit's WZ code-letters on the fuselage.

SPITFIRE

DR ALFRED PRICE

PILOTS' STORIES

The History Press

Henry Cozens leading six of No. 19 Squadron's new Spitfires in formation for the benefit of an official photographer aboard a Blenheim. The squadron number had been painted on the fighters' tails shortly before this flight, and it would be removed soon afterwards. (If you count only five Spitfires, there is another hidden behind the fourth in order away from the camera.)

First published 2012

The History Press
The Mill, Brimscombe Port
Stroud, Gloucestershire, GL5 2QG
www.thehistorypress.co.uk

© Dr Alfred Price 2012

The right of Dr Alfred Price to be identified as the Author of this work has been asserted in accordance with the Copyrights, Designs and Patents Act 1988.

British Library Cataloguing in Publication Data.
A catalogue record for this book is available from the British Library.

ISBN 978 0 7524 6734 4

Typesetting and origination by The History Press
Printed in India

CONTENTS

INTRODUCTION

My aim in writing this book has been to set down, for posterity, a selection of accounts taken from the transcripts of the numerous interviews I conducted with Spitfire pilots. I have long believed the adage that 'if you really enjoy doing a task, you cannot reasonably call it work', and for me, writing this book was certainly not 'work'. How could it be, when it was an honour to be in the presence of the interviewees? I was then able to speak to them individually and seek answers to my detailed questions. For an aviation writer and enthusiast, life doesn't get any better than that.

Without exception, the pilots interviewed for this book relate that Reginald Mitchell's little fighter was a sheer delight to fly. Its responsiveness to the controls was legendary, 'like pulling on a pair of gloves' was the most repeated description, and those same pilots also spoke of their association with the Spitfire with pride and infectious enthusiasm. No form of warfare can be ever regarded as 'clean', but surely one of the least dirty is that of the fighter pilot who sallies forth into the sky to defend his homeland and protect his loved ones.

Last but by no means least, I should like to acknowledge the invaluable assistance I received from John Page and Graham Homan, who gave freely of their time and expertise in the preparation of this work.

Alfred Price,
Uppingham, Rutland

FOREWORD

by Wing Commander R.R. Stanford-Tuck DSO DFC (1916–1987)

This foreword was originally written for the author's 1974 volume, which included a selection of the stories included in this collection.

▲ ▲ ▲

When Alfred Price invited me to write a foreword for this book I was, of course, honoured; but I had the passing thought 'Oh dear, another air book to wade through'. My fears were quite unfounded. As soon as I had read the first few pages I was held by it and read on almost non-stop till I had finished with Maffre's excellent 'Spitfire Swansong'.

I think the average member of the public during the war thought of Spitfire pilots as being carefree, beer-swilling types, rather like the rugger club members one could see being very noisy in any pub on a Saturday night. In fact, with a very few exceptions, nothing could have been further from the truth. Wartime flying and especially air combat in Spitfires was a very cold, calculating, 'cat and mouse' affair. Woe betide any fighter pilot who was casual or who daydreamed – he would very soon 'cop it up the back end', or one of his pals would. However, in spite of their deadly business, the Spitfire pilots had one great advantage, their aircraft, which they came to love in that strange way that men will love their cars or boats. I got my hands on a Spitfire for the first time on a crisp morning in December 1938. It belonged to No. 19 Squadron at Duxford. From the first moment I sat in the cockpit, going through all the instruments, cockpit checks, take-off and landing procedures etc., I thought 'If it comes to a war, this is the girl for me'. Later that day, after my first flight, I felt this even more and for the first time in any aircraft I felt I was really part of it.

Just over a year later the tremendous thrill of getting my first Me 109 over Dunkirk justified my high opinion of the handling and fighting qualities of the Spitfire. As the years went past she carried me through countless combats and difficult situations and gave of her utmost every time it was demanded. She was a true thoroughbred.

I was so enthralled reading this book and recalling the memories it brought back of the airmen I had known, the flying, and the wonderful spirit which existed in those years, that I was very tempted to write considerably more; but that is not my part in this book. All I can say, with sincerity, is that this is a fine book about a fine aircraft and fine men, and I add my thanks to Alfred Price for asking me to write these few words.

1

THE PATH TO THE SPITFIRE

The year 1931 saw the Supermarine Aircraft Works at Southampton riding the crest of a wave, firmly established as a world leader in the design and production of high-speed racing seaplanes. In September of that year the Supermarine S.6B won the coveted Schneider Trophy outright for Britain, with a flight round the circular course at an average speed of 340mph. A few months later a sister aircraft advanced the world absolute speed record to 379mph. Later still in that same year, an S.6B with a modified Rolls-Royce R engine raised the world absolute speed record to 407mph. To realise any of those feats in a single year would have been a magnificent achievement for any aviation company, but to accomplish all three was an absolute triumph for Supermarine and its talented Chief Designer, Reginald Mitchell.

Yet although the design and production of the racing floatplanes had advanced the cause of high-speed flight, it would take some years before the various lessons could be incorporated in service equipment for the RAF. The racing seaplanes had been tailor-made to perform one specific task – achieving the highest possible speed over the measured course, and alighting on the water safely afterwards. Little else mattered. These aircraft had short endurance, poor manoeuvrability and very poor visibility for the pilot in his cramped cockpit. Also, since the RAF had won the Schneider Trophy outright, there was no chance of anyone else running a challenge in the foreseeable future.

After the excitements of the previous year, the focus of the company's workforce returned to the production of the Southampton, Scapa and Stranraer twin-engined, long-range maritime patrol flying boats, to meet orders for the RAF and foreign air forces. Also in the autumn of 1931, and with a good deal less fanfare than had attended the activities of the racing floatplanes earlier in the year, the Air Ministry in London issued Specification F.7/30 for a new fighter type to equip its home defence squadrons. At that time the fastest fighter in the RAF inventory was the Hawker Fury, a biplane with a maximum speed of 207mph. As aviation experts pointed out, when the Fury reached its maximum speed in level flight it was flying at barely half as fast as the Supermarine S.6B had gone during its final record-breaking run.

Those who drafted the specification for the new fighter did not specify exact performance or other requirements. Instead, the various design teams were told to meet certain minimum requirements and do the best they could offer in terms of speed. The F.7/30 laid down the following requirements for the new fighter:

The highest possible rate of climb
The highest possible speed above 15,000 feet (ft)
A good view for the pilot, particularly during combat
Good manoeuvrability
Be capable of easy and rapid production in quantity
Ease of maintenance
An armament of four .303 inch (in) machine guns and provision to carry four 20 pound (lb) bombs.

When specification F.7/30 was issued, Great Britain was in the grip of a financial slump. Times were hard for the nation's industries, and none more so than the aviation industry. There was intense competition to secure what might prove to be a lucrative order from the RAF, and perhaps foreign governments as well. Seven aircraft companies submitted design proposals for eight fighter prototypes to meet the F.7/30 requirement. Five of the aircraft were biplanes: the Bristol 123, the Hawker PV3, the Westland PV4, the Blackburn F.7/30 and the Gloster SS37. The other three entries were monoplane designs: the Vickers Jockey, the Bristol Type 133 and the Supermarine Type 224.

At that time the most powerful British aero engine available for installation in fighters was the Rolls-Royce Goshawk inline, which generated 660 horsepower (hp). On that power no aircraft was going to go much faster than 250mph, and at that

The Supermarine 224 was Reginald Mitchell's first attempt to build a fighter aircraft, for his entry in the F.7/30 design competition. Although the Type 224 was roundly defeated in that contest, it would serve as a vitally important stepping stone to the aircraft that later became the Spitfire.

speed the advantage of the monoplane over the biplane was by no means certain. Indeed, the consensus amongst the leading British designers at that time was that the biplane was slightly the better, as was shown by the greater proportion of biplanes entered for the F.7/30 competition (five against three). In the all-important matter of rate-of-climb, a good biplane would usually show a clean pair of heels to a good monoplane, and it was considerably more manoeuvrable.

The Supermarine submission to the competition was an all-metal monoplane designated the Type 224. Power was from a Rolls-Royce Goshawk engine developing 660hp. The Type 224 made its first flight in February 1934, when it demonstrated a top speed of 238mph and took eight minutes to climb to 15,000ft.

The engine employed an evaporative cooling system, using the entire leading edge of both wings as a condenser to convert the steam back into water. However, the system did not work well, and when the pilot ran it at full throttle for any length of time the engine was liable to overheat. Flight Lieutenant (later Group Captain) Hugh Wilson was one of the RAF pilots who tested the aircraft. He told the author: 'We were told that when a red light came on in the cockpit, the engine was overheating. But the trouble was that just about every time you took off that red light came on – it was always overheating!'

If the aircraft was to make a combat climb at full throttle, when it reached 15,000ft the condenser in each wing would be full of steam. Then the relief valve at each wing would open, and a line of excess steam would trail behind each wing. Once that happened the pilot had to ease back on the throttle and level the aircraft, to allow the engine time to cool down before he could resume his climb. For an aircraft intended to go into action at the end of a rapid climb, the requirement to level off to cool the engine would have been be a major limitation in combat. Even when it sat on the ground the Type 224 made enemies, as ground crewmen soon learned the folly of resting a hand on the steam condenser in either wing before it had cooled down after a flight.

The Type 224 did not show up well against its competitors, either. The winner of the F.7/30 competition was a biplane of conventional layout, the Gloster SS.37. It had a maximum speed of 242mph, giving it a small advantage over the Supermarine Type 224, but for its time the Gloster fighter possessed a superb rate of climb: it reached 15,000ft in six and a half minutes – a full one and half minutes ahead of the Supermarine design. Moreover, it was a far more manoeuvrable than the Type 224. The SS.37, with modifications, would enter RAF service later in the decade as the Gladiator.

Beverley Shenstone joined the Supermarine design team as an aerodynamicist in 1934, by which time the Type 224 was of no further interest either to the RAF or to Supermarine. During a discussion of the Type 224 with the author, Shenstone commented:

> When I joined Supermarine, the design of the Type 224 was virtually complete and I had little to do with it. As is now well known, that fighter was not successful. My personal feeling is that the design team had done so well with the S.5 and the S.6 racing floatplanes, which in the end reached speeds of over 400 mph, that they thought it would be child's play to design a fighter intended to fly at little over half that speed. They never made that mistake again!

Towards the end of 1934, Rolls-Royce began bench testing a new 27 litre (l) V-12 engine designated the PV XII (later named the Merlin). It passed its 100-hour type test while running at 790hp at 12,000ft, and aimed at an eventual planned output of 1,000hp. In November 1934 the board of Vickers, the parent company of Supermarine, allocated funds for Mitchell and his team to commence preliminary design work on a completely new fighter powered by the PV XII engine. The proposal aroused

immediate interest at the Air Ministry, and in the following month the company received a contract to build a prototype fighter to the proposed new design from Supermarine. The new fighter received the designation F.37/34.

The incorporation of the new Rolls-Royce engine into the proposed new Supermarine fighter opened up an entirely new range of performance possibilities for the new machine. With speeds well over 300mph now in prospect, Mitchell could use his hard-won experience in drag reduction in high-speed aircraft. Nevertheless, it was first necessary to make some changes to the airframe to enable it to accommodate the new engine. The PV XII engine weighed about one-third more than the Rolls-Royce Goshawk engine it was to replace, so to compensate for the forward shift of the centre of gravity, the sweepback of the leading edge wing had to be reduced. From there it was a relatively minor step to incorporate the elliptical wing that would be the most recognisable feature of the new fighter. Beverley Shenstone told the author about the process by which this change came about:

> The elliptical wing was decided upon quite early on. Aerodynamically it was the best for our purpose because the induced drag, that which is caused in producing lift, was the lowest when this shape was used: the ellipse was an ideal shape, theoretically a perfection. There were other advantages so far as we were concerned. To reduce drag

Close-up of the Type 224, showing the relatively high drag method of construction used in this aircraft.

The F.37/34 prototype K5054 pictured at Eastleigh Airfield, Southampton, on 5 March 1936, shortly before it took off on its maiden flight.

we wanted the lowest possible wing thickness-to-chord ratio, consistent with the necessary strength. But near the root, the wing had to be thick enough to accommodate the retracted undercarriage and the guns; so to achieve a good thickness-to-chord ratio we wanted the wing to have a wide chord near the root. A straight-tapered wing starts to reduce in chord from the moment it leaves the root; an elliptical wing, on the other hand, tapers only very slowly at first, then progressively more rapidly towards the tip... The ellipse was simply the shape that allowed us to carry the thinnest possible wing, with sufficient room inside to carry the necessary structure and the things we wanted to cram in. And it looked nice.

At this time most major air forces – the Royal Air Force included – operated fabric-covered biplane fighters with open cockpits and fixed undercarriages. Compared with that, the new Supermarine fighter was a revelation: a cantilever monoplane constructed almost entirely of metal, with a supercharged engine, an enclosed cockpit and a retractable undercarriage.

The overwhelming credit for the fighter now taking shape in the drawing office at Woolston must of course go to Reginald Mitchell and his small design team, and the Rolls-Royce engineers at Derby struggling to improve the power output and reliability of the PV XII engine. Yet there were others, some working for the government, who also deserve a share of the credit.

One of the few design stipulations in the F.7/30 specification was that the armament should comprise four Vickers .303in machine guns. Squadron Leader Ralph Sorley, working at the Operational Requirements section at the Air Ministry, cast doubt on that score. He argued that the four Vickers .303in machine guns, each firing at a rate of 850 rounds per minute (rpm), would lack the punch to destroy the fast all-metal bombers then about to enter service in the major air forces. Sorley, an experienced military pilot, believed that in any further conflict fighter pilots would find it extremely difficult to hold their gun sight on a high-speed bomber for more than a couple of seconds. Unless a lethal blow could be administered in that time, the bomber would escape. Sorley later wrote:

> By 1934 a new Browning gun was at last being tested in
> Britain which offered a higher rate of fire [1,100rpm]. After
> much arithmetic, I reached the answer of eight [Browning
> guns] as being the number required to inflict the required
> two-second burst. I reckoned that the bomber's speed
> would probably be such as to allow a pursuing fighter just
> one chance to attack, so the bomber had to be destroyed in
> that vital two-second burst.

Sorley's arguments convinced the Deputy Chief of the Air Staff, Air Vice-Marshal Edgar Ludlow-Hewitt, that the new fighter would need to carry eight of the new rapid-firing Browning guns, rather than four slow-firing Vickers guns. In April 1935 Sorley visited the Supermarine works to ask whether there was room in the wings of the new fighter to accommodate the revised armament. Mitchell passed the question round his design team and the answer came back in the affirmative: it would indeed be possible to fit the additional four guns into the fighter's wings.

By mid-1935 the main design parameters for the revised fighter had largely been settled, and metal was being cut. However, there remained one important aspect: how to cool the PV XII engine. The initial thought was that the evaporative cooling system should be retained, despite its miserable performance when fitted to the Goshawk engine of the Type 224. The alternative, to use a conventional cooling system with external radiators, would impose a severe drag penalty.

Selecting an effective method for cooling the engine was no trivial matter. When the PV XII ran at full power, it produced

K5054 pictured in the hangar at Eastleigh in May 1936, after it had been painted in the Supermarine Company's trademark light blue colour scheme overall.

an amount of heat roughly equivalent to 400 1-kilowatt electric fires running simultaneously. Unless that heat could be dissipated, the engine would overheat and was liable to suffer damage. Fortunately, Fred Meredith, a scientist working at the Royal Aircraft Establishment at Farnborough, had been experimenting with a novel type of ducted radiator to overcome just this problem. The airflow entered a duct at the front of the device, where its cross-sectional area was progressively narrowed. This reduced the velocity of the air in the duct and increased its pressure. The heated air then passed through the radiator matrix, where it picked up additional heat. Then the heated air passed through a divergent duct at the rear of the device. Thus the ducted radiator acted rather like a low-powered ramjet engine: the air entered the duct and was compressed, then it passed through the radiator matrix where it was heated, before finally emerging from the rear of the duct with an increased velocity. The system produced relatively little thrust, but by removing a source of drag it justified its value. Reginald Mitchell immediately saw the merits of the scheme, and redesigned his new fighter to carry a Meredith-type ducted radiator positioned under the starboard wing.

On the 990hp from the latest version of the Merlin (as the PV XII engine was now named) it was predicted that the new

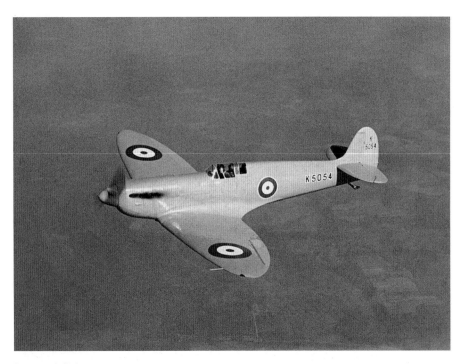

During early flights, pilots had complained that the rudder horn balance was over-sensitive in operation, and by this flight it had been reduced in size.

and system checks. Then the fighter was dismantled and transported by road to the nearby airfield at Eastleigh (now Southampton Airport). Following reassembly, the fighter underwent further engine runs and checks early in March. When these were completed, on the fifth of that month an official from the Aeronautical Inspection Directorate made a detailed examination of the aircraft and pronounced it fit to fly.

On the afternoon of 5 March 1936 the new Supermarine F.37/34 fighter, serial number K5054, was made ready for its maiden flight from the airfield at Eastleigh. Captain J. 'Mutt' Summers, chief test pilot of the Vickers parent company, climbed into the cockpit, strapped in and started the engine. When he was satisfied that the cockpit instruments gave the expected correct indications, he waved away the chocks. Then he gave a burst of power to get the little fighter moving across the grass. One of a small group of professionally interested spectators present was Jeffrey Quill, who told the author:

'Mutt' taxied around for a bit then, without too much in the way of preliminaries, went over to the far side of the airfield, turned into wind and took off. With the fine pitch prop the new fighter fairly leapt off the ground and climbed away. It then passed out of our sight but I know what Mutt would have been doing. First, he would have needed to confirm that the technical people had worked out the stalling speed correctly, so that he could get back on the ground safely. To that end he would have taken it to a safe altitude, about 5,000ft, and tried a dummy landing to find the best approach speed and make sure that when it stalled the aircraft did not flick on to its back or do anything unpleasant like that. Probably Mutt did a few steep turns to try out the controls. Then, having checked that everything really important was all right, he landed and taxied in.

fighter should be able to reach a maximum speed around 350mph. On 26 November 1935 Air Commodore R. Verney, Director of Technical Development at the Air Ministry, visited the Woolston factory and penned a brief memorandum on the state of the work at that time:

1. The fuselage is nearly completed, and the engine installed. The wings are being plated, and some parts of the undercarriage still have to be finished. I like the simple design of the undercarriage very much, also the flush riveting of the surfaces of the fuselage and wings. The glycol radiator is in the starboard wing, with controlled inlet cooling. Tubular honeycomb oil coolers are set forward under the engine.
2. As far as I can see it cannot be flying this year, but it should be early in January. It is in many ways a much more advanced design than the Hawker [Hurricane], and it should be a great deal lighter.

By the end of February 1936 assembly work on the new fighter was almost complete. It was now wheeled on to the hard standing beside the Woolston works for engine running

For reasons lost in time, that first flight lasted only eight minutes before Summers returned to Eastleigh. For the maiden flight the fighter was fitted with a fine pitch propeller, to give it optimum performance at the low-speed end of the performance envelope. Summers was keen to have a coarse pitch propeller fitted, so he could take the aircraft to the higher speed end of its performance envelope. On the following day, 6 March, Summers took the fighter up for its second flight lasting twenty-three minutes.

Early in April the Spitfire went into the hangar at Eastleigh for some minor work. The rudder horn balance was too large and needed to be smaller, carburettor air intake was lowered slightly to give an increase in ram air pressure, and the aircraft needed painting. Ernie Mansbridge, in charge of flight testing the aircraft, told the author of a problem that arose with the last of these:

The finish was put on by the same people at Derby who did the Rolls Royce cars. We asked Rolls what they did to get such a finish on their cars. They put us in touch with the firm that did it for them, some of that firm's people came down to Eastleigh and they had the prototype for three or four days. They put filling in the various joints and rubbed it all down, put more filling on and rubbed it down again. Then they applied the paint, they really did a very good job.

It had sounded like such a good idea to get the experts who painted Rolls-Royce cars to perform the task on the Spitfire prototype, but in the event the idea backfired. Ernie Mansbridge again:

In flight the wings of an aircraft flex, a car body does not. Because of this flexing we soon had cracking of the finish. And this became more serious during high-altitude trials, when the filling would shrink in the cold. After a bit the wing surface on the prototype took on an appearance rather like crazy paving. It became a continual problem for us, to patch up the paintwork as best we could.

Shortly afterwards the Vickers parent company bestowed a name on its new fighter aircraft: 'Spitfire'. By all accounts Reginald Mitchell was less than enthralled with the choice. Jeffrey Quill heard him comment: 'It's the sort of bloody silly name they would give it!'

On 26 May Mutt Summers delivered K5054 to the RAF test establishment at Martlesham Heath. Flight Lieutenant (later Air Marshal, Sir) Humphrey Edwardes-Jones was to be the first RAF test pilot to fly the aircraft, and when he landed he had orders to report his impressions on the new fighter by phone to the Air Ministry in London. After the Spitfire had been refuelled, Edwardes-Jones took off in the new fighter. He told the author:

Men behind the Spitfire: left to right: 'Mutt' Summers, Chief Test Pilot at the Vickers parent company; Major Harold Payn, Assistant Chief Designer; Reginald Mitchell, Chief Designer; S. Scott Hall, Air Ministry Resident Technical Officer; Jeffrey Quill, Chief Test Pilot at Supermarine.

I took off, retracted the undercarriage and flew around for about 20 minutes. I found that she handled very well. Then I went back to the airfield. There was no air traffic control system in those days and I had no radio. As I made my approach I could make out a Super Fury some way in front of me doing S turns to lose height before it landed. I thought it was going to get in my way, but then I saw it swing out to one side and land, so I knew I was all right. But it had distracted my attention at a very important time. As I was coming in to land I had a funny feeling that something was wrong. Then it suddenly occurred to me: I had forgotten to lower the undercarriage! The Kaxon horn, which had come on when I throttled back with the wheels still up, was barely audible with the hood open and the engine running. I lowered the undercarriage and it came down and locked with a reassuring 'clunk'. Then I continued down and landed. Afterwards people said to me 'You've got a nerve, leaving it so long before you put the wheels down.' But I just grinned and shrugged my shoulders. In the months that followed I would go quite cold just thinking about it: supposing I had landed the

'Mutt' Summers landing the prototype at the Society of British Aircraft Constructors' display at Hatfield in June 1936.

first Spitfire wheels up! I kept the story to myself for many years afterwards.

Once down, I rang the number at Air Ministry, as ordered. The officer on the other end said, 'I don't want to know everything, and obviously you can't tell me. All I want to know now is whether you think the young pilots and others we are getting in the Air Force will be able to cope with the aircraft.' I took a deep breath – I was supposed to be the expert, having jolly nearly landed with the undercarriage up! Then I realised that it was just a silly mistake on my part and I told him that if there were proper indications of the undercarriage position, in the cockpit, there should be no difficulty. On the strength of that brief conversation the Air Ministry signed a contract for the first 310 Spitfires on 3 June, eight days later.

A few days later the Spitfire underwent further speed trials at Martlesham, which established its maximum speed as 349mph at 16,800ft. For the Royal Air Force, the new British fighter appeared at exactly the right time. In Germany the newly forming Luftwaffe was building up rapidly and its own high-performance monoplane fighter, the Messerschmitt Bf 109, was about to enter large-scale production.

The test programme at Martlesham Heath continued until 1 August, when the prototype returned to Eastleigh for the installation of military equipment. These included the eight .303in Browning machine guns, as well as a reflector sight and a radio. Several minor modifications were also incorporated,

including a new oil cooler, the installation of a spin recovery parachute and the latest version of the Merlin engine which now developed an extra 60hp. The new fighter resumed testing early in December 1936, and the first item on the agenda was to test the fighter's ability to recover from spins, as the centre of gravity was moved progressively rearwards. The fear was that the aircraft might enter a flat spin and fail to recover using the usual stick-forwards-and-opposite-rudder technique. To avoid that possibility the Spitfire carried a makeshift spin recovery system, as Jeffrey Quill describes:

> The small parachute, about 3ft in diameter, was folded and housed in a box about 9in by 6in by 2in, fitted in the cockpit on the right side. From the parachute a steel cable ran out between the front of the canopy and the windscreen, then to the base of the fin where it was attached to a ring bolt. To stop it flapping about in the airflow, the cable was held down at regular intervals with sticky tape. If the aircraft got into a flat spin and would not come out using the normal recovery procedure, the idea was that I should slide back the canopy, grab the folded parachute and toss it out on the side opposite to the direction of the spin (taking care not to let the cable pass across my neck if the parachute had to be tossed to the left!). The parachute would then stream out behind the tail and as it opened it would yank the aircraft straight, thereby providing what was in effect a much more powerful rudder. Once the parachute had pulled the aircraft straight, it could be jettisoned.

Quill tested the parachute and jettison system on 11 December, and the arrangement worked as intended. In the days to follow he flew the fighter seven times, with the centre of gravity moved progressively aft between each flight. He put the fighter into a spin in both directions and each time it recovered normally, without using the parachute.

Early in 1937 Reginald Mitchell was diagnosed as suffering from cancer. The treatment he received failed to relieve his condition, and in June of that year he died at the tragically young age of 42. By then Mitchell's legacy to the nation, potentially the most effective fighter aircraft in the world, had proved its capabilities beyond reasonable doubt. At that time the word 'potentially' was appropriate, however, for the series of tests had revealed that the prototype Spitfire had a major

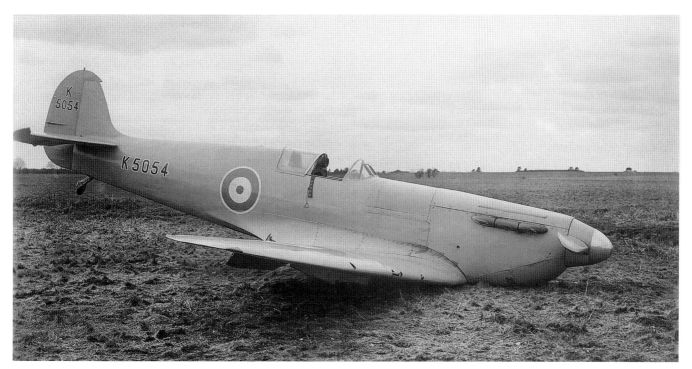

Left: On 22 March 1937 Flying Officer Sam McKenna was airborne from Martlesham Heath in the Spitfire when the Merlin engine suffered a failure of the lubrication system. The pilot made a skilful wheels-up landing and the aircraft incurred minimal damage.

Below: Following the repair work, K5054 was fitted with a radio (note the aerial mast mounted behind the canopy). The aircraft was also painted in the dark green and dark earth scheme now required by the RAF, as the political situation Europe deteriorated. The aircraft resumed flying on 9 September 1937.

shortcoming. At low and at medium altitude its eight Browning machine guns had successfully fired their complements of 300 rounds over the North Sea. Then, in March 1937, an RAF pilot took the fighter to 32,000ft for what was to be the final, high-altitude firing test. It ended in a fiasco: one gun fired 171 rounds, another fired eight, yet another fired four, and the remaining five guns failed to fire at all. That was bad enough, but as the fighter touched down the jolt released the breech blocks of three guns that had not fired. Each one then loosed off a round in the general direction of Felixstowe!

The cause of the problem was the guns freezing up at high altitude, and the solution was to duct hot air from the engine coolant radiator to the gun bays. Getting this solution to work was no easy matter, however. In July 1938 the problem would still be present in the first production Spitfires about to be delivered to the RAF. During a closed meeting at the Air Council the Chief of the Air Staff, Marshal of the Royal Air Force Sir Cyril Newall was moved to comment that: 'If the guns will not fire at the heights at which the Spitfires are likely to encounter enemy bombers, they will be useless as fighting aircraft.' The problem of guns freezing up remained

until October 1938 when, following a series of modifications, all eight guns fired their complements of ammunition at high altitude. Subsequent production Spitfires incorporated

K5054 continued flying until 4 September 1939, when it was seriously damaged in a landing accident at Farnborough. The pilot, Flight Lieutenant 'Spinner' White, was killed.

the design changes, and these were fitted retrospectively to earlier aircraft.

During the early summer of 1938, production Spitfires began to emerge from the Supermarine assembly hangar at Eastleigh in growing numbers. The prototype's part of the fighter's test programme came to an end. The hand-built prototype differed greatly from the production aircraft, and it went to Farnborough where it served as a high-speed 'hack' used to test various new features.

On 4 September 1939, the day after Great Britain declared war on Germany, the prototype suffered serious damage in a fatal landing accident at Farnborough. That was before people nursed sentimental ideas about preserving historic aircraft. Although the Spitfire prototype could have been repaired, nobody in a position of authority thought it worth the effort and it was scrapped. The prototype had cost the British taxpayer £15,776. Rarely has government money been better spent.

2

SPITFIRE INTO SERVICE

by Henry Cozens

During the summer of 1938 the first Spitfires were issued to an RAF squadron, No. 19 at Duxford. Henry Cozens commanded the squadron at that time and his account of the introduction of the new high-performance monoplane into service conveys well the mood in the RAF at that time.

In December 1937, I was promoted to squadron leader and posted to take command of No. 19 Squadron based at Duxford, near Cambridge. At that time we flew the Gloster Gauntlet, a biplane with an unimpressive performance compared with the sort of opposition we were likely to meet if it came to a war with Germany. I heard a buzz that the first of the new Spitfire fighters were to be issued to a squadron based at Catterick in Yorkshire. I thought it might be possible to change this, so I got in touch with one of my friends at Fighter Command Headquarters and asked him whether he thought the idea of sending the first of these new fighters so far north was sound. There was bound to be a lot of Air Ministry interest in the aircraft and Catterick was rather a long way from London; and besides, it was a notoriously small airfield. Might not Duxford, a larger airfield much closer to London, be more suitable? My questions must have prompted the correct line of thought because a few weeks later I heard that my own squadron, and No. 66 which shared Duxford with us, would be the first to receive Spitfires.

On 4 August 1938, amid much excitement, we received the first of the new aircraft: Spitfire K9789. I made my first flight in her on the 11th. At that time there were no pilots' notes on the Spitfire, no conversion courses and, of course, no dual-control aircraft. I was shown round the cockpit, given a cheerful reminder to remember to extend the undercarriage before I landed, wished 'Good Luck', and off I went.

After flying the Gauntlet, my first impression of the Spitfire was that her acceleration seemed rather slow and the controls were a lot heavier than I had expected. Thinking about it afterwards, I realised why: the Gauntlet took off at about 70mph and was flat-out at about 220mph; the Spitfire took off at about the same speed but could do well over 350mph – in other words the speed range was much greater, and although the acceleration was in fact greater it took somewhat longer to reach its maximum speed. Moreover, as she neared the top end of her speed range, the Spitfire's controls became beautifully light.

On August 16th, I collected the second Spitfire for Duxford, K9792. Nos 19 and 66 Squadrons were ordered to carry out the intensive flying trials using these two aircraft; our instructions were to fly them both to 400 hours as rapidly as possible and

The first Spitfire delivered to an RAF unit was the third production aircraft K9789, which arrived at No. 19 Squadron based at Duxford on 4 August.

On 14 May 1938 the first production Spitfire, K9787, made its maiden flight with Jeffrey Quill at the controls. That aircraft, and also the second production machine K9788, would remain at Supermarine to test various features of the new fighter.

report our findings. The two squadrons set about the task with enthusiasm and the two aircraft were airborne almost continuously from dawn to dusk; alone, I amassed twenty-four flying hours in the Spitfire before the end of August. We had a few adventures. I remember one fine afternoon seeing a Spitfire taxiing in and, as usual, the ground crew were all out watching her. Suddenly one of the undercarriage legs started to fold. In no time people were running towards the aircraft from all directions and they grabbed the wing and managed to hold it up until the propeller stopped. The precious fighter escaped damage.

During these intensive flying trials, Air Chief Marshal Sir Hugh Dowding, the Commander-in-Chief (C-in-C) of Fighter Command, visited us at Duxford. I showed him over the Spitfire and then we went to my office. When we were alone together he told me the position regarding this aircraft, if it came to a war. He said that the Hurricane was a great success and it could take on the Junkers 88 and the other German aircraft; but the Messerschmitt 109 was more than a match. So his question was: could the Spitfire take on the 109? If it could, then Fighter Command was prepared for war. If it could not, then we should have to think again.

As the intensive flying trial progressed I became convinced that the Spitfire could indeed take on the Messerschmitt 109 – and any other fighter then in existence. But that was not to say that she was perfect. For one thing the engines of these first Spitfires were difficult to start: the low-geared electric starter rotated the propeller blades so slowly that when a cylinder fired there was usually insufficient push to flick the engine round to fire the next. There would be a 'puff' noise, then the propeller would resume turning on the starter. Also, the early Merlin engines leaked oil terribly; it would run from the engine, down the fuselage and finally got blown away somewhere near the tail wheel. Yet another problem was what we called 'Spitfire Knuckle': when pumping up the undercarriage it was all too easy to rasp our knuckles on the side of the cockpit. There was a further problem for the taller pilots, who were always hitting their heads on the inside of the low cockpit canopy.

When we were about halfway through the 400-hour trial, I had a chat with Squadron Leader Fuller-Good who commanded 66 Squadron and we agreed that we had learned just about all we could from the exercise. I felt that if the First World War was anything to go by, no fighter was likely to last

in action for anything like 400 hours. All we were now going to find out was how to wear out two perfectly good Spitfires. So together we wrote an interim report on the new fighter and off it went. That set the wheels in motion, for a few weeks later we received a high-powered deputation from the Air Ministry, Fighter Command Headquarters, Supermarine, Rolls-Royce and goodness knows where. We discussed the shortcomings at length and they promised to do what they could to overcome them. I remember that my own bandaged 'Spitfire Knuckle' made a particularly strong impression on the Supermarine team. The improvements we asked for were all incorporated in our own or later marks of the Spitfire. The simpler things like the bulged cockpit canopy to make life easier for the taller pilots and the faster starter motor we received quite quickly. The improved oil seals for the Merlin took a little longer and leaking oil did remain something of a problem throughout the Spitfire's service life. The later Spitfire Mark I's (Mk I) had an engine-driven hydraulic system to raise and lower the undercarriage, which did away with the need to pump and the resultant 'Spitfire Knuckle'.

During the early days we tried several different types of airscrew on the Spitfire. The original two-bladed, fixed-pitch wooden propeller was designed to give its best performance envelope at high speed, but this produced serious disadvantages at the lower speeds; for example, during take-off it almost stalled. We tried to get over this at first with a three-bladed propeller with a finer pitch, then with a three-bladed, two-pitch propeller with one setting for take-off and another for high speed. I did not like the two-pitch propeller at all. It was far too easy to leave it in coarse pitch for take-off and that could give rise to a dangerous situation. There was no halfway house: the answer was the constant speed propeller, which automatically gave the correct pitch settings for all airspeeds. Early in 1939 I flew a trial with one of these and I remember being much impressed with the improvement in acceleration and general handling at low

Squadron Leader Henry Cozens commanded No. 19 Squadron when it received its first Spitfires, in August 1938. He is depicted as a Flight Lieutenant, in the Royal Air Force full-dress uniform of the 1930s. His career as a fighter pilot had began on Sopwith Snipes in 1923, and before he retired he would fly Meteors and Vampires.

Right: A pair of Spitfires of No. 66 Squadron being refuelled at Duxford. Although concentrating aircraft in this way made the refuelling task easier, the first attacks on airfields would teach units the value of dispersal.

Below right: Spitfire K9987 was delivered to No. 66 Squadron shortly before the outbreak of war. By 3 September 1939 the RAF had accepted delivery of 306 Spitfires. Of these, 187 formed the full equipment of ten squadrons (Nos 19, 41, 54, 65, 66, 72, 74, 602, 603 and 611). A further eighty-three were distributed as follows: at maintenance for the installation of operational equipment, seventy-one; employed on trials at the makers or at various service test establishments, eleven; allocated to a training unit, one. The remaining thirty-six Spitfires had been written off in accidents.

Spitfires of No. 19 Squadron flying in the standard RAF battle formation employed at the beginning of the war.

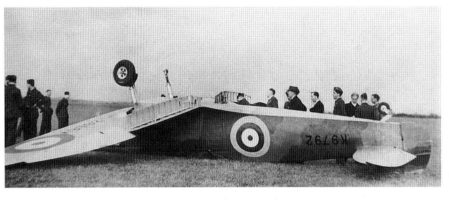

speeds. Fortunately, by the opening of the Battle of Britain, the operational Spitfires all had constant speed propellers.

Throughout the late summer and autumn of 1938 we received Spitfires at the rate of about one per week, and the year was almost over before we were at our full strength of sixteen aircraft. Until we were up to strength and fully operational with Spitfires, we held on to our earlier Gauntlets and still flew them from time to time.

Jeffrey Quill, the senior test pilot at Supermarine, was a frequent visitor to Duxford to see how we were getting on. One of the points he was a little anxious about was the size of the flaps on the Spitfire. Did we think they were too large for so light an aircraft? I agreed that they were a bit fierce, but I told him: 'Sooner or later people are going to hang things on this aircraft. I don't know what they will be, but I am certain that it will happen. And with the performance improvements planned by Supermarine the Spitfire is not going to get any lighter, is she?' He agreed that she would not, so we thought it better to leave the flaps alone and see what happened. As everybody now knows, the Spitfire more than doubled in weight during her development life; and to the very end the flaps were the same as they were in 1938.

When the Spitfire first arrived at Duxford they had lacked guns, but during the months that followed guns were fitted. I had my first experience of firing on 3 November, at the range at Sutton Bridge; as it happened, it was a night sortie. I had expected a few sparks from each gun, but I was in no

Top: The first Spitfire written off. On 3 November 1938, Pilot Officer G. Sinclair was landing at Duxford at the end of his first flight in a Spitfire, K9792, when a faulty port axle stub sheared on landing. Sinclair was unhurt.

Above: Spitfires and Hurricanes massed on the ground at RAF Digby. The occasion was a multi-squadron formation flight over Midlands cities, to publicise Empire Air Day on 20 May 1939. Also, more importantly, it was intended to boost civilian morale as the war clouds gathered.

Six of the original Spitfire pilots who flew with No. 19 Squadron: Flying Officers Pace, Robinson, Clouston, Banham, Ball and, seated, Thomas.

way prepared for the fireworks display which came from each wing: the long tongues of flame leapt out about 10ft in front of each gun. And the recoil of the eight fast-firing Browning machine guns, after the two Vickers guns I had been used to in the Gauntlet, was unexpectedly severe; it slowed down the aircraft as though one had put the brakes on.

In January 1940 I left Duxford to take up a staff appointment. By then the Royal Air Force had more than a dozen squadrons fully equipped with the Spitfire, and several others were about to receive it. We on No. 19 Squadron had introduced the type into service and, I am proud to say, we did it without losing a man.

FIRST ENCOUNTER

By Horst von Riesen

On 16 October 1939 Spitfires of Nos 602 and 603 Squadrons were scrambled to intercept a small force of German bombers attacking shipping in the Firth of Forth. For the first time, the new RAF fighter was to go into action against the enemy. Two of the German bombers were shot down, one of them being credited to Squadron Leader E. Stevens, the commander of No. 603 Squadron. During the same engagement Pilot Officers Morton and Robertson, also of No. 603 Squadron, reported intercepting an enemy aircraft 'thought to be a He 111' over Rosyth and pursuing it out to sea at very low level. When they finally broke off their attacks the bomber's starboard engine was observed 'not running'.

In fact the German bombers involved in the day's attack on the Firth of Forth were not Heinkel 111s, as was widely reported in British accounts of the action, but Junkers 88s. And Horst von Riesen should know – because he was one of those on the receiving end!

I n the autumn of 1939 I was a young lieutenant serving with I.Gruppe of Kampfgeschwader 30 (I./KG 30), based at Westerland on the island of Sylt. At that time we were the only unit in the Luftwaffe equipped with our fast new long-range dive bomber – the Junkers 88.

Initially our activities had kept us well clear of the British defences. But on the morning of 16 October one of our reconnaissance aircraft spotted the battle cruiser HMS *Hood* entering the Firth of Forth. We received orders to attack her, if we could catch her in open water; but at that stage of the war both sides tried hard to avoid causing civilian casualties and we had strict orders that if she was in harbour we were either to attack other warships outside, or else return with our bombs.

Nine of our aircraft were bombed-up and took off, but when we arrived over Rosyth we found *Hood* safely in dock – where we were not allowed to harm her. Just to the east of the Forth Bridge there were some small warships, however, and I decided to attack one of these. I selected one and carried out a diving attack, but scored only a near-miss.

Then, as I was climbing away, my radio operator suddenly shouted over the intercom that there were several fighters about 2 kilometres (km) away, diving on us. I looked in the direction he was pointing and as soon as I saw them I knew that I would need all the speed I could possibly squeeze out of my Junkers if we were to escape. I pushed down the nose

and, throttles wide open, dived for the sea. But it was no good. The Spitfires, as we soon recognised them to be, had the advantage of speed and height from the start and they soon caught up with us. As I sped down the Firth of Forth just a few metres above the surface, I could see clearly the splashes from the shells from the shore batteries, as they too joined in the unequal battle.

Although the Spitfire pilots reported the bombers they engaged on 16 October 1939 as Heinkel 111s, they were in fact Junkers 88s. During the action two German bombers were shot down and others, including Horst von Riesen's, suffered damage.

Leutnant Horst von Riesen had a memorable brush with Spitfires on 16 October 1939.

I had only one ally: time. Every minute longer the Junkers kept going meant another 7km further out to sea and further from the Spitfires' base; and I had far more fuel to play with than they did. Finally, however, the inevitable happened: after a chase of more than twenty minutes there was a sudden 'phooff' and my starboard motor suddenly disappeared from view in a cloud of steam. One of the enemy bullets had pierced the radiator, releasing the vital coolant and without it the motor was finished. There was no alternative but to shut it down before it burst into flames.

My speed sagged to 180km/h (112mph) – almost on the stall when flying asymmetric – and we were only a few metres above the waves. Now the Junkers was a lame duck. But when I looked round, expecting to see the Spitfires curving in to finish us off, there was no sign of them. They had turned round and gone home.

Even so, we were in a difficult position. With that airspeed there lay ahead of us a flight of nearly four hours, if we were to get back to Westerland. During our training we had been told that a Ju 88 would not maintain height on one engine – and we were only barely doing so. Should we ditch there and then? I thought no; it was getting dark, nobody would pick us up and we would certainly drown or die of exposure. An alternative was to turn round and go back to Scotland, and crash-land there. One of my crew suggested this but one of the others shouted over the intercom, 'No, no, never! If we go back there the Spitfires will certainly get us!' He was right. The thought of going back into that hornets' nest horrified us. So we decided to carry on as we were and see what happened. We preferred to risk death from drowning or the cold, rather than have to face those Spitfires again.

Gradually, as we burnt more fuel and the aircraft became lighter, I was able to coax the Junkers a little higher. The remaining motor, though pushed to the limit, continued running and finally we did get back to Westerland.

So it was that I survived my first encounter with Spitfires. I would meet them again during the Battle of Britain, over the Mediterranean and during the Battle of Sicily. It was not a pleasant experience.

Now I thought I was finished. Guns were firing at me from all sides, and the Spitfires behind seemed to be taking turns at attacking. But I think my speed gave them all a bit of a surprise – I was doing more than 400 kilometres per hour (km/h) (250mph), which must have been somewhat faster than any other bomber they had trained against at low level – and of course I jinked from side to side to make their aim as difficult as possible. At one stage in the pursuit I remember looking down and seeing what looked like rain drops hitting the water. It was all very strange. Then I realised what it was: those splashes marked the impact of bullets being aimed at me from above!

FIRST SPITFIRE RECONNAISSANCE FLIGHTS

In August 1939, shortly before the outbreak of the Second World War, Flying Officer Maurice 'Shorty' Longbottom penned a memorandum on strategic aerial reconnaissance. In it he stated:

> ... this type of reconnaissance must be done in such a manner as to avoid the enemy fighters and AA [anti-aircraft] defences as completely as possible. The best method of doing this appears to be the use of a single small machine, relying solely on its speed, climb and ceiling to avoid detection.

Longbottom's idea was to produce an unarmed high-speed, high-flying reconnaissance aircraft that could dart into enemy territory, take the required photographs and dart out, all with a minimum of fuss and avoiding the defences whenever possible. Today this concept is firmly accepted and it would raise scarcely an eyebrow, but in 1939 it was a radical departure from the accepted line of thinking. At that time most long-range reconnaissance aircraft were adapted bomber types, which retained their defensive armament so they could fight their way to and from their targets. Yet, as Longbottom pointed out, those guns and their gunners imposed a weight penalty which brought the aircraft within reach of the very defences it needed to avoid if it was carry out its mission effectively.

The ideal aircraft for long-range reconnaissance, Longbottom believed, was a high-speed, single-seat fighter, and he suggested the Spitfire. It could be stripped of its guns and radio, and fitted instead with cameras and additional fuel tanks. He argued that the removal of the guns, radio and items of unnecessary equipment would reduce the weight of the Spitfire by 450lb. With its high power-to-weight ratio, the Spitfire fighter could get airborne carrying an additional 480lb, which meant that the aircraft could get airborne with 930lb of lifting capacity that could be devoted to cameras and extra fuel. Such a modified Spitfire would be able to carry three times as much fuel as the standard fighter version, giving it a theoretical range of 1,500 miles.

Longbottom's paper ascended the chain of command and was well received, but initially little could be done about his proposal. The RAF was desperately short of Spitfires and almost all were allocated to Fighter Command for the defence of Britain. The change of heart came in the autumn of 1939, with the realisation that the Blenheims carrying out

Flight Lieutenant Maurice 'Shorty' Longbottom, second from the right, who wrote the original paper suggesting the use of the Spitfire in the photographic reconnaissance role. With him are other pilots who flew with No. 221 Squadron in France in 1940. (Tuttle)

The scene at Seclin near Lille on 18 November 1939, as Flight Lieutenant 'Shorty' Longbothom prepared to get airborne to make the first attempt to photograph the German Siegfried Line defences in front of Aachen. LAC Fred Hunt, crouching under the starboard wing, described to the author the plane's unusual colour scheme. It was painted overall with a delicate shade of pale bluish green which, under certain light conditions, appeared to have pinkish tinge. On the ground this made the aircraft conspicuous, but once it was airborne the Spitfire merged well into the sky background. Fred Hunt continued: 'The planes were very highly polished between every sortie. Much time was spent polishing them with wax furniture polish. Because of the considerable secrecy afforded to these reconnaissance missions, most of the pre-flight preparations took place in the hangar. At the last moment the Spitfire was pushed outside and one of the ground crew ran the engine to warm it up. Then the engine was stopped, the tanks were filled to capacity top, the pilot got in and took off. When it landed after the mission, the Spitfire was immediately pushed into the hangar to get it out of sight.'

daylight photographic reconnaissance over Germany were too vulnerable for the task. Even during shallow penetration missions, these aircraft suffered severe losses. Fighter Command was persuaded to part with a couple of its precious Spitfires and these were sent to Heston airfield, north of London, for conversion. There, a secret reconnaissance unit, codenamed the `Heston Flight` and commanded by Wing Commander Sidney Cotton, prepared the Spitfires for their new role. Appropriately, 'Shorty' Longbottom was one of the first officers posted to the new unit.

The two Spitfires received only the minimum of modification for the reconnaissance role, and there was no time to fit additional fuel tanks. Each aircraft had a vertical camera mounted in each wing, in place of the guns and ammunition boxes. The aircraft were then 'cleaned up' to give the last ounce of speed: the empty gun ports were sealed off, then all joints were filled with plaster of Paris and rubbed down to give a smooth finish. Cotton then had the Spitfires painted in a very pale shade of green, which he thought would make them least conspicuous when observed from below. The reconnaissance unit was then given the cover name 'No. 2 Camouflage Unit' to conceal the reason for the planes' unusual colouring.

In mid-November 1939 one of the modified aircraft was detached to Seclin, near Lille, to carry out an operational trial. On the 18th, Longbottom, newly promoted to flight lieutenant, flew the first Spitfire reconnaissance mission to photograph the German city of Aachen and the nearby fortifications. As he made his photographic runs at 33,000ft the pilot found navigation more difficult than expected. When his pictures were developed, they showed the countryside on the Belgian side of the frontier to the south of Aachen. Longbottom adjusted his technique, and on his next flight, four days later, he successfully photographed the Belgian-German border to the east of Liege.

For most of the six weeks that followed, heavy cloud cover precluded high-altitude photography of enemy territory, but at the end of December 1939 the skies cleared, allowing the two Spitfires to resume operations. They photographed Aachen, Cologne, Kaiserslautern, Wiesbaden, Mainz and parts of the Ruhr industrial area. These flights demonstrated that as a vehicle for photographing enemy territory the Spitfire was the best type available. Between the start of the war and the end of 1939 Blenheims had flown eighty-nine reconnaissance sorties

The Belgian village of Bulligen (centre, two thirds of the way up) as photographed during the first successful Spitfire reconnaissance sortie on 22 November 1939. Taken from 33,000ft, the picture reveals little ground detail.

into German airspace, of which sixteen (18 per cent) failed to return. Due to these high losses, and the frequent harassment from the defences, only forty-five of the Blenheim sorties (about half) yielded useful photographs. In contrast, by the end of 1939 the two Spitfires had flown fifteen sorties without a single loss, and ten (two-thirds) of the sorties had yielded useful photographs. Of the five abortive Spitfire sorties, four were due to cloud cover at the target and only one was due to fighter interference. The flights proved the soundness of Longbottom's concept for high-performance, unarmed reconnaissance operations, and Air Chief Marshal Dowding was persuaded to release a dozen more of his precious Spitfires for conversion to the reconnaissance role.

Although these initial flights had established the feasibility of Longbottom's concept, much still remained to be done. Even after the prints had been blown up to the extent the grain of the film allowed, photos taken from 33,000ft using the Spitfires' F.24 cameras produced pictures of too small a scale to show troop activity. Roads, railways, villages and major fortifications could be picked out, but anything smaller was likely to be missed. The answer was to fit improved

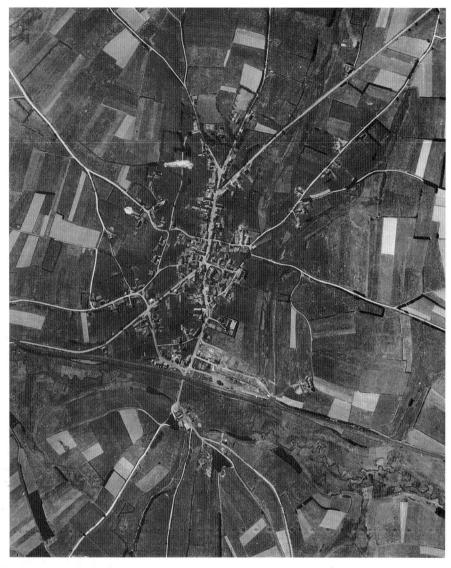

Compare the previous photograph with this one taken at about the same altitude, using an F.52 camera introduced later in the war. The latter shows much more ground detail, and illustrates well the advances made in reconnaissance equipment during the period.

cameras with longer telephoto lenses, which would give better definition of ground features. Also, additional fuel tanks were needed to extend the Spitfires' range. During the early months of 1940, progressive increases in fuel tankage enabled the reconnaissance Spitfires to penetrate deeper into enemy territory. In January 1940 the first of the improved photographic reconnaissance Spitfires was ready for operations. This was designated the PR IB, and to distinguish it from the earlier variant it was renamed the PR IA. The new variant carried one 8in focal length camera in each wing, giving a one-third improvement in the scale of the photographs. Also, to increase its range the PR IB carried an extra 29 gallon (gal) fuel tank in the rear fuselage. In February 1940, 'Shorty' Longbottom demonstrated the effectiveness of the new variant when, operating from Debden in Essex, he returned with photographs of the important German naval bases at Wilhelmshaven and Emden.

Early in 1940 the operations in France were reorganised and a new unit, No. 212 Squadron, formed at Seclin to fly Spitfire reconnaissance missions. During operations with the PR IAs, Cotton's light green camouflage scheme was found to be unsuitable for use at high altitude. Accordingly the new Spitfires were painted in a medium blue scheme which proved more effective

In March 1940 the Spitfire PR IC appeared, with an additional 30gal blister tank under the port wing. Counterbalancing this were a pair of 8in lens cameras in a similar blister under the starboard wing. With an additional 29gal tank in the rear fuselage, this version carried 59gal more fuel than the fighter version. On 7 April, Longbottom took the prototype PR IC to Kiel and brought back the first photographs of the port taken since the outbreak of war.

Just over a month later, on 10 May 1940, German forces launched their powerful Blitzkrieg attack on France, Holland and Belgium. In the following hectic weeks No. 212 Squadron flew numerous sorties to chart the relentless progress of the German Panzer columns across France, although the Spitfires' photographs could do nothing to avert the defeat that followed. Yet, by keeping Allied commanders aware of the growing peril, they allowed preparations to be launched in time for the successful evacuation of large numbers of troops from Dunkirk. It is no exaggeration to say that the reconnaissance Spitfires played a major part in preventing that defeat from turning into an irretrievable disaster. When its position in France was no longer tenable, No. 212 Squadron withdrew to England and shifted its operations to Heston.

BAPTISM OF FIRE

By Colin Gray

During the so-called 'Phoney War', the period prior to the opening of the German offensive in the West on 10 May 1940, Spitfire fighters had occasionally been in action against German bombers operating off the coasts of England and Scotland. Though they did not encounter enemy fighters until a few days after the offensive began, Allied troops were forced to withdraw within range of the Spitfire squadrons based in southern England. During the final week of May and the beginning of June, Royal Air Force Fighter Command endeavoured to cover the evacuation of

This and previous page: The 600th production Spitfire, serial P9450, pictures undergoing its production test flight with Jeffrey Quill at the controls, in April 1940. Note the black underside of the port wing, contrasting with the white underside for the starboard wing. Its purpose was to provide a simple means of national identification, to avoid 'friendly fire' incidents involving fighters or AA gun batteries.

Allied troops from Dunkirk. In the course of these operations, Spitfires found themselves in action against enemy fighters of equivalent performance for the first time; now the Royal Air Force's premier fighter type had to show that it could take punishment, as well as dish it out.

Pilot Officer Colin Gray, a New Zealander flying Spitfires with No. 54 Squadron based at Hornchurch, first went into action on 24 May against an enemy formation near Calais and was credited with one Messerschmitt 109 damaged. On the following day his unit escorted a squadron of Fleet Air Arm Swordfish, who were attacking German ground troops advancing east of Dunkirk. The lumbering biplanes and their

escorts reached the target without interference from enemy fighters, completed their attack and turned back for England. As their charges headed out to sea with no enemy aircraft in sight, the Spitfires, freed of the requirement to escort them further, headed south looking for trouble. They soon found it, and in the action that followed Colin Gray's inexperience almost cost him his life.

Suddenly we found ourselves in amongst a gaggle of 109s. I opened fire at one of them, but stopped when I noticed smoke coming back over my wings. That shook me – I thought somebody was firing at me. I pulled round hard

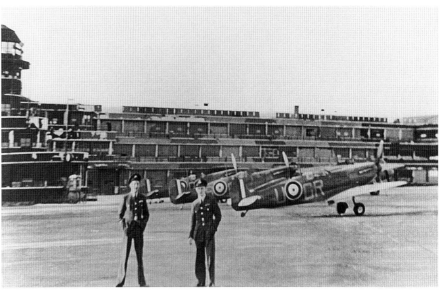

but there was nobody there – what I had seen was cordite smoke blowing back from my own guns. I looked back at the Messerschmitt and saw Sergeant John Norwell on its tail and the German pilot baling out.

Afterwards Norwell and Gray were each credited with a half share in the destruction of the Messerschmitt, but as the German fighter plunged earthwards Gray allowed his gaze to follow his falling enemy too long. The error nearly cost him his life.

Suddenly there was one hell of a row, like somebody running a bar along a piece of corrugated iron. The stick was knocked out of my hand and ended up in the left hand corner of the cockpit, and my aircraft flicked into a spiral dive. I grabbed the stick and hauled back on it, the Spitfire responded immediately and started to climb. I looked behind but didn't see anyone, the German pilot had not repeated my mistake of following me down. I selected 12 pounds [emergency boost] and continued my climb; the airspeed indicator read 240mph and I thought 'This is bloody marvellous!' [the normal speed for a Spitfire in a steep climb was about 190mph indicated]. But then, as I continued the climb, the Spitfire began to shudder and it seemed as if it was going to stall. I couldn't understand it – the airspeed indicated still read 240mph. I eased the stick forwards, but still it read 240mph… Then I realised what had happened: my pitot head [air speed sensor mounted under

the port wing] had been shot away, the needle had dropped to the 240mph position on the dial under gravity…

I levelled out and took stock of the situation. One cannon shell had gone through the port aileron; that was what had knocked the stick out of my hand and sent the aircraft into the violent spiral dive which shook off the Messerschmitt. The airspeed indicator was out and there was no air pressure or hydraulic pressure, which meant that I had no flaps or brakes and I couldn't lower the undercarriage using the main hydraulic system. As I approached Hornchurch I blew down the undercarriage using the emergency carbon dioxide system, and saw the 'undercarriage down' sticks push up through the wings and two green lights come on to indicate that the wheels were down and locked.

The landing was very difficult. With the flaps up one came in at a different attitude than usual and, of course, I had no idea of my airspeed (the indicator still read 240mph!). The first time, I came in too fast. The station commander at Hornchurch, Wing Commander 'Daddy' Bouchier, was watching my performance and was overheard to say 'The silly young bugger, he's going too fast. He'll never get in!' He was right. I got my wheels almost on the ground, realised I was not going to make it and took off again. The second time I stood well back from the airfield, and dragged the aircraft in at just above stalling speed. That time I landed, and as

Above and above left: Historic photos taken at Le Bourget, Paris, on 16 May 1940. They show the de Havilland Flamingo airliner which conveyed Prime Minister Winston Churchill to France, to discuss the request for more RAF fighters to be sent to join the battle following the German breakthrough at Sedan. The three Spitfires of No. 92 Squadron escorted the Prime Minister's aircraft throughout the visit.

The Dunkirk evacuation saw the start of combat operations by Spitfires, and revealed that the new fighter could take punishment as well as dish it out. This was the condition of the Spitfire flown by Pilot Officer Oswald Pigg of No. 72 Squadron, who regained their base after a dogfight over Dunkirk on 2 June.

I touched down the elevator cable finally parted and the control column collapsed back into my stomach.

On examination of the Spitfire afterwards it was found that a cannon shell had gone through the inspection hatch in the rear fuselage and exploded inside. Splinters from the shell had slashed their way out of the skinning, leaving it looking like a cheese grater. The air bottles had been knocked out, so were the batteries. There were bullet holes up and down the fuselage and, of course, the cannon shell through the aileron. From the entry and exit holes of the bullets it was clear the Messerschmitt had dived on me from the right and above; it had been a very neat piece of deflection shooting.

The Spitfire was put up on trestles and people from Vickers were invited to come and look at it, to see how much it had suffered. It was the first Hornchurch aircraft that had been fairly well clobbered, and still got back. Soon there would be many others.

Colin Gray went on to become one of the most successful RAF fighter pilots of the Second World War and ended the conflict as a wing commander, credited with twenty-seven and a half aerial victories. Yet, of the many actions in which he fought, the most memorable was that on 25 May 1940 when lack of experience so nearly put a premature end to his career as a combat pilot.

AN EVEN MATCH

During the early war period, from September 1939 to May 1940, the Spitfire fighter squadrons all remained in Britain and there was no opportunity to go into action against there opposite numbers in the Luftwaffe. The lull in the West came to an abrupt halt on 10 May, however, when the Germans launched their great offensive into Holland, Belgium and France. Soon there was no need for the Spitfire squadrons to go overseas to meet the enemy; instead, the land battle was being fought on territory within their limited radius of action from airfields in south-east England. From 12 May, when No. 66 Squadron's Spitfires mounted a patrol over The Hague, the new fighter was committed to action in steadily greater numbers. At last the Spitfire was to come face to face with its Luftwaffe counterpart – the Messerschmitt Bf 109E.

The initial encounters between these two adversaries were usually inconclusive, though they did demonstrate that they were obviously closely comparable in performance. Also during that May, in the still-peaceful skies over the Royal Aircraft Establishment at Farnborough, a Spitfire Mk I and a captured Bf 109E fought a series of mock combats as part of a trial intended to compare the strengths and weaknesses of each. To provide a fair picture of the capability of each aircraft they were flown in pre-planned tactical exercises. The Messerschmitt was positioned ahead of the Spitfire and its pilot attempted to shake off his pursuer by means of a horizontal speed run, through four tight turns in each direction, a dive and then a steep climb. Afterward the two aircraft changed positions and repeated the procedure, then engaged in a short free-play fight.

In level flight, the maximum speeds of the two aircraft were about equal. During the turns, flown at speeds between 90–220mph, the Spitfire had little difficulty in keeping behind. Nor did the dive present the pursuer with any great problem. When the Messerschmitt was pulled out of the dive and into a steep climb at low airspeed, however, the Spitfire – whose optimum climb rate was achieved at a flatter angle but a higher airspeed – had difficulty in following. Furthermore, even when the Spitfire could follow, its pilot found it almost impossible to hold the gunsight on the target.

When the Spitfire was in front, it was a clear that in a turning match at medium altitude and in the middle of its speed range, it was easily the better aircraft. Also, with its superior rate of roll it could shake off the pursuer by means of a flick half-roll and a quick pull out of the subsequent dive. The Messerschmitt pilot found the latter particularly difficult to counter, because when he rolled after the Spitfire his speed built up rapidly in the steep dive and his elevator became so heavy that a quick pull out was impossible. Of course, these advantages could be exploited only if the Spitfire was flown to its limits. During subsequent trial flights there were several occasions when the Messerschmitt succeeded in remaining on the tail of the Spitfire merely because the latter's pilot lacked experience and failed to tighten his turn sufficiently for fear of stalling and spinning.

Manoeuvrability at medium speeds is only one of many factors which could be turned to advantage in air combat, however. Two points emerged from the trial whose significance was to be confirmed again and again during the great air battles soon to follow. The first was that when the Messerschmitt pilot performed a sudden bunt (pushing the control column sharply forwards so the aircraft entered 'zero G' flight conditions) and the Spitfire tried to follow, the latter's engine would splutter and lose power because the normal float-type carburettor fitted to the Merlin ceased to deliver fuel. The Messerschmitt's Daimler Benz engine, on the other hand, had direct fuel injection and did not suffer from this failing. Many a Messerschmitt pilot saved himself by adopting this manoeuvre to shake off a British fighter on his tail. Later, Spitfire pilots learned to half-roll and pull through when following a bunting Bf 109, using an aileron turn to get back upright when they were established in the dive. It was

The Messerschmitt Bf 109E, which equipped virtually the entire complement of Luftwaffe single-engined fighters throughout 1940.

not an ideal solution but it did enable a good pilot to maintain the pursuit.

The second point was that during diving manoeuvres at high speeds the controls, and particularly the ailerons, of both aircraft became progressively heavier. At 400mph the Spitfire's rate of roll was about the same as that of the Bf 109, with both pilots having to pull as hard as they could on the stick to get one-fifth aileron movement and both aircraft requiring about four seconds to roll through 45 degrees. Under these conditions the Spitfire ceased to have any clear advantage in manoeuvrability. German pilots soon discovered that if they kept their speed up and evaded during combat, the Spitfire pilot would find it hard to bring his guns to bear.

One important lesson failed to emerge from the Farnborough trial, which was that the German fighter had the edge in combat at altitudes above 20,000ft. Before the fighting began, many experts considered high-altitude dogfighting to be so unlikely as not to warrant a trial. They would soon learn otherwise.

Overall, however, the Spitfire Mk I and the Messerschmitt Bf 109E matched each other fairly evenly. If they fought, victory would usually go to the side that was the more alert, that gained and held the initiative, that understood the strengths and weaknesses of his own and his opponent's aircraft, that displayed the better teamwork and which, in the last resort, could shoot more accurately.

SPITFIRES IN CAPTIVITY

The Spitfire received its baptism of fire while providing air cover for Allied troops retreating to, and being evacuated from, the area around Dunkirk. There was fierce fighting over the evacuation area, with heavy losses on both sides. In the course of the actions between 21 May and 4 June, more than sixty Spitfires were lost in action.

The first Spitfire to fall into German hands intact was K9867 ZP-J of No. 74 Squadron, which force-landed at Calais-Marck airfield on 23 May, while the area was held by Allied troops. When German troops captured the airfield on 26 May, the Spitfire was still there.

For the Spitfire squadrons the worst single day during the Dunkirk evacuation was 11 June, when twelve aircraft were lost. One of those forced down, P9317 ZD-A of No. 222 Squadron, made a wheels-down landing at Le Touquet airfield held by German troops, and became the second intact Spitfire captured by the enemy.

Since November 1939 a few Spitfires modified for photographic reconnaissance had been operating from bases in France. In February 1940 these aircraft were incorporated into No. 212 Squadron, with a detachment based at Seclin, near Lille. No. 212. Squadron flew throughout the Battle of France, and withdrew to England with most of its aircraft and personnel in June. It left behind one Spitfire intact, however: P9331, a PR 1B which had suffered a glycol leak during a mission on 7 June and landed at Rheims/Champagne. The aircraft was still there four days later, when German troops occupied the area.

The fourth Spitfire to fall intact into German hands had been the first of all to arrive in France: Spitfire 01, the 251st production aircraft, which had been delivered to the French Air Force in June 1939 for evaluation. This aircraft was at that service's test centre at Orleans/Bricy when German troops overran the airfield on 18 June. Thus, by the third week in June 1940, four Spitfires had fallen into German hands. We know that at least one of them was taken to the Luftwaffe test centre at Rechlin and made airworthy.

Below left: The first Spitfire captured intact by German forces was K9867, ZP-J of No. 74 Squadron. This aircraft suffered damage in action and landed at Calais-Marck on 23 May 1940, when the airfield was held by Allied forces. It was still there three days later when that airfield was over by German troops. (Barbas)

Below: The second Spitfire captured was P9317, ZD-A of No. 222 Squadron, which made a forced landing at Le Touquet airfield, which had recently been taken by German forces. (Barbas)

Above: The third Spitfire captured intact was P9331, a photographic reconnaissance PR 1B of No. 212 Squadron based at Seclin. As described earlier, this aircraft landed at Rheims/Champagne on 7 June when it was in French hands, but was there still when the airfield was captured by German troops a few days later.

Above right: The fourth Spitfire captured intact by German forces had been purchased by the French Air Force before the war. Designated No. 01 in that service, it was at the test centre at Orleans/Bricy when German forces overran the area. (Gentilli, Willis)

Prior to the Battle of Britain, the German fighter ace Hauptmann Werner Moelders test-flew both a Spitfire and a Hurricane. He later wrote:

It was very interesting to carry out the flight trials at Rechlin with the Spitfire and the Hurricane. Both types are very simple to fly compared with our aircraft, and childishly easy to take-off and land. The Hurricane is very good-natured and turns well, but its performance is decidedly inferior to that of the Me 109. It has strong stick forces and is 'lazy' on the ailerons.

The Spitfire is one class better. It handles well, is light on the controls, faultless in the turn and has a performance approaching that of the Me109. As a fighting aircraft, however, it is miserable. A sudden push forward on the stick will cause the motor to cut; and because the propeller has only two pitch settings (take-off and cruise), in a rapidly changing air combat situation the motor is either overspeeding or else is not being used to the full.

Werner Moelders' remarks were probably not intended to be a fully objective assessment of the British fighter, though he put his finger on two weaknesses of the early Spitfires. At the time he made his remarks one of the weaknesses was in the

process of being cured: under a crash programme all Spitfires in frontline units were being retrofitted with constant speed airscrews, thus overcoming the problem of the earlier two-pitch propeller. The problem of the motor cutting out when the plane was bunted would be more difficult to cure, however, and would remain with the fighter for some time to come.

Oberleutnant Hans Schmoller-Haldy of Jagdgeschwader (JG) 54 also had the chance to fly a captured Spitfire at about this time, and he was rather more impressed with it as an adversary. He told the author:

My first impression was that it had a beautiful engine. It purred. The engine of the Messerschmitt 109 was very loud. Also, the Spitfire was easier to fly, and to land, than the Me 109. The 109 was unforgiving of any inattention. I felt familiar with the Spitfire from the very start. That was my first and lasting impression. But with my experience with the 109, I personally had the impression, though I did not fly the Spitfire long enough to prove it, that the 109 was the faster, especially in the dive. Also, I think the pilot's view was better from the 109. In the Spitfire one flew further back, a bit more over the wing.

For fighter-versus-fighter combat, I thought the Spitfire was better armed than the Me 109. The cannon fitted to the 109 were not much use against enemy fighters, and the machine guns on top of the engine often suffered stoppages. The cannon were good if they scored a hit, but their rate of fire was very low. The cannon had greater

range than the machine guns. But we were always told that in a dogfight one could not hope to hit anything at ranges greater than 50 metres, it was necessary to close in to short range.

After the Battle of Britain, two Spitfires, or one Spitfire repainted in two different sets of British markings, featured in a series of propaganda photographs taken by the Luftwaffe. One of these aircraft carried the spurious squadron code G-X and featured an unusual layout of roundels: Type B (red/blue) markings on the upper surface of the wings well inboard of the usual position, and larger Type B markings on the fuselage. The other Spitfire had Type B markings in the usual place on the upper wing surfaces, but featured over-sized Type A1 (red/

white/blue/yellow) markings on the fuselage and carried no squadron code letters.

It is difficult to establish with certainty the identities of the Spitfires flown in British markings by the Luftwaffe, though it is possible to state which they were not. One give-away is the radio mast: both Spitfires which appeared in the German photographs were fitted with the pointed mast introduced early in 1940. That rules out the first aircraft captured, K9867, and the French Spitfire 01, both of which were fitted with the early type cylindrical mast. It also rules out the photographic reconnaissance aircraft P9331, which had no radio mast at all. That reduces the list to P9317, N3277 and X4260, with P9317 as the most likely contender because she was the first one captured and the one with the least damage.

Propaganda photos taken during the mock combats employing captured enemy aircraft. The successful German offensive in the spring of 1940 culminated in the occupation of Holland, Belgium, Luxembourg and much of France. By its end the Luftwaffe possessed large numbers of foreign aircraft in a flyable or near flyable condition.

BATTLE OF BRITAIN FIGHTING TACTICS

The following paper, excerpts of which are presented here, was issued by the Air Tactics Branch of the Air Ministry in July 1940. Its purpose was to familiarise fighter pilots with the lessons learned during the aerial fighting so far. It was the most recent tactical paper on air fighting available to Royal Air Force fighter pilots during the Battle of Britain period. The paper provided a tactical framework within which pilots could make their own decisions in combat, and was not intended to lay down hard-and-fast rules.

HINTS AND TIPS FOR FIGHTER PILOTS

Most of our fighter experience in the war has been gained during the battles resulting from the invasion of Holland, Belgium and France. Under these conditions patrols were working either from aerodromes on the Continent which were subjected to continual attacks and which had often to be evacuated, or from aerodromes in south-east England under improvised arrangements.

Some of the hints, therefore, are more applicable to such conditions than to home defence fighting, but they have been retained, because although France has ceased to be a belligerent, and her aerodromes are closed to us, the distance between our own country and aerodromes occupied by the Germans is now so short that home defence operations are likely to have many of the features which we have been accustomed to connect only with Continental operations.

DUTIES

Fighter pilots may be called upon for the following duties:

(a) Home Defence. In this case fighters will be opposed to formations of enemy bombers usually escorted by fighters. Our patrols will normally be sent off to meet specific raids, the composition and strength of which may be known before interception takes place.

(b) Offensive Patrols over the Continent. These patrols will normally be despatched to areas in which enemy aircraft can be expected to be congregated. The strength and composition of the enemy forces will not be known before interception takes place. All types of enemy aircraft may be encountered.

(c) Escort of Bomber or Reconnaissance Missions. In this case your duty is to ensure the safety of the aircraft which you are escorting and not to be drawn off in pursuit of aircraft which do not directly threaten them.

ENEMY FORMATIONS

Although the enemy may adopt any type of formation, the following are those normally met:

(a) Bombers in vics [standard V-shaped formations] of three, five or seven aircraft; vics in line astern, often stepped up to the rear or to the flank. Fighter escort is usually 3,000 to 4,000ft above and astern, or above and between the bombers and the sun. Fighters normally adopt a large vic formation of nine or twelve aircraft. One or more of these vics may be employed stepped up and behind each other.

(b) Bombers sometimes form a double vic, i.e. one vic inside another or a vic with one or more aircraft in the 'box' so as to give concentrations of defensive fire.

(c) Ju 87 dive bombers are sometimes met with in no particular formation, particularly just before they deliver their attack. Under these conditions they form a large jumbled mass.

DEFENSIVE TACTICS OF ENEMY BOMBERS

Enemy bombers when attacked may:

(a) Close into tight formation.

(b) Form a circle.

(c) If their formation is broken, dive to ground level and jink.

(d) Make for the nearest cloud.

Pilot Officer David Glaser of No. 65 Squadron in his Spitfire. Note the 'blinker' fitted in front of the cockpit to shield the pilot's eyes from the glare of the exhaust flames during night flying.

(e) Ju 88 has a habit of slowing up when attacked so that the fighter will overrun it and become a target for the rear guns of the Ju 88.

(f) Sometimes also a flank aircraft of an enemy formation, which is not being engaged, will drop back to attack with crossfire a fighter attacking another aircraft of the formation.

TACTICS OF ENEMY ESCORT

The enemy escorting fighters normally maintain their formation and position until our fighters start to attack the enemy bombers. Enemy fighters then immediately peel off in ones or twos in succession and dive very steeply upon our fighters. They open fire in the dive but do not usually attempt to remain on the tail of our fighters; instead, they continue their dive straight past and below and then climb up again into position for another attack.

TACTICS TO BE EMPLOYED AGAINST ENEMY FORMATIONS

Fighters should never rush in to attack a formation immediately after it is sighted. It is absolutely essential that the situation should be weighed up so that the most profitable method of attack can be decided upon, and also so that the disposition of the enemy fighters which are escorting the bombers may be studied. It must be remembered that the main aim is to shoot down the bombers; experience has proved that this cannot be done and that our fighters will be at a tactical disadvantage unless the enemy fighters are neutralised.

On finals for landing, following a curved approach to enable the pilot to keep the airfield in sight… Throttle back… Hood open and locked, side door in the half-cock position to prevent the hood slamming shut in the event of a mishap… brake pressure checked… undercarriage down below 160 mph… two green lights and indicator bars out… mixture rich… propeller pitch lever fully fine… flaps down below 140mph… Over the hedge at 85mph indicated… ease the stick gently back to hold it off the ground as the speed falls away… 64mph and it stalls gently on to the ground.

If, therefore, we have a strong force of fighters, at least a quarter of them must be detached to take up the attention of the enemy fighters so that, while they are thus occupied, the remainder of our fighters can attack the enemy bombers without interruption.

If, however, our fighters are numerically inferior to the enemy escorting fighters, some form of stratagem must be employed. Suggested methods are:

(a) Attack or feint attack with small part of our force against the enemy fighters so as to draw them off.

(b) That the fighter should make a feint attack upon the bombers, thus bringing down the enemy fighters against him. Close watch should be kept upon the fighter as it dives and just before it arrives within range, its attack should be avoided by quick manoeuvre. Time may thus be gained for a very quick attack upon the bombers before the next fighter arrives within firing range.

(c) A detachment manoeuvre above or to the flank of the enemy fighters to give warning by radio when enemy fighters start their attacking dive.

(d) Even a small detachment which reaches a position above the enemy fighters will often cause them to desert the bombers.

(e) If interference from enemy fighters can be temporarily neglected, a flight of five (see para f) aircraft can use the 'astern attack from the beam'. Aircraft take position in line astern, 800 yards [yd] to port of the enemy bomber formation, and ahead and 1,000ft above, on the order 'turn to right in astern. Going down', the flight turns in simultaneously. Nos 1 and 2 deliver a full beam attack, Nos 3 and 4 a quarter attack, fighters break away to the left and downwards, reform line astern to port of the formation, and repeat the manoeuvre.

(f) Our fighters have generally attacked enemy bombers from astern. The introduction of armour in enemy bombers may force us to attack from the beam and even from directly ahead. Such attacks are more difficult to deliver but have been frequently adopted and when properly executed, have been extremely successful.

DO NOTS

(a) Do not go into the middle of a vic of enemy bombers. If you do this they can concentrate the fire or their rear guns upon you. Attack them from the flank and if possible, from both flanks simultaneously.

(b) When you are going into the attack, do not give the enemy a chance of a deflection shot at you. As far as you can, keep your nose on the enemy, and approach in his blind spots as much as possible.

(c) Do not fire a long burst if enemy fighters are about; two seconds is long enough. Then break away quickly to ensure that an enemy fighter is not about to attack you. If all is clear, then you can immediately renew your attack upon the bomber.

(d) Do not break away by means of a climbing turn. This gives an easy shot to the enemy rear gunner. Break away outwards and downwards at as high a relative speed as possible.

(e) If the enemy forms a circle, do not attack it in a hesitating manner. When you attack a circle go straight into it without hesitation as soon as you can find a gap.

(f) Do not forget that enemy fighters can reach practically any part of this country. Never relax your vigilance.

PATROLLING

(a) Make certain before leaving the ground that you thoroughly understand the orders for the patrol and what you are expected to do.

(b) If your patrol is ordered to take off at a fixed time, be ready in plenty of time so that you can sit quietly and calmly in your aircraft, collecting your thoughts, before you have to take off.

(c) In choosing a height for your patrol, always try to patrol higher than the enemy.

(d) Never patrol in tight formation. Two-five spans is a comfortable distance which allows you to search around without fear of collision.

(e) The rear aircraft or section of any fighter formation must always be in a position to watch the sky astern of the formation and to give warning of attacks by enemy fighters. If aircraft are in a single composite formation, the rear two aircraft should continually 'weave', i.e. swing across and exchange places with each other so that they can keep this watch to the rear. All aircraft in the formation, however, should try to assist in watching the whole sky.

(f) A useful patrol formation for a squadron is sections in line astern, stepped up, the third section to a flank and the rear section acting as look-out to the rear. Alternatively, aircraft have successfully patrolled in flights of five, each five forming an independent unit under its own leader. The look-out is provided by Nos 4 and 5 crossing over above the formation. On sighting the enemy formation, No. 4 or 5 dives down in front of the leader, indicating the position of the enemy by clock code over the R/T. As soon as he is in front of the formation, he turns off in the direction of the enemy. When the formation leader spots the enemy, he reassumes the leadership. If more than one flight of five operates together, No. 1 flight takes position above and to the flank of No. 2 Flight, each flight providing its own look-out.

(g) The same section should not be detailed to act as look-out for the whole period of the patrol because its 'weaving' tactics use up considerably more petrol than normal straight flying.

(h) Do not patrol continuously along the same track. This will allow enemy fighters to anticipate your movements and obtain a favourable position for a surprise attack on you.

(i) When patrolling, change your height and course continuously to avoid anti-aircraft fire.

(j) If you are patrolling, as you should, with a portion of your force acting as an upper guard, this guard should regulate its movements so that it can immediately go to the assistance of the lower formation when required.

(k) Never leave your formation unless ordered to do so.

ENEMY DECOY TACTICS

If you see a lone bomber apparently without any particular employment, he will almost certainly be a decoy, and fighters, 4,000ft above and probably hidden in the sun, are waiting for you to attack him. A favourite trick of enemy fighters is to allow one or two of their number to lead you just under clouds. When they have got you in that position, enemy fighters in superior numbers dive out of the clouds to attack you.

Always expect that enemy fighters are in the offing and are waiting for you to take some unguarded action.

ENEMY FIGHTER TACTICS

(a) Me 109s and Me 110s normally fly in squadron formations of twelve.

(b) Enemy fighters always like to be in superior numbers and to have the advantage of height and sun. Unless they have these advantages, they will not usually stay to fight, but will make a quick diving attack hoping they have you at a disadvantage and will then use their speed to escape.

(c) German fighters often work in pairs. If you get on the tail of one, the other immediately tries to get on your tail.

(d) When attacked, German fighters will very often dive vertically away from you. It is not usually worthwhile to follow them especially if they are faster in the dive than you are. If you are over German territory he may try to lead you over a FLAK [anti-aircraft] battery.

(e) The Me 110, after he has attacked, will often pull up into a stall turn, so that he may have a look round to see where he should go next. If you can catch him at the top of his zoom, he is very easily shot down.

(f) The Me 110 will often make a head-on attack at you, and open fire with cannons at long range. He does not like to hold on to this attack to close range.

DOGFIGHT HINTS

(a) Formations quickly become broken up in a dogfight. Aircraft of sections should try, as far as possible, to keep together for mutual support.

(b) If you hear the sound of firing, turn immediately. The sound almost certainly comes from an enemy fighter which is attacking you from astern.

(c) Turn sharply and slightly downwards. Hurricanes and Spitfires are more manoeuvrable than German fighters and they will have difficulty following you in your turn. The Me 109 is particularly bad at a sharp turn to the right.

(d) If you are involved in a head-on attack, remember the rule of the air: when you have to break away to avoid collision, turn to the right.

(e) Never waste ammunition. The golden opportunity may come when your ammunition is finished.

(f) Be especially careful at the moment you break off a combat. Take evasive action immediately because you are especially liable to attack at this moment. A useful manoeuvre to break off a combat is a dive using full aileron. Regain height as soon as possible.

(g) If your engine stops dive straight down to make the enemy think that he has 'got' you. Manoeuvre without engine gives the game away and the enemy likes to concentrate on the 'lame duck'.

(h) If you have to bale out, half-roll on to your back, open the lid, undo your straps and push the stick forward.

(i) Never fly straight, particularly if you are alone. Keep continually turning from side to side so that you can keep a look-out behind you. If the sun is bright and is behind you, it is advisable to make a 360-degree turn at short intervals so that you can make quite certain that the sky is clear in all directions.

(j) Beware of the Hun in the Sun.

The object in night fighting is to 'stalk' the enemy and to reach firing position without being observed. The following points should be noted:

(a) Under normal conditions of darkness, aircraft which are not illuminated by searchlights can best be spotted when they are between 40-deg and 60-deg above you.

(b) Cockpit and instrument lighting should be reduced to the barest minimum to assist you in searching for the enemy, and to prevent your own presence being revealed.

(c) The illuminated ring sight should be dimmed so it is only just visible.

(d) Before opening fire the aircraft must be positively identified as an enemy. This is best achieved from a position below him.

(e) The following method of attack is recommended by Fighter Command. Having reached a position below the enemy and regulated your speed to his, slightly raise the nose of your aircraft without increasing the throttle opening; you will thus rise behind the enemy. Keep below his slipstream – if you have difficulty in holding your aircraft out of the slipstream it is usually an indication that you have reached too great a range.

(f) The range at which the enemy is engaged should be as short as possible; in no circumstances should it be greater than 150yd.

GENERAL HINTS

(a) If there is a chance that enemy fighters may be about, look well before you take off, turn quickly, be especially careful while circling the aerodrome before landing and do not make a long straight approach.

(b) Light AA guns from the ground are accurate and effective up to 4,000ft. The most dangerous heights for heavy AA guns are between 4,000ft and 8,000ft.

(c) Watch that your oxygen fittings do not come adrift.

(d) Do not leave your transmitter on 'send'. If you do, you make communication impossible for the whole formation and you may ruin the patrol.

(e) Remember to turn on your sight, and cine-camera on, if you have one.

(f) If you have been in action, test your hydraulic system for possible damage before you get back to your home aerodrome.

(g) If you see white or greyish smoke pouring out of an engine of the enemy aircraft, it probably means that you have damaged his cooling or oil circulation. You should therefore switch your aim to the other engine. Black smoke may indicate either that the engine has been damaged or that the pilot is overboosting. There are indications that the enemy will try to produce smoke artificially so as to deceive you, so you must use your judgement as to whether you have caused sufficient damage to make it impossible for him to return to his base.

FINALLY

Remember that the closer the range, the more certain you are of bringing down the enemy. Remember also that everyone tends to underestimate range and that when you think you are within 200yd of the enemy you are probably still 400yd away.

9

BETTER FITTED FOR THE FIGHT

Between the outbreak of war and the start of the Battle of Britain, the Mark I version of the Spitfire underwent several detailed improvements to make it a more capable fighting aircraft. In this section we examine the changes, and their effects on the fighter's performance.

In the spring of 1940, to improve the performance of its fighters, the RAF introduced 100 octane petrol instead of the 87 octane fuel previously used. In the case of the Merlin IIs and IIIs fitted to the Spitfire Mk I, this gave no improvement at or above the engines' full-throttle altitude set at 16,500ft. Below that altitude, however, the new fuel gave a valuable increase in power. Supercharger boost could be increased from +6½lb to +12lb without causing detonation in the cylinders, and this increased the maximum speed of the Spitfire by 25mph at sea level and 34mph at 10,000ft. Up to full-throttle height the fighter's climbing performance was also improved.

A further significant improvement in performance, in particular during take-off and in the climb, came with the installation of constant speed de Havilland or Rotal airscrews in place of the earlier two-pitch type: when fitted with one of the new propellers the Spitfire Mk I's rate of climb was increased by about a half and the take-off distance was reduced by about a third.

Other modifications made to the Spitfire at this time, although they improved its fighting ability, detracted from performance. To protect the pilot and other vital parts of the plane, shaped steel plates were installed behind and beneath the pilot and in front of the fuel and glycol tanks; in total the sections of steel armour weighed 73lb. A thick slab of laminated glass was fitted on the front of the windscreen to protect the pilot's head and the sheet of light alloy covering the fuel tanks was thickened to 10SWG (Standard Wire Gauge), or about 3mm (sufficient to make rounds impacting at a shallow angle ricochet off).

Another important addition was the installation of IFF (Identification, Friend or Foe) transponder equipment.

Although it imposed a weight and performance penalty, this equipment was essential to enable the aircraft to identify itself on the screens of radar stations along the coast of Great Britain, on which the RAF's fighter control system depended. The various modifications added about 335lb to the Spitfire, and brought its all-up weight to around 6,155lb. Moreover, some of the changes increased drag and so reduced the plane's top speed: for example, the slab of toughened glass mounted in front of the windscreen cost 6mph, the IFF wire aerials from the fuselage to the tip of each tailplane shaved off another 2mph. The maximum speed usually quoted for the Spitfire Mk I is 362mph at 18,500ft; however, that figure referred to K9787, the first production aircraft with an all-up weight of 5,819lb. By the summer of 1940 the maximum speed of a fully-equipped Mk I was somewhat lower, about 350mph at the same altitude.

One further modification introduced before the Battle of Britain needs also to be mentioned here, and while it would give a significant improvement in the fighter's ability to manoeuvre effectively in combat, the weight and performance penalties were negligible. During comparative flight tests of a captured Messerschmitt Bf 109 against contemporary RAF fighters, it was discovered that in the German fighter the seat was more reclined than in British fighters. As a result, the pilot could pull more 'G' (gravitational acceleration) without blacking out. To adjust the seating position in British fighters would have incurred a major modification programme, but a simpler solution was readily to hand. A Spitfire was modified with two-step rudder pedals, the lower step for normal flight and the upper step for use in high 'G' manoeuvres, i.e. in combat. Flight Lieutenant Robert Stanford-Tuck of No. 92 Squadron was asked to take the modified Spitfire through the

FIG.3 SPITFIRE

Above and right:
Close-up of the canopy, showing the laminated glass slab in front of the windscreen. The latter became a standard fitting to all fighter versions of the aircraft. Note the push-out panel on the port side of the canopy, to allow the pressure inside the canopy to be equalised with that outside, should there be difficulty in opening the canopy at high speed.

Opposite: Spitfire cockpit showing some of the changes made during the early war period. In front of the windscreen is Barr and Stroud GM 2 reflector gunsight, which replaced earlier and less effective ring-and-bead sight. In the bottom left of the cockpit is the port two-step rudder pedal. In normal flight the pilot placed his feet on the lower steps. Before he entered combat the pilot lifted his feet on to the upper steps, to raise his legs. This gave the body a more horizontal posture, and raised the pilot's ability to withstand the effects of 'G'.

repertoire of combat manoeuvres to determine the advantages and disadvantages of the modification. The questionnaire he was asked to fill in, and his answers to it, are reproduced here.

QUESTIONNAIRE ON AUXILIARY RUDDER PEDALS

You are requested after an extended and fair trial to express your views freely on the merits or disadvantages of the auxiliary rudder pedals.

Q1 Is the rudder easy to manipulate in manoeuvre using upper steps?
A1 Yes, comparatively so, as one only wants to use at higher speed and consequently very little rudder is required.

Q2 Have you proved that it raises your 'blacking out threshold' and enables you to do tighter turns.
A2 Yes, as when one is trying to shoot with heavy stresses on the body, the head can still be in the firing position relative to sight but knees are well up in the stomach, tightening muscles.

Q3 Is the upper step a comfortable position?
A3 For any period, definitely no. But for a short dogfight of, say, 20 minutes, it is not at all uncomfortable.

Q4 Is there any disadvantage in having the auxiliary step fitted?
A4 Absolutely none that I have found. It interferes in no way with any manoeuvres one might wish to do.

Q5 Any other comments?
A5 I have tried out these extra pedals over quite a long period now, and cannot find one single disadvantage in having them fitted, but on the other hand every advantage as outlined.

On the strength of Tuck's recommendation, the two-step rudder pedals were installed in all new Spitfires, and existing aircraft were retrofitted with them. During the Battle of Britain this relatively minor modification would enable Spitfire pilots to engage in manoeuvring combat more effectively than would otherwise have been the case.

10

BATTLE OF BRITAIN SQUADRON COMMANDER

Donald MacDonell joined the Royal Air Force in 1932 and trained as a pilot at Cranwell. After receiving his commission he was posted to No. 54 Squadron equipped with Bristol Bulldogs. In 1935 he was seconded to the Fleet Air Arm and flew Nimrod fighters from the aircraft carriers Courageous and Glorious. In 1937 he qualified as a flying instructor, and the following year was posted as a flight commander to the flying school at Drem. In 1939 he was promoted to squadron leader and posted to the Directorate of Training in the Air Ministry. In July 1940, when the Battle of Britain was in its opening stages, he was appointed officer commanding No. 64 Squadron at Kenley equipped with Spitfire Mk Is.

When MacDonell assumed command of No. 64 Squadron the unit was flying daily patrols to escort convoys passing through the Straits of Dover. With increasing frequency the Spitfires encountered Junkers 87 dive bombers escorted by Messerschmitt Bf 109s, but although the squadron's pilots had several close shaves and some of its aircraft suffered damage, the unit went through most of July 1940 without the loss of an aircraft or pilot.

All of that changed on the afternoon of the 25th, however, during the series of hard-fought actions over Convoy CW8 off Folkestone. At the head of his squadron, MacDonell reached the convoy as the Junkers 87s of II/StG 1 completed an attack on the ships and were heading south at low altitude in a gaggle. Coming down fast, the Spitfires closed rapidly on their prey:

> I picked out one of the Stukas and went after it. The German rear gunner was firing back and I felt a 'thump' as my Spitfire was hit. Then I opened up at him with my eight guns. As my rounds struck home, bits fell off the Stuka then suddenly it rolled on its back and dived into the sea.

His glycol system damaged, MacDonell headed to Hawkinge with a badly overheating engine. The redoubtable Merlin kept going until the fighter was passing over the airfield boundary, then it finally packed up, although MacDonell was able to make a normal landing. During that action No. 64 Squadron lost two Spitfires: the pilot of one was killed, that of the other suffered injuries from which he later died.

Squadron Leader Don MacDonell commanded No. 64 Squadron during the Battle of Britain.

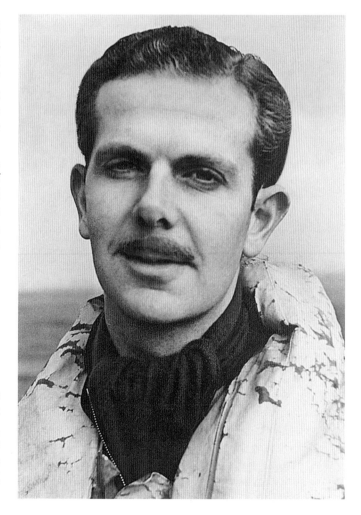

In a similar action four days later MacDonell gained his second victory, again a Junkers 87, followed a few minutes later by a Messerschmitt Bf 109. One of the unit's Spitfires suffered damage during this engagement.

In times of war a fighter squadron is a close-knit unit, and MacDonell found that among pilots the attitude towards rank was quite different from what he had known before the war:

In wartime, it was inevitable that democracy should creep into a small fighting unit like a Spitfire squadron. Having been in the service since 1932, at first I found it strange to hear the NCO pilots calling junior officer pilots by their Christian names or nicknames. I did not stop it – the most important thing was to maintain morale.

Among the pilots discipline was a bond, self-imposed by a common purpose. I was the only 'Sir' on the squadron. That sort of democracy was restricted to the air crew, however. The NCO ground crew had been in the service a long time and they maintained the old standards. They served their pilots with a technical and emotional devotion which was quite outstanding.

In wartime, fighter formations were led by the most experienced pilot, regardless of rank:

Flying experience was what mattered most. On one occasion I had to go to Group Headquarters, one of the flight commanders was suddenly ordered to move from Leconfield to Wittering. A flight sergeant was the most experienced pilot available, so he led the squadron. That would never have happened in peacetime.

August brought hectic activity for the squadron, with numerous combat scrambles and long periods at readiness in between. MacDonell was credited with the destruction of two Me 109s on the 5th, another on the 8th, one on the 11th and two more on the 15th. No. 64 Squadron's days settled into a routine, if 'routine' is the appropriate word for a period in which the risk of death was ever-present.

At Kenley, No. 64 Squadron's dispersal area was at the north of the airfield, at the opposite side from the hangars and administrative buildings. The Spitfires were parked in the E-shaped earth-and-brick revetments beside the perimeter

Kenley Airfield under attack from low-flying Dornier 17s of Kampfgeschwader 76, on 18 August. The unserviceable Spitfire in the revetment, belonging to No. 64 Squadron, suffered minor damage.

track, and from time to time the ground crews would start the engines of the planes at readiness to warm the oil and ensure they could take off immediately.

When we were at readiness the pilots would be relaxing at the dispersal area – reading, chatting, playing cards. Each Flight had a separate crew room, so no pilot was too far from his Spitfire. I would be out of my office, wearing flying kit and Mae West, with the Flight I was to lead on that day. Each pilot's parachute was laid out on the seat of his aircraft, with the straps laid over the armour plating at the back of the cockpit.

Every time the telephone rang there would be a ghastly silence. The orderly would answer it and one would hear something like: 'Yes, Sir … Yes, Sir … Yes, Sir … Sgt Smith wanted on the phone.' And everyone would breathe again. If the call was for the squadron to scramble, the orderly would shout 'SCRAMBLE!' at the top of his voice and every pilot would dash for his plane.

By the time I reached my Spitfire the mechanic would have started the engine. He got out of the cockpit and I got in, and he helped me strap into my parachute. Then he passed the seat straps and helped me fasten them. When I gave the thumbs up he would shut the side door, jump to the ground and run round in front of the port wing. Meanwhile

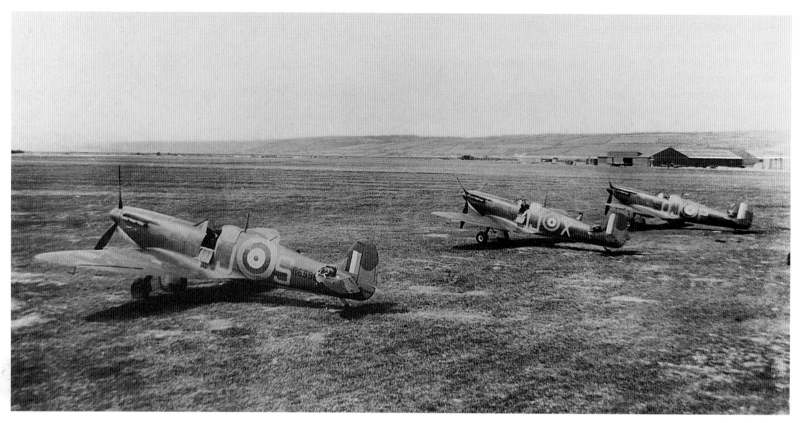

Spitfires of No. 92
Squadron at readiness.

I tightened my various straps, pulled on my helmet and plugged in the R/T lead. After checking that the engine was running properly, I would wave the ground crew to pull away the chocks, open the throttle, and move forward out of my blast pen.

After a fast taxi across the grass to the take-off position I would line up, open the throttle wide and begin my take-off run. The rest of my pilots followed me as fast as they could. The whole thing, from the scramble order to the last aircraft leaving the ground, took about a minute and a half.

As soon as we were off the ground and climbing, I would inform operations 'Freema Squadron airborne' ['Freema' was No. 64 Squadron's radio callsign]. The sector controller would come back and tell me where he wanted me to go and at what altitude. While the squadron was forming up I would climb in a wide spiral at low boost, until everyone was in place. Then I would open up to a high-throttle setting to get to altitude as fast as possible. In the spiral climb I would

always edge to the north; the enemy formations always came from the south or south-east, and it was important to avoid climbing below the enemy's fighter cover. As well as keeping watch for the enemy, I would be watching the station-keeping of my squadron. If anyone was beginning to straggle I would throttle back a little.

With the long periods on standby, flying two, three or more operational scrambles each day and sometimes a night patrol as well, by nightfall the pilots were usually extremely tired. Between 25 July and 15 August the squadron lost five Spitfires and five pilots – two killed, two wounded and one taken prisoner. Their replacements came from the training schools and MacDonell had the task of preparing them for action:

During the Battle of Britain one had to take every opportunity to train new pilots. Young pilots would arrive on the squadron with only six or seven hours' flying time on the Spitfire. One or two practice sorties could make all the difference to their ability to survive in combat. When we were at thirty minutes available, I might ring operations and ask permission to take one of the new pilots into the air for 'follow my leader' practice. If one could take them up one could point out their failings and tell them 'You won't survive ten minutes in battle if you fly like that!' The object was to tell them why and lead them round, not to frighten them.

No. 64 Squadron was heavily engaged on 16 August and MacDonell was shot down, as he describes:

We had been sent up against a raid by fifty or sixty Heinkel 111s, with a free-hunt of Messerschmitt 109s in front and a close escort of Messerschmitts above. There was a certain amount of cloud at about 8,000ft. We had been scrambled late and broke cloud to find ourselves beneath and behind the Heinkels, which had turned round after dropping their bombs. I split my squadron, and told the other Flight to attack the bombers from the starboard side. I went in with my wingman, intending to attack the bombers from below and do as much damage as we could.

We got in very close to the Heinkels and knocked one down, then we attacked two others and clearly damaged them. Then we were out of ammunition. There was a tremendous return fire from the bombers, so we broke off and dived for cloud. But by then the covering Messerschmitts were charging after us and just before we reached the cloud there was a frightful crash as my Spitfire was hit. The aircraft went out of control and I was forced to bale out. The Spitfire flown by my No. 2, Pilot Officer P. Simpson, took eight hits from cannon shells but he managed to get it back to Kenley.

I came down in the garden of a little cottage near Uckfield, about a mile from where my Spitfire crashed. I released the parachute and was wandering around, when from an Anderson shelter there emerged a very frightened householder pointing a 12-bore shotgun at me. Then his wife came out of the shelter and said 'I think he's one of ours, darling'.

Once it was clear MacDonell was not an enemy, he was taken into the house and given a large brandy.

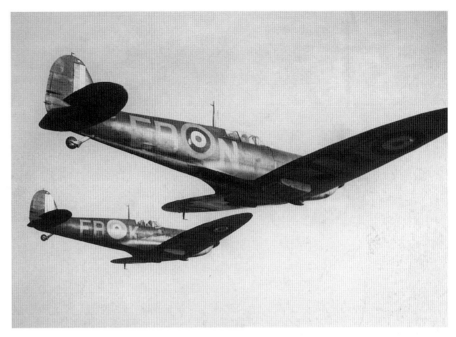

A pair of Spitfires of No. 41 Squadron.

At this time the German offensive against Fighter Command's airfields and radar stations was in full swing. Two days later, on 18 August, Kenley was attacked. As the raiders came in over the coast, eight Spitfires of No. 64 Squadron were scrambled and ordered to patrol over base at 20,000ft. They were in position when suddenly the Kenley sector controller, Squadron Leader Anthony Norman, called over the radio 'Bandits overhead!' To MacDonell the warning sounded rather odd:

Instinctively I looked up, but there was only the clear blue sky above. I thought 'My God! Where are they?' Then I looked down and could see bombs bursting on the airfield. Realising the enemy planes were below us, I gave a quick call: 'Bandits below. Tally Ho!' Then down we went in a wide spiral at high speed, keeping a wary eye open for the inevitable German fighters.

As the descending Spitfires reached 15,000ft they passed a formation of Dornier Do 17s surrounded by a melee of Hurricanes and Messerschmitt Bf 110s. These Dorniers were in the process of turning for home, having released their bombs on Kenley in a high-altitude attack coordinated with the earlier one from low altitude.

There was an awful lot going on, with aircraft flying in all directions. As we were descending, a squadron of Hurricanes came past us going towards the Dorniers. There was a lot of R/T chatter, everybody was very excited.

I dived beneath one of the enemy aircraft, which I took to be a Dornier, and pulled up to attack it from astern and underneath. I opened fire from about 300yd. The starboard engine was hit, then the port engine emitted puffs of black smoke. I thought the pilot had been hit, or the elevators damaged, because the aircraft stood on its tail, stalled, then went into a spin. I remember thinking 'How amazing, that an aircraft can stall so soon after its engines were damaged'. Rather foolishly I hung around, spellbound, watching it go down. Then I realised that there were better things to do, and pulled away. I did not see it crash but there was a lot of smoke and I didn't think it would get very far.

In fact the 'Dornier' was a Messerschmitt Bf 110 of Zerstorergeschwader (ZG) 26, piloted by Oberleutnant Rudiger Proske. The speed and angle of MacDonell's approach had taken the German crew by surprise and Proske was unaware of the Spitfire's presence until his aircraft shuddered under the impact of hits. The accurate burst damaged both the Messerschmitt's engines and wounded the rear gunner. In no position to fight back, the German pilot decided to 'play dead'; he released the stick and let the plane fall out of control. It was a convincing demonstration, as MacDonell testifies. Proske let the Messerschmitt spin through 6,000ft then, seeing that no British fighter was following, he regained control, levelled out and headed for the coast. Both engines were losing power however, and, just short of the coast, first one engine then the other juddered to a stop. The German pilot had made a wheels-up landing on farmland near Lydd, which wrecked the aircraft.

While Proske was limping away from Kenley, MacDonell was again in action. He found a Junkers 88 which had become separated from its formation, and made two firing runs on it before his ammunition ran out. The last he saw of the bomber, it was emitting smoke from the port engine and was under attack by a Hurricane. Almost certainly this was the bomber which came under attack from several British fighters that afternoon, and which crashed soon afterwards near Sevenoaks.

The co-ordinated attack on Kenley had inflicted severe damage, and the station's fighter squadrons were ordered to land elsewhere.

We received the order 'Pancake Bye-Bye One' [Bye-Bye was the codename for the emergency landing grounds, which had refuelling and rearming facilities]. 'Bye-Bye One' was Redhill, and five of us landed there. I was worried about our three other planes – I thought they had come to grief. The Spitfires were rapidly refuelled but rearming was another matter – at the landing ground they had plenty of ammunition but it was not belted-up.

After about half-an-hour I phoned Kenley operations and told them the aircraft were refuelled, but it would take the rest of the war to get them rearmed! They told us to return to Kenley, taking care to avoid the bomb craters. When we arrived we saw the three missing Spitfires, they had all landed safely.

Only one of No. 64 Squadron's aircraft suffered damage that day, caused by a bomb which exploded near the revetment in which it was parked. On the next day, 19 August, No. 64 Squadron left Kenley and moved to Leconfield in Yorkshire to rest, re-form and train its replacement pilots. At the end of October the unit returned to the south, this time to Biggin Hill. By then the Battle of Britain was in its closing stages, however, and there was little further action. On 11 November MacDonell engaged a Me 109 and reported having damaged it. On the 29th he engaged another of these fighters and shot it down.

That was MacDonell's final victory and it brought his victory score to eleven and half. On 13 March 1941, while leading his squadron as top cover for a daylight raid by Blenheims in the Pas de Calais area, Donald MacDonell was shot up by a Me 109. He managed to get halfway across the Channel, but then his engine seized and he was forced to bale out. After about half-an-hour in the sea he was picked up by a German patrol boat and taken to Le Havre. He spent the remainder of the conflict as a prisoner of war.

11

THIRTEEN DAYS IN AUGUST

By Dennis Armitage

During the Battle of Britain Dennis Armitage was a flight lieutenant and junior flight commander with No. 266 Squadron. Here he gives us his memories of Fighter Command's greatest battle.

During the initial stages of the battle, the squadron was based at Wittering in the Midlands as part of No. 12 Group, and saw little action. For the unit the period of quiet came to an abrupt end during the early morning darkness of 9 August, when it received orders that at first light it was to move to Northolt for a short detachment. Led by Squadron Leader Rodney Wilkinson, twelve Spitfires took off from Wittering at 0600hrs and headed south. On the way the weather deteriorated, however, with banks of low cloud concealing the ground. Unable to find Northolt, the squadron headed north until there was a break in the overcast skies and the Spitfires put down at the first airfield it came to, at Hatfield.

This was most sporting because someone had thought of the brilliant idea of stringing quantities of barbed wire up and down the aerodrome. At that time Hatfield was used for ground training only, except for occasional test-flights by de Havilland. The idea of the barbed wire was that it would upset any airborne divisions which might arrive from Germany. But in practice it was amazingly ineffective. Even with the Spitfire, a machine which was notoriously nose-heavy on the ground, only one of the first section to land upended. And even that I think was due to a feeling that there was something peculiar about those yards of barbed wire trailing behind the aircraft which caused the pilot to make a too sudden an application of the brakes. After that and a few belated red Very lights, hundreds of boys appeared – air cadets who were doing their ground training and had been hurriedly kicked out of bed – and stood in two great lines to mark out a 'secret' landing run which had been left clear for de Havilland. The rest of us plonked down one at a time without further incident.

It was still only 0630hrs but someone rustled up some breakfast for us and over this we had a good healthy argument, which our CO won in the end, about whether anyone had thought of sending out warning signals about the barbed wire. By 0800hrs the clouds had cleared and we flew on to Northolt, refuelled and settled down to wait. We were told we should return home at 1500hrs; at 1500hrs we were told to wait till 1700hrs; at 1700hrs to wait till 1800hrs; and at 1800hrs we were told to take off for Tangmere.

The eleven of us – the twelfth man, of course, had been left behind at Hatfield – arrived there without further incident. We parked our aircraft, arranged to borrow ground crews from a Hurricane squadron stationed there, ate, had a drink or two and so to bed – pyjama-less.

Spitfire flown by Pilot Officer 'Pedro' Hanbury of No. 602 Squadron.

A section of three
Spitfires of No. 19
Squadron gets airborne.
All three units were
heavily committed
during the September air
battles.

No. 266 Squadron's Spitfires remained at Tangmere for the next two days, during which its ground personnel arrived from Wittering. No sooner had the unit collected itself, than orders came in to prepare for yet another move, to Eastchurch on the 12th.

> The CO, the senior flight commander and I were summoned to a most secret meeting. We were informed that we had been given special duties escorting Fairey Battles [bombers] across the Channel to bomb concentrations of 'E-boats' which were now assembling along the French and Dutch coasts. It sounded horrid for the lads in the slow Battles, although not so bad for us. We were to operate from Eastchurch, on the Isle of Sheppey in the Thames Estuary, which would be ready for us the next day. In the meantime, in view of the greatly increased activity round Portsmouth, we might be called on to patrol the aerodrome if necessary but under no circumstances were we to engage the enemy if we could possibly avoid it – they wanted to be sure there would be a full squadron to go to Eastchurch on the next day.

The orders to keep out of action were smartly superseded a couple of hours later, when a large force of Junkers 88s attacked Portsmouth at midday. No. 266 Squadron scrambled twelve Spitfires and in the action that followed it claimed four enemy aircraft destroyed, two probably destroyed and nine damaged. Two if its Spitfires were lost and one pilot, Pilot Officer Dennis Ashton, killed. After refuelling at Tangmere, the unit's remaining aircraft took off for Eastchurch as planned.

> We arrived at Eastchurch to find two squadrons of Battles and another half squadron of Spitfires [No. 19] had arrived earlier that day, and after dinner flight commanders and above were summoned to a conference of war.
>
> We were told the general scheme, and apparently only two things were lacking. One was a special information service which was going to tell us where to find the fruitiest targets, and the other snag was that [the Battles] had not got any bombs. However, the group captain had reason to hope that both these things would be added unto us after lunch the next day. In the meantime he suggested we might all have a really good night's rest – breakfast at 0930hrs and another conference about 1000hrs. It was actually 0705hrs when the first bomb arrived. Not ours!

The attack on Eastchurch was carried out by Dornier 17s and caused severe damage to the airfield buildings. No. 266 Squadron lost one airman killed, and one officer and five airmen injured. One of its Spitfires suffered damage.

> We held a brief council of war and decided to station six Spitfire pilots permanently in their machines. Until the raid we had every reason to expect we should get warning of the approach of the Luftwaffe – why we did not we never

discovered – but there was no radio station at Eastchurch and our own R/T sets were, of course, no use until we were airborne, so with the telephone wires down communications were sticky.

Fortunately the [other] aircraft were practically undamaged, but unfortunately all of our spare ammunition boxes had gone up with our hangar where they were stored – fully loaded - which helped to make the fire interesting.

On the following day, 14 August, the squadron moved to Hornchurch. 15 August was one of the hardest-fought days of the Battle of Britain and No. 266 Squadron was heavily engaged. The unit claimed three enemy aircraft destroyed and one damaged, but lost two pilots killed. Armitage himself had a narrow escape and suffered leg injuries:

There had been the usual shemozzle which had eventually sorted itself out into one or two Spits, and three or four 109s buzzing round in tight circles. I had just had the pleasure of seeing the three that I had been closeted with diving down towards the sea with one of them smoking nicely. Another 'possible', perhaps even a 'probable', but not a 'confirmed' because I was not silly enough to follow him down in case there was another waiting for me up in the sun – and there was. I have no idea how he slipped under my tail, but suddenly I heard a loud bang, something hit me in the leg, and there was a fearful noise of rushing air. Under these circumstances one's reactions are automatic, even though one has no idea what the Dickens has happened. I whipped into a vertical turn, looking fearfully up towards the blazing sun and then, as confidence returned, I spotted what was probably the cause of the trouble diving away, already some 5,000ft below. I realised that the noise was simply due to my Perspex hood having been blown out and, that apart, my left leg was quite numb from the calf down. I put my hand down gingerly to feel if my foot was still there and, reassured on this point, I headed for home.

On landing I found a cannon shell had exploded inside the fuselage, the spent head of the shell having found its way under the armour plating behind the seat and struck me on the leg. One of the elevator control wires was hanging on by a single thread and another cannon shell had just caught my port wing tip.

The next day, 16 August, was even worse for No. 266 Squadron. During a combat with Me 109s near Canterbury, Squadron Leader Wilkinson, Sub Lieutenant Greenshields (a Fleet Air Arm officer seconded to the RAF) and Pilot Officer Bower were killed; Flight Lieutenant S. Bazley, the senior flight commander, baled out with burns; and Pilot Officer Sodden was injured and his Spitfire wrecked during a crash-landing. One enemy aircraft was claimed destroyed and three probably destroyed.

In the course of just two days' fighting the unit had lost its three senior officers and five other pilots killed or injured; seven Spitfires had been destroyed and two damaged. Dennis Armitage, as senior surviving officer on the squadron, was now in charge. With his engineering warrant officer he surveyed the damaged Spitfires in the hangar, amongst them the one in which he had been injured.

One of the EO's [Engineering Officer's] pet rules was the one about non-cannibalisation of aircraft. Many a time we had waited and waited with three or four unserviceable machines in the hangar, when all but one could have been put into the air by pinching the necessary parts from the remaining machine. But now things were different; we went to any lengths to get a machine flying again, patching and making-do in a thousand ways. And our straight-backed EO did not hesitate to cast aside his life-long principle, though I think it still hurt him to do so. And incidentally, for a whole month, he himself worked from dusk till dawn without a break, and most of the daylight hours as well.

The jagged hole in the fuselage was nearly a foot in diameter. The EO shook his head and with one accord our eyes strayed towards another machine in the hangar with a badly damaged starboard wing. I nodded and he nodded – no words passed but I knew that the starboard wing, the only undamaged part of my airframe, would be transferred by dawn.

On the evening of 17 August No. 266 Squadron took delivery of seven new Spitfires to make up the aircraft lost during the previous two days' fighting. There were no replacement pilots, however, and by now the unit was desperately short. Two days later, led by Armitage, the squadron was withdrawn to the Midlands to reform. It had indeed been a difficult thirteen days in August.

12

FIGHTER COMMAND SPITFIRE UNITS, 14 SEPTEMBER 1940

This section gives the order of battle of operational Spitfire units in RAF Fighter Command at 1800hrs on the evening of 14 September 1940. The following day would see the climax of the Battle of Britain. To provide a full picture of Fighter Command's strength, Spitfires held in reserve in maintenance units, those serving with operational training units and the number produced during the preceding week are also included. The first figure denotes aircraft serviceable, while unserviceable aircraft are shown in parentheses.

NO. 10 GROUP, HQ BOX, WILTSHIRE

Middle Wallop Sector
No. 609 Squadron: 15 (3) Middle Wallop
No. 152 Squadron: 17 (2) Warmwell
St Eval Sector
No. 234 Squadron: 16 (1) St Eval

Group total: 48 (6)

NO. 11 GROUP, HQ UXBRIDGE, MIDDLESEX

Biggin Hill Sector
No. 72 Squadron: 10 (7) Biggin Hill
No. 92 Squadron: 16 (1) Biggin Hill
No. 66 Squadron: 14 (2) Gravesend
Hornchurch Sector
No. 603 Squadron: 14 (5) Hornchurch
No. 41 Squadron: 12 (6) Rochford
No. 222 Squadron: 11 (3) Rochford
Tangmere Sector
No. 602 Squadron: 15 (4) Westhampnett

Group total: 92 (28)

NO. 12 GROUP, HQ WATNALL, NOTTINGHAMSHIRE

Duxford Sector
No. 19 Squadron: 14 (0) Fowlmere
Coltishall Sector
No. 74 Squadron: 14 (8) Coltishall
Wittering Sector
No. 266 Squadron: 14 (5) Wittering
Digby Sector
No. 611 Squadron: 17 (1) Digby
Kirton-in-Lindsey Sector
No. 616 Squadron: 14 (4) Kirton-in-Lindsey
No. 64 Squadron: 7 (3) Leconfield and 6 (3) Ringway

Group total: 86 (24)

NO. 13 GROUP, HQ NEWCASTLE, NORTHUMBERLAND

Catterick Sector
No. 54 Squadron: 15 (2) Catterick
Usworth Sector
No. 610 Squadron: 14 (5) Turnhouse

Group total: 44 (12)

Spitfires at Operational Training Units (OTUs) – 14 September: 26 (24)
Spitfire production during week prior to 14 September: 38
Spitfires held at Maintenance Units – 14 September:

Ready for immediate use: 47
Ready in four days: 10

Opposite: Illustrating the mixed origins of the men who fought with the RAF during the Battle of Britain are these four pilots of No. 19 Squadron. From left to right: Pilot Officer W. 'Jock' Cunningham from Glasgow, Sub Lieutenant 'Admiral' Blake, a Fleet Air Arm pilot on loan to the RAF; Flight Lieutenant F. Dolezal, a Czech who had been in his own country's air force before the German occupation, who escaped and joined the French Air Force, escaped again and was now flying with the RAF; and Flying Officer F. Brendan, a New Zealander.

13

THE SPITFIRE IN ACTION, 15 SEPTEMBER 1940

On the evening of 14 September, Fighter Command's Spitfire squadrons possessed 270 serviceable aircraft, plus a further seventy that were unserviceable. The Hurricane squadrons possessed 509 serviceable aircraft (plus ninety-five unserviceable). Thus Spitfires made up just over 34 per cent of the Command's force of modern, single-engined day-fighters. The average serviceability of the Spitfires was 79 per cent and the Hurricanes 84 per cent.

A major factor in Fighter Command's success during the large-scale engagements on 15 September was the exemplary performance of the RAF fighter control organisation. During the engagement around noon, against a raid on London, eight squadrons of Spitfires and fifteen squadrons of Hurricanes were scrambled; all except one squadron of Hurricanes made contact with the enemy. During the second and much larger attack on London that afternoon, ten squadrons of Spitfires and eighteen squadrons of Hurricanes were scrambled; all made contact with the enemy.

Spitfires from eleven squadrons went into action on 15 September: Nos 19, 41, 66, 72, 92, 152, 222, 602, 603, 609 and 611 Squadrons. Significantly, eight Spitfire squadrons would see no action on that day: Nos 54, 64, 65, 74, 234, 266, 610 and 616 Squadrons. The latter were assigned to Nos 10, 12 and 13 Groups, responsible for the defence of the west and north of the country, and were based too far from the capital to go into action in its defence.

In the course of the day's fighting eight Spitfires were lost out of 192 sorties that engaged the enemy, a loss rate of 4.2 per cent. Twenty-one Hurricanes were lost out of 327 sorties that were engaged, giving a loss rate of 6.4 per cent. Thus a Spitfire that made contact with the enemy was 66 per cent more likely to survive such contact than a Hurricane. Nine out of 184 returning Spitfires had battle damage (4.8 per cent), as did twenty-three out of 316 returning Hurricanes

(7.2 per cent). Compared with the Hurricane, the Spitfire's superior performance made it a more difficult opponent for enemy fighters and its smaller size made it less likely to take hits from the bombers' return fire.

During the two main engagements under consideration, fifty-five German aircraft were destroyed. In addition, one German plane appears to have been lost to accidental causes. Ground anti-aircraft fire was a contributory factor in four of the losses, though in each case fighters also had a share in the victory. Of the fifty German planes that fell to fighter attack, many were attacked by both Spitfires and Hurricanes. As a result it is not possible to draw valid conclusions from this action regarding the relative merits of the Spitfire and the Hurricane as destroyers of enemy aircraft. On average, one German aircraft was shot down for every ten Spitfires and Hurricanes that made contact with the enemy.

During the day there were numerous violent and confused combats between the opposing fighters in the area east of London. Few of these manoeuvring combats lasted more than about twenty seconds, however: any pilot concentrating his attention too long on one enemy fighter ran the risk of being blasted out of the sky by another. On this day the author has found only one recorded instance of a protracted combat between individual fighters. Squadron Leader Brian Lane commanded No. 19 Squadron with Spitfires, part of Douglas Bader's Wing. When the Wing was split up Lane was attacked by a Me 109, but avoided the enemy fire before curving after the Messerschmitt to deliver his riposte:

He saw me as I turned after him and, putting on full inside rudder as he turned, skidded underneath me. Pulling round half-stalled, I tore after him and got in a short burst as I closed on him before he was out of my sights again. That German pilot certainly knew how to handle a 109 – I have never seen one thrown about as that one was, and felt certain that his wings would come off at any moment. However, they stayed on, and he continued to lead me a hell of a dance as I strove to get my sights on him again. Twice I managed to get in a short burst but I don't think I hit him, then he managed to get round towards my tail. Pulling hard round I started to gain on him and began to come round towards his tail. He was obviously turning as tightly as his kite could. I could see that his slots [on the leading edge of the wings] were open, showing he was nearly stalled. His ailerons were obviously snatching too, as first one wing and then the other would dip violently.

Giving the Spitfire best, he suddenly flung out of the turn and rolled right over on his back passing across in front of me inverted. I couldn't quite see the point of his manoeuvre unless he hoped I would roll after him, when, knowing no doubt that my engine would cut [due to the float-type carburettor fitted to the Merlin engine] whereas his was still going owing to his petrol injection system, he would draw away from me. Either that or he blacked out and didn't realise what was happening for a moment, for he flew on inverted for several seconds, giving me the chance to get in a good burst from the quarter. Half righting himself for a moment, he slowly dived down and disappeared into the clouds still upside down, looking very much out of control.

The sweat was pouring down my face and my oxygen mask was wet and sticky about my nose and mouth. I felt quite exhausted after the effort and my right arm ached from throwing the stick around the cockpit. At speed it needs quite a bit of exertion to move the stick quickly and coarsely in violent manoeuvres.

Afterwards, Lane would claim the enemy fighter 'probably destroyed'. This claim does not link with any known German loss, however, and no Me 109 came down on land within 20 miles of Dartford where the combat was reported to have taken place. As has been said, long manoeuvring combats were a rarity. More usually, fighter pilots engaging their enemy counterparts would follow the adage of 'get in fast, hit hard and get out'.

14

'THE INJUSTICE OF IT ALL'

By Bob Oxspring

On 25 October the Battle of Britain was in its closing stages, though at the time the participants had no way of knowing that this was the case. Bob Oxspring was a newly promoted flight lieutenant on No. 66 Squadron, then based at Gravesend. Soon after breakfast he was scrambled and ordered to take his Flight of six Spitfires to patrol over Maidstone at 30,000ft. The Luftwaffe had been putting in occasional fighter sweeps and fighter-bomber attacks during this period, and this was to be one of those attacks.

When we arrived over Maidstone there was nothing to be seen, however. From the ground we received orders to orbit and wait. It was nearly half an hour later that the 'bandits' did show up: six Messerschmitt 109s. For once we had a perfect set-up: we were up-sun, we had a 2,000ft drop on them and the numbers were exactly equal. It did not often turn out like that during the Battle of Britain.

I told my pilots to take one each, and down we went. But the Germans were wide awake and I watched my man, the leader, suddenly barrel round and pull his fighter into a steep dive. I had been half expecting it and I tore down after him almost vertically, gaining slowly but surely. I had him cold. It never occurred to me to watch my own tail – after all, we had covered all six Messerschmitts. Well, confidence is that nice warm feeling you have just before you slide over the banana skin. I was in range and just about to open fire when, suddenly, my Spitfire shuddered under the impact of a series of explosions. In fact, those six Messerschmitts had been covering a seventh, a decoy aircraft a couple of thousand feet beneath them; their idea had been to bounce any of our fighters having a go at it. And the German leader had taken me right in front of the decoy, who got in a good squirt at me as I went past.

He must have hit my elevator controls, because the next thing I knew my Spitfire was pulling uncontrollably into a tight loop; a loop so tight that the 'G' force squeezed me hard into my seat and I blacked out. As I went down the other side of the loop the aircraft straightened out and I could see again. But as the speed built up the jammed elevators again took effect and up I went into a second loop. Obviously the time had come for me to part company with that Spitfire. But first I had to get the hood open and that was not proving easy: the only time I could reach up and see to do it, was when the 'G' was off; but I was screaming downhill fast and the hood would not budge.

I thought my time had come and I remember thinking of the injustice of it all: hit just as I was about to blow that Messerschmitt out of the sky! I have no idea how many loops the Spitfire did before I was finally able to slide back the hood. But it was not a moment too soon, because the oil tank was on fire and flames were spreading back from the engine. I threw off my seat harness and stood up, but I found I could go no further because I still had my helmet on and it was attached firmly to the aircraft. By now I was getting pretty desperate and I wrenched the helmet off with all my strength.

The next thing I knew I was falling clear of my aircraft, head-down and on my back, at an angle of about 45 degrees. I had no idea how high I was, so I pulled the D-ring right away. I knew it was a mistake, as soon as I did it.

When the parachute began to deploy, I was in just about the worst possible position. I remember watching, an interested spectator, as the canopy and the rigging lines came streaming out from between my legs. One of the lines coiled round my leg, and when the canopy developed I found myself hanging upside down. I had never parachuted before, but from my sketchy instruction I was fairly certain that head-first was not the optimum position to be in when I hit the ground!

I grabbed a handful of slack rigging lines on the opposite side to my entangled leg, and started to climb up hand over hand. After a lot of kicking and pulling I managed to get my leg free. With a sigh of relief I sank back into my harness, right way up.

Now I had time to think about what was happening around me. The first thing that struck me was the quietness; the only sounds were the spasmodic bursts of cannon and machine-gun fire and the howls of the engines, coming from the battle still in progress high above: it seemed an age since I had been part of it. But my own troubles were not over yet.

Gradually it began to dawn on me that the straps leading up from my harness, instead of being comfortably clear of my head on either side, were tangled together and chafing my ears and face. And higher up the rigging lines were also tangled, preventing the canopy from developing to its fullest extent. That meant that I was falling much faster than I should have been; and struggle as I might, I could not get the lines untangled. I went down past a cloud and seemed to whizz by: it was not going to be a happy landing. It was the only time I ever needed to use a parachute, and this had to happen!

Gradually I got lower, and I could make out trees and farmhouses and curious faces raised skywards. At about 500ft the wind carried me across some high-tension cables and even though I was hundreds of feet above the wires I could not resist the instinct to lift my feet up. Still I was coming down much too fast. The one thing I needed most of all was a nice soft tree, to break my fall. And there in my line of drift, in answer to my prayers, was a wood full of them.

Just before I hit I covered my face with my arms and came to rest amid the crack of breaking twigs. When the noise stopped I cautiously lowered my arms, and looked around. My parachute canopy was draped across a couple of trees and I was bouncing up and down between the trunks like a yo-yo. I was about 20ft up, suspended above an asphalt road.

At about my level, just out of reach, was a small branch. By doing a sort of Tarzan stunt, swinging back and forth from side to side, I was able to get closer and closer until in the end I was able to grab hold of it. Gingerly I pulled myself up and on to a thicker bough, before letting go of my harness. By this time quite a crowd had begun to collect underneath the tree; and at first there seemed to be some doubt about my nationality. But the vehemence of my Anglo-Saxon demands for help soon satisfied everyone that I was, in fact, British. Some Home Guard men made a human ladder by sitting on each others' shoulders and with their aid I managed to clamber down to mother earth. It had indeed been a memorable day.

Pilot officer 'Bogle' Bodie of No. 66 Squadron had an enemy machine-gun round strike his laminated glass windscreen, without penetrating it, during one of the September battles.

15

FEEDING THE GUNS

Representing those who played an essential part in winning the Battle of Britain, yet who never left the ground, is Fred Tandy. An armourer, his task during the battle was to ensure that when a pilot had the enemy in his gun sight and pressed the firing button, the battery of guns performed the final act in the long chain of events between the order to take off and the destruction of an enemy. In this section he recounts the rearming of the Spitfire's eight Browning guns.

I joined No. 616 Squadron with Spitfire Mk Is at Leconfield in January 1940, as an aircraftman 1st class [AC1] straight out of training. We were young and very keen and whenever there was an aircraft available we used to practice rearming again and again to try to reduce the time needed. Initially it took a team of four armourers about twenty minutes to carry out this task. Then somebody worked out a way of using a canvas loop to pull the first round of the new ammunition belt through the breech of the gun; this was important, because it meant that we could now rearm the Spitfire without having to remove the top covers from the gun bays. As a result of continual practice, and with twelve covers to remove instead of the original twenty, we cut the original twenty-minute rearming time down by more than half.

By the start of the Battle of Britain, rearming had become a slick operation. As the Spitfire taxied in after its sortie, we armourers would be watching the canvas strips doped over the gun ports: if these had been blown off it meant the guns had been fired and rearming was necessary. If this was the case and the aircraft was required to fly again immediately, the team of armourers would be waiting at the dispersal area. Each man carried an ammunition box loaded with 300 rounds of .303 ammunition under each arm. During the battle it was usual to load two of the guns with armour-piercing ammunition, two with incendiary and four guns with ball ammunition. Four out of the last twenty-five rounds in each box of ball ammunition were tracer, to warn that he was nearly out.

Even before the propeller had stopped turning there would be two armourers under each wing, busily undoing the scores of half-turn Dzus fasteners securing the gun panels and the ammunition box covers. Once these covers were off, the next

Fred Tandy (right) pictured when serving as an armourer with No. 616 Squadron.

step was to have a quick look into the breech mechanism of each gun, to check that there had been no stoppage and that the gun was serviceable: if the breech block was stopped in the rear position, it meant that the pilot had ceased fire; if it was stopped in the forward position, it meant that he had not run out of ammunition; if there had been a stoppage, the breech would usually be in the forward position with a live round 'up the spout'.

Unless the gun was unserviceable, the breech mechanism would be pulled to the rear position if it was not there already, then the belts from the used ammunition boxes could be pulled clear, and the boxes themselves could be removed and placed on the ground out of the way. Now the guns were safe and one armourer on each side would start to swab out the gun barrels from the front, to clean away the crumbs of burnt cordite; for this he would use a cleaning rod, with first a piece of oily and then a piece of clean 'four-by-two' flannel. Meanwhile the second armourer in the pair would be clicking the full ammunition boxes into place from underneath the wing, and threading the canvas straps round the first round in each one through the feed ways. With a firm pull on each one in turn, he would bring the first round in each new box up against the feed stops. Then he would cock the gun using either a special wire cocking tool or, more usually, his forage cap. Cocking brought the first round out of the belt on to the face of the breech block and at the same time released the canvas loop which could then be pulled clear. The armourer

would look up into the gun from underneath to check that the round had actually fed on to the face of the breech block, then press the manual release to bring the block forwards to feed the round into the chamber: the rear-sear-retainer-keeper spring would hold the firing pin clear of the round, so there was no risk of the gun going off at this stage. But I would point out that it was considered very bad manners if you carried out this stage of the rearming process while the other fellow was still working on the gun barrel from the front!

Now the only essential task remaining was to re-fit the gun and ammunition box covers to the underside of the wing. If there was time before the next take-off we would dope pieces of fabric over the firing ports, to keep the heat in and prevent the guns freezing up at high altitude. To save time we sometimes used ordinary medical sticking plaster for this purpose. If the grass was wet, the Spitfire was notorious for throwing mud and water on to the undersides of the wings during the take-off run. To prevent this moisture getting into the gun bays via the link and cartridge case ejector slots, we would dope pieces of newspaper over them.

At the end of a day's fighting we would take the recoils out of the guns and clean them properly. Or, if the Spitfire had been stood down from immediate readiness to, say, thirty minutes, we would remove one recoil mechanism at a time for cleaning.

On the Spitfire our responsibilities as armourers did not end with the guns. Each morning we had to change

Nobody who worked on the Spitfires' Browning guns will ever forget the knuckle-rasping hand-slashing experience of having to feel one's way round the cramped gun bays with their sharp edges and numerous pieces of locking wire. The picture shows the Browning gun installation as seen from behind and the rear. The braided cable running underneath the gun carried high pressure air to fire the gun.

Armourers at Duxford rearming a Spitfire of No. 19 Squadron. The fabric patches covering the gun ports have been blown away, indicating that the guns had been fired. The armourers under the near wing have removed two of the used ammunition boxes and are in the process of removing the other two.

From the beginning of 1940 it was clear that British fighters needed a weapon with more punch than the 303in machine gun, if they were to remain effective. The weapon of choice was the French Hispano 20mm cannon, seen here in prototype form, to be fitted in place of all eight Browning machine guns. During the early stages of the Battle of Britain No. 19 Squadron was re-equipped with cannon-armed Spitfires. But initially the Hispano cannon proved so unreliable that it had to be withdrawn from front line service to allow its faults to be rectified.

the 'colours of the day' in the Plessey six-barrelled signal cartridge discharger. And each time the guns were fired we had to fit a new film magazine into the G42 cine-camera located in the port wing root. Finally, for security, we had to check the two 4in diameter parachute flares fitted in their long chutes just behind the cockpit; these were sometimes used during night flying.

In 1940 there was a tremendous sense of 'belonging' to one's fighter squadron. Three ground crewmen were allocated to each Spitfire: a fitter, a rigger and an armourer. It was a matter of great distress if anything happened to 'their' pilot, yet in spite of quite severe losses in pilots, morale was sky-high. At Kenley during the Battle of Britain we could see the combats being fought overhead; we could see the enemy aircraft being shot down and we knew that we on the ground had our own vital part to play in bringing this about. For a young lad of nineteen, they were stirring times.

The most vulnerable areas of enemy bombers were the fuel tanks. If one suffered damage the fuel might spill out and catch fire. Alternatively, the bomber might be left without sufficient fuel to regain friendly territory. Either way, the bomber was doomed. Yet time and again German twin-engined bombers proved able to absorb large numbers of hits from .303in machine gun rounds. On occasions bombers – like this Dornier 17 – returned from France with the scars from more than a hundred hits from .303in rounds, indicative of a series of attacks from short range. A major factor that assisted the bombers' survivability was the provision of self-sealing fuel tanks. The basic tanks were made of compressed cellulose fibre, with a wall thickness of 2mm. To that was added the self-sealing covering comprising an outer covering of 3mm-thick unvulcanised rubber, two layers of lightly vulcanised rubber, .5mm thick, and an outer covering of highly vulcanised rubber, .3mm thick. If a shell fragment or a rifle calibre bullet pierced the wall of the tank, the fuel would begin to leak out. But when the petrol came into contact with the tank's layers, it set up a chemical reaction with the unvulcanised rubber, which caused it to swell and seal off the hole.

PHOENIX RISING FROM THE ASHES

By the summer of 1940 the production of Spitfires was increasing by the week. That August a total of 163 of these fighters were issued from the Southampton factories at Woolston and Itchen, and the huge Castle Bromwich plant near Birmingham which had commenced production two months earlier.

Then, on 26 September, the Luftwaffe launched its long-expected blow against Spitfire production. On that day a force of fifty-nine Heinkel 111s of StG55 delivered devastatingly accurate attacks on the Supermarine factories at Woolston and Itchen. Both works were wrecked.

Yet although the factory buildings had suffered heavy damage, most of the all-important machine tools and production jigs had survived. Moreover, the final assembly hangars and airfield at Eastleigh were untouched. Lord Beaverbrook, the newly appointed Minister for Aircraft Production, inspected the damage and declared that the

The gutted remains of the Woolston factory building after the devastating Luftwaffe attack on 26 September 1940.

buildings were damaged beyond economical repair. He ordered that both factories be cleared of everything useful, and be abandoned. Instead, the production operation was to be divided into several smaller units that would be dispersed across surrounding area. Beaverbrook then requisitioned a floor of the Polygon Hotel in Southampton, and installed the Supermarine works manager, James Bird, and his staff to draw up plans for the dispersal operation. Len Gooch later described the process:

> My first action was to obtain large-scale Ordnance Survey maps of the counties of Wiltshire, Hampshire and Berkshire. From calculations made of existing areas of factories already in use and scaled up to meet the increased output, we prepared a plan whereby 25 per cent of the output was to be made in towns with aerodromes, namely the Southampton area using Eastleigh Airport, Salisbury using High Post and Chattis Hill aerodromes, Trowbridge using Keevil aerodrome and Reading using Henley.

In each of these towns he planned to set up wing and fuselage jigs, which were made into major assemblies ready for marrying together at the aerodromes. Thus the planners intended to set up four Spitfire production lines to replace the previous one. The detail and sub-assembly work was also sub-divided, and transferred to a large number of requisitioned premises in the areas around Southampton, Winchester, Newbury, Reading and Trowbridge. To provide the necessary building space, Gooch and his staff inspected large garages, laundries, bus stations and even a works producing steamrollers. In each place where they found what appeared to be suitable premises, they returned with a member of the police. The latter presented a letter of introduction from the chief constable, without mentioning Gooch by name or the reason for the visit. If the premises were required, Gooch reported

Newly built Spitfires awaiting flight testing and delivery at Chattis Hill Airfield near Winchester.

Dispersed production: Sewards Garage at Southampton, one of the requisitioned properties, seen from the outside and, below, from the inside.

this to the local government requisition officer. The requisition papers were then served on the not-so-happy owners.

As soon as the sites had been taken over, the necessary jigs and machine tools were brought in. During the six weeks that followed the attack, a total of thirty-five separate premises were taken over for Spitfire production. By the end of that period sixteen sites were already in production, and the remainder were about to begin.

During the dispersal period large numbers of parts and components, particularly those coming from sub-contractors, were diverted to Castle Bromwich and helped swell production there. Thus, despite the inevitable disruption to production, deliveries of Spitfires to the RAF held up remarkably well in the months following the attacks: September 156; October 149; November 139; and December 117. Overall, the bomb damage, coupled with the enforced dispersal of production, resulted in the loss of about ninety Spitfires to the end of the year. Yet at the end of the process, the Supermarine phoenix that arose from the ashes at Woolston and Itchen was far less vulnerable than it had been before. Furthermore, the Luftwaffe never again attempted to launch a large scale daylight attack on the sources of the troublesome Spitfires.

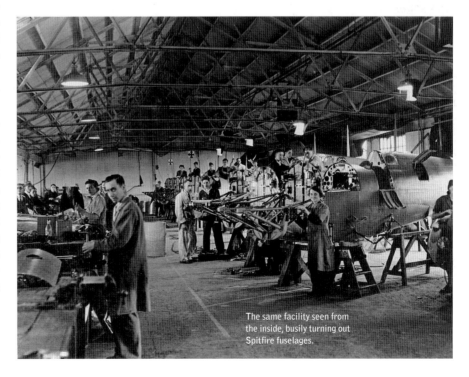

The same facility seen from the inside, busily turning out Spitfire fuselages.

Spitfire production in progress in one of the huge assembly halls at Castle Bromwich.

17

SKIRMISH OVER KENT

By the third week in December 1940 the hard-fought daylight actions of the Battle of Britain were at an end. Now air incursions by day over southern England were restricted mainly to lone reconnaissance aircraft trying to sneak through the defences to photograph targets. Flying fast, high and alone, these aircraft presented fleeting targets. To catch them the Spitfire squadrons had to expend a disproportionate effort, as can be seen from the attempt on the morning of 21 December 1940.

That morning there were blue skies over much of southern England as No. 64 Squadron, based at Hornchurch, received orders to send a dozen Spitfires to mount a standing patrol in the Maidstone area. One of the squadron's pilots, Pilot Officer Trevor Gray, later told the author:

After taking off from Hornchurch we flew to the so-called Maidstone patrol line which ran from Maidstone to the south coast. Once in position we patrolled at 15,000ft, the maximum we could sustain without using our limited supply of oxygen. Then it was a case of waiting for the enemy to come to us, but there was very little activity at this time.

Five minutes after Gray and his comrades took off, the No. 11 Group controller ordered a further dozen Spitfires, from No. 611 Squadron based at Southend, to join them on the patrol line. One fighter returned early with engine trouble, but the remaining twenty-three flew up and down the patrol line in separate formations, engines throttled back to conserve fuel. This was the position at 1109hrs, when Leutnant Helmut Fischer and his radio-operator, Unteroffizier Kurt Schaefer, of the 7th (Long Range Reconnaissance) Staffel of Lehrgeschwader (LG) 2 took off from Grimbergen, near Brussels, in their Messerschmitt 110 and headed for Southend. The clear skies over the south of England had been reported earlier in the day by German weather observation aircraft,

and indicated near-perfect conditions for high-altitude reconnaissance. Fischer's orders were to reconnoitre shipping in the Thames Estuary, then to photograph Detling airfield.

Oberleutnant Helmut Fischer, the 7th (Long Range Reconnaissance) Staffel of Lehrgeschwader 2.

Unusual photograph of Spitfires, taken by the vertical camera carried by a Bf 110 reconnaissance aircraft. It was taken during the high speed chase across Kent on the morning of 21 December 1940, and shows a gaggle of Spitfires, of either No. 64 or No. 611 Squadron, climbing to intercept the German reconnaissance aircraft. The aircraft were flying south-south-east, having just passed over Snodland near Chatham.

Stripped of armour and all its forward-firing armament except for two machine guns, the Messerschmitt rose swiftly to its penetration altitude of 33,000ft. Once there, Fischer levelled out and allowed his speed to build up to the maximum speed for continuous cruise, 350mph. The German aircraft quickly covered the 60-odd miles from the Belgian coast to Margate, where the crew observed a twenty-ship convoy in the estuary. Kurt Schaefer tapped out a coded message to report the find. The Messerschmitt continued up the Thames Estuary with Fischer and Schaefer systematically scanning the sky around them for any sign of enemy fighters trying to intercept the lone intruder. If the threat could be seen in time there was a good chance the Messerschmitt could outrun the opposition.

The intruder continued along the Thames Estuary to as far as Southend without interference, then it swung south to photograph Detling airfield. However, as luck would have it, Detling lay directly in the path of the Spitfires' patrol line. For some reason the Spitfire pilots had received no radio warning from the ground on the presence of the German aircraft in the area; the first they knew of it was when they saw the long white condensation trail high above. Trevor Gray takes up the story:

> We had been on patrol for some time when we noticed a condensation trail above us, heading south. Squadron Leader Don MacDonell, the squadron commander, led us after it. When he saw we were not gaining on it fast enough he ordered us to break formation – then we could go after it at the speed of the fastest Spitfire and rather than the slowest.

In each of the twenty-three Spitfires the pilot pushed his throttle 'through the gate' for emergency combat power and headed after the intruder at maximum climbing speed. The relatively tight cruising formations dissolved quickly, as the fastest aircraft in each squadron began to pull away from the slower ones.

By this time Kurt Schaefer had spotted the gaggles of Spitfires climbing to intercept, and started a running commentary on their relative positions. Fischer pushed his throttles wide open and headed south, trying to keep himself between the sun and the enemy fighters. In this way he hoped to present as difficult a target as possible, while setting up a lengthy high-speed chase which would run the single-engined fighters short of fuel before they could get into a firing position. Afterwards the German pilot reported:

By increasing revolutions on both engines to 2,500rpm and retracting the glycol radiators, I increased speed and at the same time gained more height. Meanwhile I saw two fighters break away from the formation and gain altitude rapidly. The radio operator gave me a running commentary of the altitude and range of the pursuing fighters. In a very short time (4–5 minutes) a couple of Spitfires reached a position about 150 metres above me and started the attack.

At the controls of the leading Spitfire was Trevor Gray, who managed to get 500yd behind the enemy aircraft. Unable to close the range further, he loosed off a series of bursts at long range. The fire was accurate and almost immediately the Messerschmitt's radio operator was mortally wounded. Other rounds smashed away part of the hydraulic system, the aircraft began to trail oil and the port undercarriage leg flopped out of its housing. Fischer hauled his aircraft round in an attempt to drive off the tormentor, but had to break away when another Spitfire swung into a threatening position behind him. With yet other enemy fighters nearing his altitude, it was obvious there was no future for Fischer where he was. He rolled the Messerschmitt on to its back and pulled it into a steep dive, to build up his speed rapidly. Then he rolled the wings level and continued for the coast in a high speed descent. Hard on his heels Trevor Gray followed, firing short busts whenever he had the enemy in his gun sight. This continued until the Spitfire's ammunition was exhausted, and it peeled away.

Now there were more than a dozen Spitfires in an extended stream edging towards the diving Messerschmitt, the fastest at the front of the queue and slowest at the rear. A total of five Spitfires were now edging their way towards the Messerschmitt, but now the latter had gained an unexpected ally.

During the rapid descent from the cold air at high altitude to air with a higher moisture content lower down, frost now began to form on the inside of the canopies and windscreens of several of the Spitfires.

Trevor Gray (left) and Helmut Fischer pictured in 1979, after having been brought together by the author.

After crossing the coast between Eastbourne and Bexhill, Fischer headed out to sea at full throttle, dodging in and out of the banks of haze which lay close to the surface. The high-speed chase continued for a few miles longer, before one by one the Spitfires were forced to break away as their fuel ran short. A number of the Spitfires landed at the forward landing grounds at Lymne, Hawkinge and Manston, but two more ran out of fuel and were wrecked when their pilots attempted to land on open fields.

For his part Helmut Fischer made his way towards the forward airfield at Mardyk near Dunkirk, and made a wheels-down landing. The Messerschmitt had collected thirty-two hits during the various attacks and the German pilot considered himself lucky to survive the encounter.

The action had an interesting sequel in 1979, when Helmut Fischer and Trevor Gray met for a second time. On this occasion, however, the German pilot was accorded a more cordial reception when he called with his wife at the Surrey home of his one-time opponent. The two men, who had fought each other thirty-nine years earlier, were able to speak as friends on the events of the past.

18

ACT OF CHIVALRY

At the beginning of 1941 the RAF began its campaign of mounting daylight attacks on targets in occupied Europe with light bombers and large forces of escorting fighters: Operation 'Circus'. Typical of the early operations of this type was Circus No. 5, launched on the afternoon of 26 February.

The target for Circus No. 5 was harbour installations at Calais, to be attacked by twelve Blenheims of No. 139 Squadron. The bombers crossed the French coast in formation at 17,000ft, their close escort comprising No. 1 Squadron's Hurricanes flying slightly above, No. 601 Squadron's Hurricanes a few thousand feet higher and No. 303 Squadron's Spitfires at 22,000ft. The high cover wing comprised three Spitfire squadrons: No. 74 at 24,000ft, and Nos 92 and 609 Squadrons at 26,000ft. It was hoped that this array of air power would be sufficient to deter the German fighter force from interfering with the operation. Some Messerschmitts were seen airborne,

After his capture Sergeant Howard Squire (centre right) was taken to the officers' mess at Calais/Marck Airfield and given a meal. He was then taken to see the remains of his Spitfire. Squire was the man without a hat, Herbert Ihlefeld on his immediate right.

but initially none made any serious attempt to engage. The bombers completed their attack without interference and they and their escorts withdrew without loss.

Twenty minutes behind the main formation came the Spitfires of Nos 54 and 64 Squadrons, briefed to carry out a sweep between Dover and Cap Gris Nez at 28,000ft and engage enemy fighters drawn up by the earlier incursion. This time there were some skirmishes with Messerschmitts, though no Spitfire pilot made any claim. However, one Spitfire of No. 54 Squadron, flown by Sgt Howard Squire, was shot down. This is his story of that day:

We were flying top cover, it was rather a hazy day and I saw nothing of the rest of the force or the coast of France. We were in two finger-fours – 'B' Flight in front led by Flight Lieutenant George Gribble and 'A' Flight behind led by Flight Officer Ray Charles. I was at the rear of 'A' Flight, flying wing to Flight Officer Chapman.

When we were roughly over the coast of France an aircraft suddenly flashed past my nose, in a steep dive from left to right. It came past so quickly I did not recognise the type. My first thought was that it might be a decoy, to lure us down after it. An aircraft on its own suddenly appearing like that would not have been a mistake; it was there for a purpose.

Nobody spoke on the radio, but suddenly Chapman peeled after the diving plane. That was a stupid thing to do and I hesitated briefly before following him – but my job was to guard his tail. The delay would be my undoing. Had I followed immediately, we would at least have kept together. But the delay put him that bit further in front of me, and almost immediately I lost sight of him against the haze. I continued down, looking for him.

Seeing no sign of his element leader, Squire levelled off and searched the sky above for the rest of the squadron. They, too, were nowhere to be seen. Feeling very much alone, he pulled his Spitfire round in a tight orbit to check for possible enemy fighters in the vicinity. Seeing none, and realising he could do little by himself, he decided to get out of the area as quickly as possible. He pushed his throttle 'through the gate' for maximum emergency power and headed north.

I had not gotten far when suddenly I saw red tracers streaking past my starboard side. Then there was an awful series of bangs as rounds struck my plane. In front of me the instruments in the blind flying panel disintegrated, and the wind came whistling through holes in my cockpit canopy. I looked around for my assailant but still I couldn't see where the attack was coming from. So I rolled the Spitfire on its back and pulled the stick hard into my stomach. The plane responded, there was no loss of control, but in my panic I pulled too hard and blacked out. I eased off on the stick and as the 'G' came off I was going down almost vertically into the haze – and with no altimeter to warn me how much height I had left!

Squire pulled out, he looked around for his attacker and again he saw nothing. His engine had obviously been hit, and was running very rough with a lot of vibration.

Again I turned back towards England, again tracers came past and again my Spitfire took hits. I did an aileron turn to shake off the attack, but although I searched the sky around I still could not see who was shooting at me. It was the classic case of a novice fighter failing to see what was happening around him.

To make matters worse, the Spitfire's engine began to lose power. Squire made yet another turn to search the sky around, and at last he caught sight of his enemy: eight Me 109s, four behind on his left and four on his right:

The Messerschmitts had me cornered. I turned out to sea and one of them fired a deliberate burst of tracer past my nose. Now I was convinced I was not going to get back to England, and made up my mind to crash-land wherever I could.

Herbert Ihlefeld and Howard Squire.

The Spitfire continued its descent towards the port of Calais. From 500ft Squire could see the long strip of sandy beach to the east of the town, and decided on a suitable piece of flat sand on which to set down his crippled fighter. His main flying instruments shot away, he had to fly 'by the seat of his pants'. He pulled down his goggles, slid back the canopy and braced himself for the crash-landing. As he neared the ground he throttled back, at which the engine stopped altogether.

I saw what looked like an area of fairly flat sand inland, and aimed for that. But on rounding out I saw to my horror that what had looked like an area of flat sand was in fact a series of sand dunes. As I neared the first I eased back on the stick and just clipped the top, which killed a lot of my speed. Then there was a noise like a lot of tin trays being bashed together as the Spitfire slid down the side of the dune into a patch of marshy ground. As the plane slithered to a halt foul black slime came squirting up into the cockpit, past my feet and over me.

Squire threw off his seat and parachute straps and clambered out of the cockpit, stepping off the wing into ankle-deep slime. To one side he could see figures running in his direction and

Howard Squire and
his captors, including
Herbert Ihlefeld, inspect
the remains of his
slime-spattered Spitfire
near Calais.

someone fired a shot that passed over his head. The young pilot crouched behind the tail of his plane and waited to see what happened next:

Suddenly several German soldiers arrived on the scene brandishing revolvers. I put my hands up initially but lowered them soon afterwards without anyone saying anything – it was pretty obvious I was not going anywhere!

The men, from an army artillery unit located nearby, took their captive to a bunker a few hundred yards away. There Squire asked for 'Wasser', one of the few German words he knew, and was brought a bowl of water, soap and a towel so he could clean the slime off his face and from the front of his uniform. Shortly afterwards a couple of Luftwaffe men arrived by car to collect him, one an Unteroffizier who spoke perfect England. They took the prisoner to the Officers' Mess at the fighter airfield at Calais-Marck, about four miles from the scene of the crash.

The escorts ushered Squire into the ante-room, where several officers were gathered. He was offered a chair, given a glass of schnapps and introduced to the pilot of the Messerschmitt Bf 109 that had shot him down: Hauptmann Herbert Ihlefeld, the commander of I/LG2 based at the airfield. A holder of the coveted Ritterkreuz, Ihlefeld had notched up twenty-five victories by the end of the Battle of Britain. So this was the hardened professional whose skilful flying in combat had made Squire feel a complete amateur!

Ihlefeld did not speak English, but most of the other officers did and one translated for him. He said he was very pleased he had been able to shoot down my plane without causing me serious injury. Then he nodded to the table and asked if I had expected such treatment. I said I had, because if we in the RAF had the opportunity we would do the same. Everybody smiled and one of the Germans commented 'Ah, we are all airmen here…'

After some more small-talk the intelligence officer quietly asked my squadron number. But when I refused to give it he shrugged his shoulders, grinned and said, 'Of course you don't tell me – you are a soldier, ja?' That was the end of the matter, nobody tried to ask military questions after that. I thought they might try to ply me with booze to get me to talk, but they didn't. Everyone was very correct and friendly.

Someone asked the prisoner if he was hungry and a steward brought a platter of garlic sausage sandwiches, and coffee. After he had eaten, Squire was asked if he had been hurt. During the crash-landing his left hand had taken a nasty knock and it was starting to feel tender. The British pilot mentioned this and was immediately driven back to Calais. There he received a full examination from a Luftwaffe doctor, who said the injury was not serious and would heal by itself (it later did).

From the surgery Squire was driven to one of the dispersal points at Calais-Marck, and was allowed to look round a Messerschmitt 109 from the outside. Then his captors offered to take him to have a final look at his Spitfire. Having had time to collect his thoughts after the traumatic experience earlier in the day, the British pilot realised he had omitted to carry out one important duty. The only really sensitive item of equipment in the Spitfire was the IFF set with its secret code settings. The equipment had a small destructor charge, which would fire if two plungers in the cockpit were pressed simultaneously. Now Squire's spirits rose: if only his captors would allow him to lean into the cockpit, he might be able to set off the destructor…

However, when Squire arrived at the Spitfire he found it swarming with the enemy soldiers and airmen, including Ihlefeld and several of the officers he had met at the airfield. Technicians had already removed several items of equipment, from the aircraft including the all-important IFF set. He was too late to carry out his plan.

From the crash site Squire was driven back to Calais-Marck, where soon after his arrival he heard an animated discussion begin in German. Officers had arrived there from a nearby flak unit, claiming that it was they who had shot down the Spitfire. A few words from the captive settled the matter in Ihlefeld's favour.

Following more drinks, a staff car arrived to collect the prisoner. After friendly handshakes all round and farewells, Howard Squire set out to begin a captivity that would last more than four years.

Herbert Ihlefeld would continue to build his victory score, and would end the war credited with 140 victories. In July 1984, after being contacted by Winston Ramsey, the editor of *After the Battle* magazine, the German fighter ace returned to Calais to resume his acquaintance with the Spitfire pilot he had shot down forty-three years earlier. It was a fitting end to the story of chivalrous treatment afforded by an airman to a vanquished foe.

SPITFIRE RECONNAISSANCE PILOT

In December 1940, having completed his flying training, Pilot Officer Gordon Green was posted to the Photographic Reconnaissance Unit at Heston and then Benson. Six weeks and fourteen flying hours later, he was pronounced operational as a Spitfire PR pilot.

The technique of high-altitude photography from a single-seat aircraft like the Spitfire was largely a question of experience, for a great deal depended on being able to judge where the cameras were pointing. One flew alone to the general area of the target, then tipped the aircraft on its side to check one was properly lined up. Once that was done it was a question of holding the aircraft dead straight and level for the photographic run. Until one learned the art it was all too easy – if, for example, one had a bit of a bank on – to come back with a lovely line of photographs of the ground a couple of miles to one side of the intended target.

Early in February 1941 I was one of four pilots of 'A' Flight of the PRU detached to St Eval in Cornwall. We were to keep watch on the French west coast ports: Brest, St-Nazaire, Lorient, La Pallice, La Rochelle and Bordeaux. On the 13th I flew my first mission to St-Nazaire, at high altitude in a Type C, and photographed the target successfully. During the week that followed I flew three other high-altitude sorties, only one of which was successful. Cloud was (and still is) a continual problem for the photographic reconnaissance pilot. During my time on the PRU well over half the sorties flown failed to bring back photos of the targets. On 21 February I flew a Type G to Brest for a low-altitude sortie but that was not successful either. Pilots took it in turns to fly high sorties in the blue-painted Type Cs or low-altitude ones in pink Type Gs. By 20 March I had flown five high-altitude and two low-altitude sorties to the French ports, of which four of the former and none of the latter were successful.

During those early missions there was no such thing as cockpit heating in our Spitfires. For the high-altitude missions we wore thick suits with electrical heating. Trussed up in our Mae West and parachute, one could scarcely move in the narrow cockpit of the Spitfire. While flying over enemy territory one had to be searching the sky the whole time for enemy fighters. On more than one occasion I started violent evasive action to shake off a suspected enemy fighter, only to discover that it was a small speck of dirt on my Perspex canopy!

A big worry over enemy territory was that one might start leaving a condensation trail without knowing it, thus pointing

A reconnaissance Spitfire pictured in her element, flying alone and high above the earth. If the weather conditions permitted, when over enemy territory, reconnaissance pilots preferred to fly in the thin layer of sky where condensation trails form. In that way they could expect a little extra warning of the approach of enemy moving in to engage them from above.

out one's position to the enemy. To avoid that we had small mirrors fitted in the blisters on each side of the canopy, so that one could see the trail as soon as it started to form. When that happened one would either climb or descend until the trail ceased. If possible, we liked to climb above the trail's layer because then fighters trying to intercept us had first to climb through the trail's layer themselves and could be seen in good time. But on most occasions the trail's layer extended above the ceiling of the early reconnaissance Spitfires.

During the final week of March 1941 we had a great panic at St Eval: the German battle cruisers *Scharnhorst* and *Gneisenau* had been out in the Atlantic and it was thought they had put into one of the French ports. Unfortunately, however, at that time the weather was very bad and we were unable to get photographs of the ports to prove or disprove this. Then on the 28th I went out at high altitude to try to photograph Brest. I arrived overhead to find that, as usual, it was covered in cloud. But there were a few clear patches about so I decided to hold off in case one of the gaps drifted over the port. It happened after a wait of about twenty-five minutes, and I ran over the top and took my photographs. From 30,000ft all one could see was the town and the seafront,

Above: Classic low-altitude oblique reconnaissance photo taken from Spitfires. 'Into the valley of the shadow of death...' Here the German heavy cruiser *Admiral Hipper* is seen in dry dock at Brest, taken by Pilot Officer J. Chandler in January 1941.

Right: Flight Lieutenant
Tony Hill, a brave
and resourceful
reconnaissance pilot,
was killed in October
1942 in the course of
a low-altitude 'dicing'
mission.

Opposite page:
Well-known photograph
of the Wuerzburg
radar at Bruneval
near Le Havre, taken
in December 1941 by
Flight Lieutenant Tony
Hill. This photo led to
a commando operation
to capture the radar
and bring parts of it to
Britain for examination.

Below: The Spitfire
PR 1C was the main
workhorse of the PRU
during 1940 and 1941.
It carried its two 8in
focal length cameras
under the starboard wing
in a flattened blister
hinged at the front,
counterbalanced by a
30gal tank in a blister
under the port wing.

it was impossible to make out any detail or tell what warships, if any, were in port. Only after my return to St Eval, when the photo interpreters had seen my photos, did I learn that the two German battle cruisers were tied up in the port.

Two days later, on 7 April, I went out at low altitude in the same aircraft and on that occasion I was able to sneak in and photograph the port from 1,500ft, without too much trouble from the defences.

During those early missions to cover Brest we lost about five pilots fairly quickly. After the first couple had failed to return the flight commander, Flight Lieutenant Keith Arnold, asked Benson to send some reserve pilots and they duly arrived. They both took off for Brest the evening they arrived, and neither came back. It was a very sobering incident. We had the advantage of knowing just what it could be like over Brest and, most important of all, we knew when things were going wrong and when we had to turn back if we were to survive. Every German in the area knew roughly when we were coming so it needed all the cunning we could muster – approaching from a different direction each time – plus a large share of luck if one was to come through.

For the remainder of April I flew a total of eleven high-altitude and eight low-altitude missions to Brest, of which only three of the high altitude missions were successful. Then, early in May,

I returned to Benson and for the next three months flew the more normal types of reconnaissance mission at high altitude to the Channel ports and over Germany.

Looking back at my time with the PRU, I get a lot of satisfaction from the knowledge that although I played my part in the war, I never fired a shot in anger. In one sense we in the reconnaissance business had things easy. All the time it was impressed on us: bring back the photographs and, if you can't, bring back the aeroplane. An infantryman taking part in the Battle of Alamein could not suddenly decide 'This is ridiculous, I'm going home!' He just had to go on. But if we thought we had lost the element of surprise, we were not only permitted to turn back, we were expected to do so.

Right: Another coup by Tony Hill: this photograph, taken in May 1942, depicts the Giant Wuerzburg night fighter control radar at Domburg on the Dutch island of Walcheren. The man standing beside the radar gave the scale of the apparatus when the photos were analysed.

On the other hand, there were times when I knew real fear. When one was fifteen minutes out from Brest on a low-altitude sortie, one's heart was beating away and as the target got nearer one's mouth got completely dry. Anyone who was not frightened at the thought of going in to photograph one of the most heavily defended targets in Europe was not human. Whenever it was possible to see a target to photograph it, the flak could engage us: if we could see to photograph, they could see to open up at us. But throughout my time as a reconnaissance pilot my luck held. I never once saw an enemy fighter, nor was my aircraft ever hit by flak. Indeed only once during the time we were flying those missions over Brest did one of our aircraft come back with any damage, and that was only minor. It was all rather like a fox hunt – either the fox got away unscathed or else it was caught and killed. There was rarely anything in between.

Soon after the withdrawal from France, the first Spitfire PR IF joined the unit. This carried a 30gal blister tank under each wing and a 29gal tank in the fuselage, and it carried two vertical cameras mounted behind the cockpit. With 89gal of extra fuel compared with the fighter version, the PR IF gave a very useful increase in range and was able to photograph targets as far away as Berlin, taking off from airfields in East Anglia. In the months to follow the remaining PR IC variants converted to PR IF standard.

The PR IF was a great advance in range performance, but Supermarine engineers saw the converted fighter could do even better. By redesigning the internal structure of fighter's wing, the whole of the leading edge could house a large integral fuel tank holding a total of 114gal. This was a more difficult modification to embody than the other reconnaissance versions, and the work took correspondingly longer. The newer variant, designated the PR ID, carried an additional 29gal fuel tank in the rear fuselage. That gave the aircraft a total internal fuel capacity of 228gal, two and a half times greater than that of the Mark I fighter. The additional fuel tankage gave a dramatic increase in the radius of action of the reconnaissance Spitfire. It also gave rise to the unusual spectacle of Spitfires being refuelled almost at the wing tip. On 29 October 1940 a PR ID photographed the port of Stettin on the Baltic (now Szczecin in Poland) and returned after five hours and twenty minutes airborne. Other remarkable missions followed in rapid succession: to Marseilles and Toulon in the south of France, and to Trondheim in Norway.

Vertical photography from high altitude was the most used method to cover large areas or cities on clear days, but a separate technique was needed to take close-up oblique photos of small targets or if there was a layer of cloud cover. The final reconnaissance variant based on the Spitfire Mark I was the Type G, optimised for the low-altitude photographic role. This version retained the fighter's normal armament of eight .303in machine guns, to provide a self-defence capability if it encountered enemy fighters. The PR IG carried a 29gal fuel tank behind the pilot to give it a small increase in range. The camera installation in the rear fuselage comprised one obliquely mounted camera pointing at right angles to the direction of flight, and a 14in and a 5in lens camera both mounted vertically. The majority of PR IGs were painted overall in a very pale shade of pink, barely off-white (to see that colour, look at the cloud base on an overcast day).

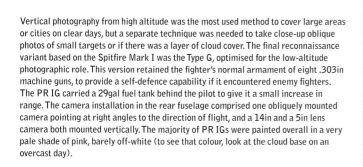

A FAIR DAY'S WORK

In July 1941 No. 1 PRU was a squadron-sized unit, with its main base at Benson near Oxford and with a detached flight at St Eval in Cornwall. Listed below are the missions flown on one day of that month, 17 July, by the unit's Spitfires. Beside the serial number of each aircraft is the letter denoting the version of reconnaissance Spitfire employed. Unless otherwise stated, all the missions were flown at high altitude.

During that day the unit's eleven serviceable Spitfires flew twenty sorties and all the aircraft returned safely. Three versions of reconnaissance Spitfire were flown by the unit: the PR IC (nine sorties flown), the PR IF (eight sorties) and the PR IG (three sorties).

The PR IG version was used for short-range, low-altitude 'dicing' missions. The two longest sorties, to Kiel in the morning and to Limoges in the afternoon, were both flown by PR IF serial X4491. This aircraft spent a total of nine hours and five minutes airborne that day, a remarkable figure.

The above section illustrates the wealth of intelligence on enemy dispositions that could be collected in a single day by just one squadron-sized reconnaissance unit.

Serial/Version	Take-off (hrs)	Time	Airborne Targets
X4494/F	0700	1.30	Brest (from St Eval)
X4491/F	0855	4.20	Kiel–Brunsbuttel–Cuxhaven
X4384/F	0915	2.25	Brest. Took off from Benson, landed at St Eval
R6900/C	0930	3.05	Airfields: Aachen, Coblenz, Dusseldorf
X4672/G	0930	2.10	Airfields: Abbeville-Amiens area (low altitude)
X4497/C	0950	3.55	Kastrup–Copenhagen
X4333/C	0950	3.05	Valenciennes–Hazebrook–Vimy–Arras
X4334/C	0950	3.00	Airfields in south-east Belgium
P9550/C	0957	4.03	Hamburg–Bremen–Emden–Delfzijl
X4492/F	0958	3.12	Amsterdam–IJmuiden
X4491/F	1400	4.45	Montlucon–Limoges
X4672/G	1400	2.00	Cap Barfleur–Dieppe (low altitude)
R6900/C	1405	2.20	Flushing, airfields in Ghent–Bruges area
X4334/C	1350	2.50	Airfields east of Paris
X4492/F	1525	2.50	Airfields in Orleans–Etaples area
P9550/C	1630	2.15	Caen–Falaise area
X4384/F	1815	1.30	Guernsey–St Malo–Rennes–Brest (from St Eval)
R7059/G	1830	2.00	Brest (from St Eval) (low altitude)
P9550/C	1915	1.15	Cherbourg
X4384/F	2020	1.15	Brest (from St Eval)

OUTCLASSED

War is no respecter of reputations. If one side introduces a much-improved new aircraft then a position of air superiority can be translated into one of air inferiority in a matter of weeks. This is what happened to RAF Fighter Command in the autumn of 1941, when the German fighter Gruppen based in France re-equipped with the new Focke Wulf Fw 190.

In June 1942 the RAF secured an airworthy example of the new German fighter and within days of its capture it underwent detained trials pitted against each of the Allied fighters it was likely to meet in action. Reproduced below are excerpts from the report by the Air Fighting Development Unit on the trial of the Fw 190 against the Spitfire Mk V. It illustrates in the starkest terms the measure of the inferiority

The captured Focke Wulf Fw 190, seen in the marking of its new owners.

of Fighter Command's principal fighter type during the third year of the war.

The Fw 190 was compared with a Spitfire VB from an operational squadron for speed and all-round manoeuvrability at heights up to 25,000ft. The Fw 190 was superior in speed at all heights, and the approximate differences are listed as follows:

SPEED
At 1,000ft the Fw 190 is 25–30mph faster than the Spitfire VB.
At 3,000ft the Fw 190 is 30–35mph faster than the Spitfire VB.
At 5,000ft the Fw 190 is 25mph faster than the Spitfire VB.
At 9,000ft the Fw 190 is 25–30mph faster than the Spitfire VB.
At 15,000ft the Fw 190 is 20mph faster than the Spitfire VB.
At 18,000ft the Fw 190 is 20mph faster than the Spitfire VB.
At 21,000ft the Fw 190 is 25mph faster than the Spitfire VB.
At 25,000ft the Fw 190 is 20–25mph faster than the Spitfire VB.

CLIMB
The climb of the Fw 190 is superior to that of the Spitfire VB at all heights. The best speeds for climbing are approximately the same, but the climb angle of the Fw 190 is considerably steeper. Under maximum continuous climbing conditions the climb of the Fw 190 is about 450ft/min better up to 25,000ft.

With both aircraft flying at high cruising speed and then pulling up into a climb, the superior climb of the Fw 190 is even more marked. When both aircraft are pulled up into a climb from a dive, the Fw 190 draws away very rapidly and the pilot of the Spitfire has no hope of catching it.

DIVE
Comparative dives between the two aircraft have shown that the Fw 190 can leave the Spitfire with ease, particularly during the initial stages.

MANOEUVRABILITY
The manoeuvrability of the Fw 190 is better than that of the Spitfire VB except in turning circles. If on the other hand the Spitfire was flying at maximum continuous cruising and was 'bounced' under the same conditions, it had a reasonable chance of avoiding being caught by opening the throttle and going into a shallow dive, provided the Fw 190 was seen in time. This forced the Fw 190 into a stern chase and although it eventually caught the Spitfire, it took some time and as a result was drawn a considerable distance away from its base. This is a particularly useful method of evasion for the Spitfire if it is 'bounced' when returning from a sweep. This manoeuvre has been carried out during recent operations and has been successful on several occasions.

If the Spitfire VB is 'bounced' it is thought unwise to evade by diving steeply, as the Fw 190 will have little difficulty in catching up owing to its superiority in the dive.

The above trials have shown that the Spitfire VB must cruise at high speed when in an area where enemy fighters can be expected. It will then, in addition to lessening the chances of being successfully 'bounced', have a better chance of catching the Fw 190, particularly if it has the advantage of surprise.

22

PRODUCTION TEST PILOT, ALEX HENSHAW MBE

Those fortunate enough to have watched Alex Henshaw display a Spitfire still talk about it, for he was an acknowledged virtuoso in the art of aerobatics in this aircraft. During his six years as a production and development test pilot he came to know the Spitfire as few others can have done – which is not surprising, considering he personally tested more than one in ten of all those built.

I learned to fly at my own expense, at the age of twenty, and in the years that followed, flying occupied most of my spare time. During the 1930s a skilful and resourceful civilian pilot with money or suitable sponsors could make a name for himself in aviation. I became enthusiastic about competition flying and enjoyed a run of successes culminating in my winning the King's Cup in 1938. In the following year I took the records for the flight from London to Cape Town and the return.

Alex Henshaw, second from right, and other works pilots walk out to test fly another batch of Spitfires.

Prime Minister Winston Churchill chatting to Alex Henshaw, when he visited the Castle Bromwich works.

When war came I accepted a job with Vickers as a test pilot. After testing Wellingtons at Weybridge, and Spitfires and Walruses at Southampton, in the summer of 1940 I became chief test pilot at the new Spitfire factory at Castle Bromwich. During the years that followed I was responsible, in addition, for flight testing the Spitfires built at Cosford and Desford, the Seafires at South Marsden and the repaired aircraft at Cowley. I remained at this work until 1946, by which time I had flown a total of 2,360 different Spitfires and Seafires – more than one in ten of all of those built.

As a production test pilot, one's task is really that of flight inspector. One has to satisfy oneself that everything works as it should and that the aircraft behaves as it should and as it was designed to. Unless there was some unforeseen snag, the flight test procedure for the Spitfire was straightforward. The procedure differed somewhat from mark to mark, so in this description I shall confine myself to that for the Mark V.

After a thorough pre-flight check I would take off and, once at circuit height, I would trim the aircraft and try to get her to fly straight-and-level with hands off the stick. The Mark V lacked aileron trim tabs and most of the new ones had a tendency to fly with one wing low. When that happened I would land immediately and taxi to one corner of the airfield, where a mechanic would be waiting. He carried a special tool

rather like a tuning fork, and on my instruction he would bend the trailing edge of the aileron on his side once, twice or thrice, up or down. Then he would go round to the other side, and similarly bend the opposite aileron in the other direction. That done I would take off again and trim the aircraft to fly hands-off, to see whether the wing dropping had been cleared; usually it had, but if it had not the process was repeated until the trim was acceptable. Sometimes, if bending alone was not sufficient, it was necessary to change the ailerons. It was a Heath Robinson system, but it worked.

Once the trim was satisfactory, I would take the Spitfire up in a full-throttle climb at 2,850rpm to the rated altitude of the supercharger blower. Then I would make a careful check of the power output from the engine, calibrated for height and temperature. Many factors could give a false reading: a leaking boost gauge line, a high ambient temperature, a faulty calibration of the rev-counter, or even an incorrectly set-up altimeter. If all appeared satisfactory, I would then put her into a dive at full power and 3,000rpm, and trim her to fly hands-off and feet-off at 460mph IAS [Indicated Airspeed). Unless this was all right, adjustments would be necessary to the elevator trim; or slight dressing down might be needed to the trailing edge of the tailplane. Personally, I never cleared a Spitfire unless I had carried out a few aerobatic manoeuvres to determine how good or how bad she was; but the extent of this depended upon how tired or how rushed we were at the time.

The production test was usually quite a brisk affair: the initial circuit lasted less than ten minutes and the main flight took between twenty and thirty minutes. Then the aircraft received a final once-over by our ground mechanics, any faults were rectified, and the Spitfire was ready for collection. Sometimes I would make more than twenty such test flights in a single day, necessary if previous bad weather had stopped flying and, with the production line going at full blast, the number of aircraft awaiting testing began to mount.

As I have said, unless there was some unforeseen snag the flight test procedure was usually straightforward. But we did get the odd problem that gave us a lot of worry before we could get it sorted out. For example, there was one Spitfire which had been returned to us with a report that she behaved all right at normal speeds, but in high-speed dives she vibrated to such an extent that it seemed about to break up; a complete wing change had been suggested. We at Castle Bromwich treated the report with some reserve; besides, a wing change was a major job and we wanted to be sure that the fault could not be cleared by less drastic measures. However, when two of my experienced test pilots confirmed the seriousness of the vibration (one had even prepared to bale out), I knew we had to take the report seriously. I took the Spitfire up and, as everyone had said, at normal speeds every dial and gauge read correctly and her performance was average for the mark. I did some mild aerobatics and still everything seemed to be normal. So I stepped up the aerobatics, and as I dived preparatory to some vertical rolls there was a sudden bang like an explosion. There was a terrible row and the Spitfire seemed to vibrate so violently that I hastily prepared to bale out. I pulled out of the dive and then, as suddenly as it had begun, the staccato noise and vibration ceased. It was all very mysterious.

I flew around for a while mulling over the matter, and finally decided to do a series of dives from high level and take down some figures, so far as I was able. I prepared myself for a possible break-up. At about 430mph in the first such dive the vibration set in again and I had to brace myself against the cockpit to take the figures I wanted. As I did so I found that I could read all the gauges quite easily; the readings were all normal. Gradually it dawned on me that while there was some vibration, the worst part of the problem was the staccato sound; and while the latter was certainly disturbing to the pilot, it appeared to be quite harmless to the machine. Momentarily I took my hands off the controls and pressed them over the ear pads of my flying helmet to damp out the sound; to my surprise and intense relief, the Spitfire seemed to be behaving like any other at that speed. I felt that I now had the key to the problem. But where was the noise coming from? I climbed the Spitfire again and took her into a third

dive, and this time I felt all round the cockpit and thought I could feel a hard persistent hammering near the engine. I was, however, sure that the banging had nothing to do with the engine or the airscrew, for these had been changed earlier without curing the problem. It seemed to be coming from the engine bulkhead – or perhaps the main petrol tank. Then it came to me with such simplicity and suddenness that I couldn't resist shouting at myself for being such a bloody fool and not guessing the reason earlier.

The top of the upper petrol tank had a thick outer covering of hard rubber self-sealer, and above it was a heavy piece of bullet-proof plating. If the self-sealer had become partially detached, as the speed built up it would flap vigorously between the armour plating and the nearly-empty fuel tank; and if that happened it would almost certainly give rise to the sort of kettle-drumming noise we had experienced. I immediately landed and had the tank top-cover removed. Sure enough, the self-sealer had come adrift. With a new fuel tank fitted, she proved to be a perfectly ordinary Spitfire.

I loved the Spitfire, in every one of her many versions. But it has to be admitted that the later marks did not handle quite so nicely as the earlier ones had done. One test of manoeuvrability was to throw her into a flick roll, and see how many times she rolled. With a Mark II or a Mark V one got two and a half flick rolls, but the later Mark IX was heavier and you only got one and a half; with the later and still heavier marks one got even less. Similarly, with the earlier versions one could take off and go straight into a half loop and roll off the top, but the later Spitfires were much too heavy for that. The essence of aircraft design is compromise and an improvement at one end of the performance envelope is rarely obtained without deterioration somewhere else.

23

SPITFIRE NIGHT FIGHTERS

In August 1941 Sergeant Peter Durnford joined No. 111 Squadron at North Weald flying Spitfire Vs, having come straight from training. He quickly became operational and took part in several convoy patrols and fighter sweeps over occupied Europe. At the beginning of November the squadron was ordered to move to Debden and, with the similarly painted No. 65 Squadron, began night-flying training sorties.

When night flying was taking place at Debden, the grass runway was marked on one side by a line of 'Glim' lamps (battery-powered portable lights). Getting airborne at night in a Spitfire was simple enough, Durnford recalled, provided the pilot learned to ignore certain distractions:

> You had to take off with the hood open, or as you went past the Glim lights their light reflected off the canopy and seemed to flash all over the place. But when you opened the throttle with the hood open a stream of exhaust sparks would swirl into the cockpit during take-off (that also happened when you took off by day with the canopy open, but then of course we you never noticed them). Initially we had a lot of glare from the circular exhaust stubs, too. The only thing to do was get airborne quickly, then throttle back and close the canopy. It was one of those things you had to get used to.

Sergeant Peter Durnford of No. 111 Squadron, pictured in the cockpit of his all-black Spitfire.

The only item of self-contained navigation equipment carried by the Spitfire was the compass. To return to Debden at the end of the sortie, pilots had to rely on VHF radio bearings and homing signals from base.

Once near the airfield you could locate the Chance light, flashing the code of the day. Knowing where it was placed (it was in a different position each night), you could then position yourself for a curved approach, and pick up the glide path indicator and the Glim lamps during the last stage of the descent.

In the Spitfire a long, straight-in, engine-on approach was difficult at night because the engine cowling blocked the view ahead and you couldn't see the runway lights. You had to make a curved approach to keep the runway in sight.

In December, No. 111 Squadron returned to North Weald for a few days, before on 23 December the unit received orders to go back to Debden. On arrival the unit's pilots learned that, with No. 65 Squadron, they were now to operate in the night-fighter role. The concern was that the Luftwaffe might resume large-scale night attacks on Britain at any time, and the two squadrons would provide a useful and additional night interception capability.

With the two squadrons established in the new role, their Spitfires were repainted in matt black overall. National markings and squadron codes were retained on the fuselage and fin, but those above and below the wings were painted over. The ground crews fitted 'fishtail' exhausts, to reduce exhaust glare during night flying.

On Christmas Eve 1941 Peter Durnford flew a one-hour and ten-minute night sector reconnaissance patrol over East Anglia. From then on the two squadrons flew patrols on nearly every evening the weather allowed.

If German bombers resumed night attacks, the two Spitfire squadrons were to employ the 'Smack' interception procedure while working in conjunction with radar-laid searchlights. When enemy aircraft were detected approaching the coast, the sector controller was to order the fighters to scramble. The Spitfires were to take off individually and climb to a pre-briefed altitude, each making for its patrol area marked by a single vertical searchlight beam. On arrival, the Spitfire was to orbit near the beam and wait. When an enemy aircraft neared the area the searchlight beam would waver for a short time, then depress to 20 degrees, pointing in the direction in which the fighter was to head.

> We would fly along the beam until another searchlight came on, pointing vertically upwards. Then it would waggle and point in the next direction we were to go. When we got close to the intruder we were to get a radio call 'Cone!', and several searchlights would switch on and cone the target with their beams. Once we had the target in sight we were to engage it.

Although the two Spitfire squadrons regularly practised the 'Smack' interception procedure, for some reason they were not allowed to test them against a friendly aircraft; the first time the pilots flew the full procedure would be against a real enemy.

In the event the Spitfires were never put to the test, however, for the expected enemy attacks failed to materialise. The final part of December 1941, January 1942 and the first eleven days of February 1942 proved particularly quiet over Britain. The Spitfire pilots never got so much as a glimpse of an enemy plane at night. The night operations continued until 12 February, when there was excitement from a quite different quarter. The battle cruisers *Scharnhorst* and *Gneisenau*, and the cruiser *Prinz Eugen*, escorted by several smaller warships and almost every German fighter in the area, were forcing a passage through the English Channel on their way back to Germany.

> We had been on readiness during the night, sleeping in the dispersal hut. There was some local flying in the morning, then we knocked off. Suddenly we were called back to readiness. The wing commander flying dashed into the briefing room and said: 'The German fleet is coming through the Channel, follow me!'
>
> He took off and we followed. We were supposed to rendezvous with the Spitfire squadrons from North Weald,

Peter Durnford's Spitfire JU-H pictured at Debden in December 1941. The aircraft was painted matt black overall, without roundels on the wings. The aircraft retained its regular fuselage and tail markings, and toned down identification letters, however.

> but the weather was terrible and we missed them. We went out over the sea, and the next thing I knew we had run into a whole lot of 109s. There was a terrific low-level scrap and our squadron was split up. I fired on a 109 and saw strikes around the cockpit, it rolled on its back and went down. Due to the very low height, 100ft or so, it must have gone in (I was later awarded a 'Probable').
>
> Then I passed over some ships which threw a lot of flak at me and my No. 2. We got separated and in the end I decided to go home, I was getting short of fuel. Visibility was poor and I had a job finding somewhere to land. In the end I put down at North Weald and just as I landed the prop stopped. I had run out of fuel, after two hours and ten minutes airborne.

Following the passage of the German warships through the English Channel, the two squadrons ceased night operations and a few weeks later their Spitfires were repainted in normal day-fighter colours. Summing up the Spitfire night-fighter operations, Peter Durnford commented:

> It has been said the Spitfire was not suitable for the night interception role. Personally, I think the suitability of the aircraft really depended on the suitability of the pilot. I enjoyed night flying and I never had any problems. I was fairly confident we could have intercepted enemy planes using the 'Smack' procedure. But some pilots had a twitch about flying at night, for them everything was wrong. As they said 'Only birds and fools fly, and birds don't fly at night'.

SORTING OUT A ROGUE

Small defects in an airframe, defects not readily apparent to the eye, can cause unusual handling characteristics in the air. When that happened to Spitfires, and all the normal cures had been tried and had failed, the experts at Boscombe Down were called in to try and find out what was wrong. This report, written early in 1941, illustrates how they cured the poor handling characteristics found on Spitfire P7525. However, even before it began to be circulated it had ceased to be of relevant interest so far as P7525 was concerned: almost immediately after the Spitfire had been put right and returned to No. 66 Squadron, she was written off in a crash after running out of fuel in bad weather.

1.0 INTRODUCTION

Complaints were made by No. 66 Squadron that the handling qualities of this aeroplane, which was representative of others in the Squadron, were bad because in spite of full forward trim the aeroplane could not be dived to more than 320mph IAS. Also, it was very left-wing low in the dive and there was insufficient rudder bias to prevent it from yawing to the left. There was a considerable amount of aileron snatch which was also a subject of complaint.

2.0 TESTS CARRIED OUT

2.1 The aeroplane was flown as received and the squadron's criticisms confirmed. It was check weighed and the centre of gravity determined; also the range of trimmer movement was checked. These measurements confirmed that the aeroplane was a normal Spitfire II so far as these points were concerned. Examination of the fin and tailplane trailing edges showed that they were swept up sufficiently to spoil the flow over the rudder and elevator and the respective trimmers. The attached photograph shows this clearly.

2.2 The trailing edges of the fin and tail plane were dressed down until the sweep up was removed. In addition, the 8in and 6in lengths of under standard-size trimming cord doped to the upper port and lower starboard aileron trailing edges respectively were removed and a single 10in length of full-size cord was doped to the upper trailing edge of the port aileron. A certain amount of the backlash present in the aileron circuit was absorbed by tightening the cables, but the remainder could not be eliminated readily because it was due to a little slackness in the hinge pins.

2.3 After these alterations the aeroplane was flown to check the handling and diving qualities. It was trimmed for full-throttle level flight, the elevator trimmer indicator then being at the normal setting of 1½ to 1¼ divisions nose down and dived up to the limiting speed of 460mph IAS. No abnormal forward pressure was required on the control column and neither yaw nor wing dropping was experienced in the dive when the normal amount of starboard bias was used. The ailerons were found to be slightly overbalanced, until at about 440mph IAS the overbalancing and snatching became disconcerting. This snatching was very apparent in tight turns and to a lesser degree when pulling out of the dives.

3.0 CONCLUSIONS

3.1 The modifications carried out on the aeroplane restored its handling qualities to normal and made it representative of other Spitfire Mk IIs, with the exception of the aileron control.

3.2 The trailing edges of all fin and tailplane surfaces of Spitfire aeroplanes should be carefully inspected to ensure that the contours are not distorted.

3.3 Aileron hinge pins should have just sufficient clearance to eliminate mechanical stiffness; the control cables should be kept taut.

Enough to make a difference. The small amount of sweep up of the tailplane, as shown, was sufficient to spoil the airflow over the rudder and elevators. This limited her diving speed to 320 IAS and produced an uncomfortable yaw to the left.

FIRST SPITFIRES TO MALTA

Until the spring of 1942, no Spitfire fighter squadron had been based outside Great Britain. Early in that year, however, the air situation in the Mediterranean reached a critical stage. The Hurricanes defending Malta were outclassed by the new 'F' version of the Messerschmitt Bf 109, and there was a serious risk that the latter might establish air superiority over the beleaguered island.

Malta's strategic importance stemmed from its value as a base for Allied bombers and torpedo-bombers which inflicted a heavy toll on the ships transporting supplies and reinforcements for the German and Italian armies in North Africa. Whenever the latter were about to launch a new offensive in the Western Desert, there was usually a series of heavy air attacks on Malta to neutralise its aerial strike forces. At the end of 1941 the combined German and Italian High Command decided to lance the Maltese abscess for all time: the island was to be seized in a combined airborne and seaborne assault.

As a preliminary to invasion, early in 1942 the Luftwaffe began concentrating units at airfields in Sicily and the number of aircraft on the island increased from 200 to more than 400. About half of the total were bombers, Junkers 87s and 88s, and more than a hundred of the latest Bf 109Fs were deployed to support their attacks. The aerial bombardment of Malta opened in January and rapidly gained in momentum, with losses on both sides.

The continued survival of Malta would depend to a large extent on the effectiveness of the island's fighter defences, but each time an RAF fighter was lost in action, its replacement required a considerable effort. The island lay 1,380 statute miles to the east of Gibraltar, well beyond the ferry range of any existing British single-engined fighter. Moreover, the strength of the enemy air forces in Sicily ruled out the delivery of fighters to the island by freighter: any attempt to do so would result in a full-scale battle, with heavy losses and little prospect of success.

The Hurricanes then on Malta had been transported by aircraft carrier to a launching point off the coast of Algeria, where they took off and flew the rest of the way. That distance, 660 miles by the shortest practical route, was about as great as that from London to Prague. For the flight each Hurricane was fitted with two 44gal underwing tanks, one under each wing. Several such operations were mounted and by the end of 1941 more than 300 Hurricanes had been delivered to the island in this way.

Now there was a requirement to send Spitfires to Malta using the same route as previously, and they too were to be taken halfway by aircraft carrier. To enable the Spitfires to cover the rest of the distance, Supermarine engineers had designed and built a batch of new 90gal jettisonable fuel tanks for carriage under the Spitfire's fuselage. Also, to prevent dust and sand getting into the engine and causing excessive wear, these Spitfires were the first production machines fitted with dust filters for their carburettor air intakes.

At the beginning of February 1942 the process of delivering the first contingent of Spitfires to Malta, codenamed Operation Spotter, was well advanced. Sixteen crated fighters were loaded on the freighter *Cape Hawk* at Liverpool. The ship also carried sixteen pilots for No. 249 Squadron and about a hundred ground crew, with Wing Commander Maclean in charge of the entire detachment.

Cape Hawk set sail from Liverpool on the afternoon of 9 February as part of an escorted convoy, and arrived at Gibraltar on 21 February. She then entered the inner harbour, where she tied up next to the aircraft carrier HMS *Eagle*. Work began to offload the crates, and by the following day all sixteen were lined up on the quayside beside the ship. There the boxes were to remain, however, for it was essential to keep the movement of the fighters a secret from the enemy as long as possible. It was known that German agents kept watch on the port from the Spanish town of Algeciras on the other side of the bay. Each day several hundred Spaniards came to work

Point of no return: Spitfire taking off from HMS *Eagle* on 21 March 1942 on Operation Picket 1, the second delivery of Spitfires to the besieged island of Malta.

on Gibraltar, returning each evening before nightfall; it was believed that some of these workers were paid by the Germans to report anything of interest they had seen at the port.

To keep secret the existence of the batch of Spitfires on Gibraltar, the crates were not opened until after dark on the 22nd. Ray Honeybone described the start of the operation:

> As the end was unbolted from the first of the large cases, a Spitfire fuselage was revealed. The fuselage with the engine in position lay in the centre, with the mainplanes mounted on the side walls. The propeller was mounted on one side wall. The drill was to drag the fuselage out of its cradle, transfer it to a set of belly jacks, manoeuvre out each mainplane in turn, fit the main and rear spar bolts, then drop and lock down the undercarriage units. This gave us a

mobile structure, to which the propeller was fitted prior to lifting the aircraft on board the carrier...

George Revell takes up the story, and explains how the need for secrecy dominated every part of the operation:

> This activity was taking place at night, but with a generous amount of lighting as Gibraltar wasn't blacked out unless an air raid alert was sounded. However, to reduce the chances of our 'friends' across the bay seeing too much, the lighting on the flight deck was kept to a minimum, particularly when the loads reached flight deck level.

Also, as each Spitfire came on board, a party of sailors at one end of the flight deck would start the engine on one of

HMS *Eagle's* Sea Hurricanes to serve as a diversion. Once it was on deck, the Spitfire was wheeled across the flight deck to the lift and taken below. The work went on throughout the hours of darkness then, as Ray Honeybone explained, as dawn approached the aircraft crates on the quay were restored to make it appear as if nothing had happened:

> To keep up the pretence of secrecy, each empty case was reassembled to make it look as though nothing had been disturbed. At first light we assembled our camp beds on the hangar floor for some much-needed sleep.

The last four of the Spitfires were hoisted on to *Eagle's* flight deck during the small hours of the 25th. Now the work of reassembling the fighters went ahead at top speed. The 'erks' were divided into eight gangs, each comprising a corporal and three men, and each gang was allocated two Spitfires to work on. Several members of the detachment had previously worked at Maintenance Units and were familiar with the repair and reassembly of Spitfires. Although these were brand new aircraft some of the parts needed to be changed. Squadron Leader Hughes, the RAF detachment commander, had no spare parts, so he had to cannibalise one of the fighters to provide spares for the rest.

Ray Honeybone described the work of reassembling the Spitfires and getting them ready for flight:

> There were coolant joints to make, hydraulic and air systems to complete, controls to connect and adjust, all the myriad jobs which on a squadron you did occasionally, one at a time as rectification, we now did all at once and in record time.
>
> A feature new to all of us was the auxiliary fuel tank which held 90gal of 100 octane fuel. These we were told were necessary to double the range of the Spitfire, so it could get to where it was going. Under the fuselage and in line with the mainplanes was a three-point mounting, the centre one of which was retractable so that the tank could be jettisoned. There was also a device consisting of a spring-loaded mushroom valve in the cockpit floor, which mated with a seating on the upper surface of the jettison tank. Mating can be a loose term in engineering, but it was necessary to arrange that the tanks stayed securely

A Spitfire being refuelled from petrol tins in one of the makeshift revetments on the island, a task being carried out by a soldier, a sailor and an airman.

> fixed to the fuselage and at the same time the mushroom valve and seat met in a perfect contact. Otherwise the fuel would not flow upwards to the carburettor. As each aircraft was brought to the stage where engines could be run, again after dark, each was towed 'topside' on deck and put through its paces. A cock provided selection from main fuel to auxiliary fuel and it seemed logical to expect that fluid should flow. But almost as soon as the cock was turned, a small red light indicated a lack of fuel pressure. And try as we may, it was a hit and miss affair to arrange the tank and valve position to work with much measure of success.
>
> After its engine had been run, and the fitters knew whether or not the slipper tank would feed properly, each fighter was given over to the armourers who jacked up into a flight attitude for harmonisation of the guns with the gun sight.

Still the slipper tanks gave considerable trouble; they were the first of their type ever made, they had been designed and manufactured in a hurry – and it showed. During the early hours of 27 February HMS *Eagle* left Gibraltar with her precious cargo, escorted by a battle group which included the carrier HMS *Argus*, a battleship, a cruiser and nine destroyers.

That first attempt to deliver Spitfires to Malta was a failure. Flight Lieutenant Stanley Grant, who was to have led the fighters to the island, explained why:

The next day, when we were well clear of land, Hughes brought the aircraft up on deck to run the engines and, above all, to test the functioning of the long-range tanks, without which the operation was not on. These first 90gal tanks had evidently been produced in a great hurry and were 'a bit of a lash-up'. The fuel was drawn up into the main tanks by suction and if there was the slightest air leak in the seal between the tank and the fuselage, there was no fuel transfer.

Hughes soon found that the seals were not satisfactory and although he and his team strove hard all that day and well into the night, he could not make them work properly. Accordingly, around midnight, with our take-off due the next morning, Hughes sent a message to the Admiral via Wing Commander Maclean, saying that the aircraft could not be allowed to take off without further extensive tests. We heard later that the Admiral nearly exploded, and sent back the message that under no circumstances could his ships hang around in daylight in the middle of the Mediterranean, within easy range of enemy bombers. The Spitfires had to take off the next morning – at all costs. But Hughes was adamant. The aircraft were, in his view, not airworthy and he could not agree to let them take off until he was certain that the drop tanks functioned properly. So the Admiral had to give in, and the whole fleet turned around and steamed back to Gibraltar.

Once back at Gibraltar, there was hectic activity to get the Spitfire's new fuel tanks to work properly. Ray Honeybone recalled:

Our worst enemy was the suction valve on the belly tanks; we had about a 95 per cent failure rate with them … In the end a man from Supermarine was flown out to Gibraltar, to help us get them to work. When I met him I put up a bit of a black, I said the man who designed that system ought to jump off Beachy Head! He said: 'Don't say that, corporal, I designed it…'

As soon as he saw one of the tanks on HMS *Eagle*, the designer was able to pinpoint the reason why so many failed to work properly. Although it was vitally important to establish a good seal between the tank and the fuselage of the fighter, there was another problem that had not been realised. At the lowest point of each tank there was a small bulbous protrusion that acted as a sump, and the fuel transfer pipe reached almost to the bottom of that sump. If the sump was dented, that could block the end of the pipe and so prevent fuel transfer. In the course of crating, uncrating, and fitting the tanks to the aircraft by people unfamiliar with them, several of the tanks had dented sumps. The remedy was to cut away the dented area and solder a patch over the cut-away area. That cured the problem, and there was a maximum effort to repair all of the damaged tanks and prove that they transferred fuel satisfactorily.

Early on the morning of 5 March, HMS *Eagle* and her covering force put to sea again. Once the ships were clear of land, the Spitfires were brought out on deck and their engines started, and this time all of the fuel tanks functioned perfectly. Then each fighter in turn was pointed in a safe direction and the armourers fired short bursts to test the guns.

Soon after dawn on the morning of the 7th, HMS *Eagle* reached the planned launching position. She turned into wind and Stanley Grant led the first of the Spitfires off the deck. At measured intervals the other fourteen followed him into the air (the 16th Spitfire, it will be remembered, had been cannibalised to provide spare parts for the others).

There was no opportunity to test fly the Spitfires after reassembly – the flight to Malta would constitute the test flight, and if any part of the work had been done incorrectly a pilot might pay for the error with his life. Moreover, since reassembly had taken place aboard the aircraft carrier, the Spitfires' compasses could not be 'swung' to determine their errors; the planes' compasses might give readings several degrees out and they were not to be trusted, especially during a long flight over the sea with few landmarks. As a result, a Blenheim bomber made a rendezvous with the carrier off Algeria, to lead the fighters the rest of the way. In spite of the difficulties, all fifteen Spitfires reached Malta safely and the next day they went into action.

Four days after his arrival on the island, on 11 March, Stanley Grant was promoted to squadron leader and appointed commander of No. 249 Squadron to operate the Spitfires. During March, HMS *Eagle* made two further deliveries of Spitfires to Malta, to bring the total delivery to thirty-one aircraft. That was barely sufficient to replace losses incurred in the increased tempo of air fighting, and clearly a much larger reinforcement of Spitfires was needed if the island was to survive its ordeal.

26

MORE SPITFIRES TO MALTA

As described in the previous chapter, HMS *Eagle* delivered a total of thirty-one Spitfires to Malta in March 1942, although this relatively meagre reinforcement could not sustain the losses of fighters. Prime Minister Winston Churchill explained this problem in a personal telegram to US President Roosevelt on 1 April:

Air attack on Malta is very heavy. There are now in Sicily about 400 German and 200 Italian fighters and bombers. Malta can now only muster 20 or 30 serviceable fighters. We keep feeding Malta with Spitfires in packets of 16 loosed from EAGLE carrier from about 600 miles West of Malta.

This has worked a good many times quite well but EAGLE is now laid up for a month by defects in her steering gear. There are no Spitfires in Egypt. ARGUS is too small and too slow and moreover she has to provide the fighter cover for the carrier launching the Spitfires and the escorting force. We would have used VICTORIOUS but unfortunately her lifts are too small for Spitfires. Therefore there will be a whole month without any Spitfire reinforcements.

2. It seem likely from extraordinary enemy concentration on Malta that they hope to exterminate our air defence in time to reinforce either Libya or their Russian offensive. This would mean that Malta would be at best powerless to interfere with the reinforcements of armour to Rommel and our chances of resuming against him at an early date ruined.

3. Would you be willing to allow your carrier WASP to do one of these trips provided details are satisfactorily agreed between the Naval Staffs? With her broad lifts, capacity and length, we estimate that WASP could take 50 or more Spitfires. Unless it were necessary for her to fuel, WASP could proceed through the Straits at night without calling at Gibraltar until the return journey as the Spitfires would be embarked in the Clyde.

4. Thus instead of not being able to give Malta any Spitfires during April, a powerful Spitfire force could be flown into Malta at a stroke and give us a chance of inflicting a very severe and possibly decisive check on the enemy. Operation might take place during the third week of April.

Three days later the US President replied in the affirmative: that the USS *Wasp* would be available to deliver the fighters to Malta. She sailed into Glasgow on the 10th, where she took on forty-seven Spitfires and their pilots; at first light on the 14th she set out for the Mediterranean.

One of those who took part in this operation, codenamed 'Calendar', was Pilot Officer Michael Le Bas of No. 601 Squadron, who now picks up the story from his viewpoint.

I arrived at Abbotsinch (an airfield near Glasgow) on the morning of 12 April to find that I had been allocated to No. 601 Squadron under Squadron Leader John Bisdee, which was preparing to go overseas; also doing the same thing were the pilots of No. 603 Squadron. Neither squadron had any aircraft or ground crew, but somebody had seen an American aircraft carrier docked at Glasgow and loading Spitfires. The favourite rumour was that we were to be shipped out to the Caribbean to provide fighter defence against an expected enemy attack in that area. It turned out to be wishful thinking!

That evening the two squadrons' air crew boarded the carrier, the USS *Wasp*, and I had the chance to look round her. She had flown off her own aircraft except for a single squadron of Wildcat fighters which sat on the deck with wings folded. Below decks, the hangar was chock-full of brand new Spitfires with some of them hanging from the ceiling on straps. The aircraft were painted in unusual colours which I later learned to be the 'sand and soil' desert camouflage. Each aircraft had four 20mm cannon and carried a 90gal drop tank, features I had never seen before.

Early the following morning, with the battle cruiser HMS *Renown* and six destroyers in company, we set sail for our unknown destination. When we were well out to sea the Royal Air Force pilots were summoned to the ship's main briefing room where the force commander, Wing Commander John MacLean, told us why we were there: we were to fly to Malta and take part in the defence of the island. With the extra 90gal of fuel in the drop tank the Spitfire V had a still-air range, allowing for fuel consumed in the take-off and climb, of 940 miles. If the drop tank was carried to the destination or 1,040 miles, it was dropped when empty. Since the still-air distance from the launch point to Malta would be about 600 miles, that left a fair margin in case we met unexpected headwinds or had to fight our way through enemy fighters to reach the island.

The extra 90gal of petrol, together weighing about 770lb, meant that the Spitfire would have to take off in the overload condition. There would be little margin for safety and no unnecessary weight could be carried. Two of the four cannon were to be left unloaded and the magazines of the others were loaded with only sixty rounds in each, less than half the normal complement. We were enjoined to take in our aircraft the bare minimum of personal kit and what we did carry had to be packed in such a way that the Spitfire could fight if necessary. Our bags were to be flown to Malta by courier aircraft later.

Squadron Leader 'Jumbo' Gracie, who had flown to Malta from HMS *Eagle* the previous month, briefed us on the take-off from the carrier. He said the technique was to rev up to 3,000rpm on the brakes, then release the brakes and select emergency boost override. All of the Spitfires had taken off from the *Eagle* successfully and with the extra length of *Wasp*'s flight deck, getting airborne from her should be 'a piece of cake'. Gracie said he would lead the Spitfires off *Wasp* for this operation; after take-off the fighters were to form up in three formations of twelve and one of eleven, each formation departing when ready.

After leaving *Wasp* we were to fly along the north coast of Algeria and Tunisia as far as Cap Bon, then head south-east to skirt round the enemy-held island of Pantalleria before heading due east for Malta. Maclean told us that he would be getting weather reports from Malta and we would not be launched unless clear skies were forecast over the entire

route. This would be important because the only navigation equipment we carried was our maps, compasses and watches; for the final part of the flight we could get radio bearings from Malta.

The US Navy air commander then told us the procedure for take-off. During the launching operation the carrier would be committed to sailing a straight course in broad daylight within easy range of enemy air bases; so obviously the sooner we were all away after the launch began, the shorter the time *Wasp* would be exposed to enemy attack.

On the afternoon before the launch the first twelve Spitfires would be taken up onto the flight deck and ranged aft, to leave room in the hangar to lower the aircraft suspended from the ceiling. At first light on the 20th the carrier would turn into wind and her own squadron of Wildcat fighters would take off to provide air cover. Then Gracie would go off, followed at short intervals by the remaining Spitfires on the deck. As the last aircraft began its take-off run, the Spitfire in the hangar nearest the lift was to start its engine. The lift would then go down to pick it up and take it to the deck. As soon as possible the pilot was to taxi forwards so that the lift could go down for the next

The flight deck of USS *Wasp* on the afternoon of 19 April. Ranged ready to take off at first light the next morning are *Wasp's* own Wildcat fighters, and behind them the Spitfires of No. 603 Squadron.

Spitfire which had in the meantime started its engine. The whole operation would necessarily be complicated and our instructions were minute and detailed. Above all else, we had to follow the deck crews' instructions implicitly.

On the morning of 20 April we were roused early and after a breakfast and final briefing we boarded our aircraft. My Spitfire was one of those in the hangar and as I sat in the cockpit I could hear the roar of the engines of the aircraft on the deck above as they took off. Our Spitfires were all pointing towards the bow of the ship, which meant it was difficult to see what was going on in the rear of the hangar behind us.

After what seemed a long wait my squadron commander, John Bisdee, received the order to start his engine and it burst into life. I was to go off immediately after him. I remember being rather worried about getting my heavily laden Spitfire off the deck until suddenly the thought occurred to me: 'Bisdee weighs a good three stone more than I do; so if he gets airborne, I'll be all right!'

By craning my neck round I saw the lift come down and Bisdee's aircraft being pushed backwards on to it, then up it went. My Spitfire was pushed backwards to where his had been and I was given the signal to start my engine. No sooner had the Merlin settled down than the lift was on its way down for me. I was pushed on to the lift and up I went. Even before

the lift was fully up I received the signal to taxi forwards; the deck crewman had judged things nicely and as my Spitfire began to move forwards the lift slotted into its place in the deck. My tail wheel was hardly off it before the great slab of steel was on its way down again for the next aircraft.

Bisdee's Spitfire was already airborne; he had made it! Once I was on deck with the brakes on Maclean clambered on to my wing and reached in to the cockpit to check that my propeller was in fine pitch. He checked each Spitfire before it took off; the engine had to be started with the propeller in coarse pitch, but if it was left in that position the aircraft would not accelerate quickly enough to gain flying speed before it reached the end of the deck. When Maclean was satisfied he jumped off my wing, the deck officer began rotating his chequered flag and I pushed throttle forward until I had maximum rpm. His flag then fell and I released the brakes and pushed the throttle to emergency override to get the last ounce of power out of my Merlin. The Spitfire picked up speed rapidly in its headlong charge down the deck, but not rapidly enough. The ship's bows got closer and closer and still I had insufficient airspeed and suddenly – I was off the end. With only 60ft to play with before I hit the water, I immediately retracted the undercarriage and eased forward on the stick to build up my speed. Down and down with the Spitfire until, about 15ft above the waves, it reached flying speed and I was able to level out. After what seemed an age, but was in fact only a few seconds, my speed built up further and I was able to climb away.

Once I had a bit of height I switched to the fuel in the drop tank and was relieved that my engine continued running, which showed that the tank was feeding properly. For the launch *Wasp* had been heading south-westwards into the 15mph wind. High above and in front of me Bisbee took his aircraft in a wide orbit round the carrier so that I and the pilots behind me could get into position in formation as rapidly as possible. Once we had formed up, the twelve Spitfires turned due east for our new home.

When at our cruising altitude of 10,000ft we throttled back to 2,050rpm to get the most out of each gallon of fuel. At first the skies were clear of cloud and to the south of us we could make out the reddish-brown peaks of the mountain range which ran along the Algerian coast. As we settled down for the long flight boredom began to set in and

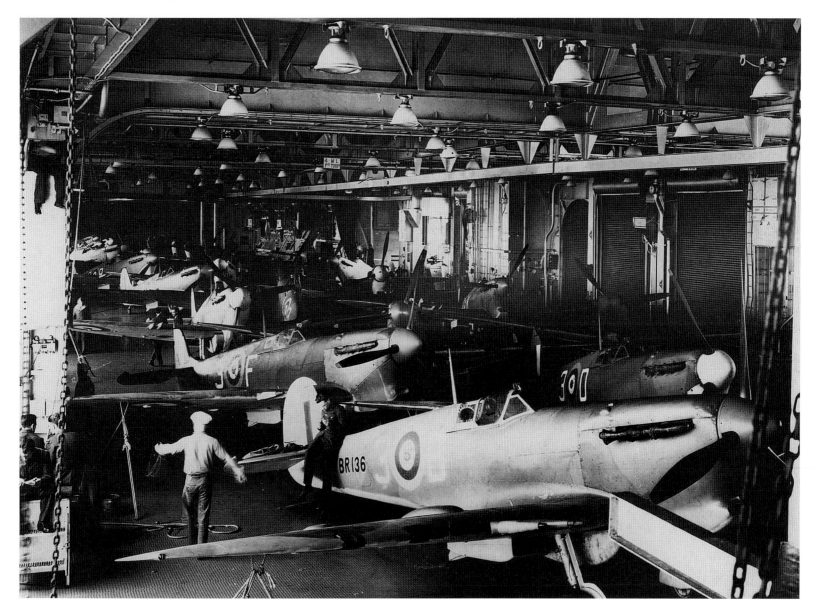

I remember being worried in case I lost concentration and would not be alert enough if we came under attack.

The sun climbed higher and higher in front of us, disconcertingly bright. At the same time the ground haze gradually thickened until it swallowed up the mountains which had provided a useful check on our navigation. Now there was no alternative but to continue on our compass heading, comforted only by the even drone of our Merlin engines.

Things were to get worse before they got better. As we continued eastwards cloud began to build up beneath us, hiding the sea and our important turning point at Cap Bon. About half an hour before we were due to reach Malta we expected to be in VHF range, so Bisdee broke radio silence

The first major reinforcement of Spitfires to reach Malta was on Operation Calendar on 20 April 1942, when the US Navy carrier *Wasp* launched forty-seven of these fighters. Forty-six of them reached the island.

Above: When the deck control officer lowered his flag, the Spitfire pilot was to begin his take-off run.

Right: Pilot Officer Mike Le Bas of No. 601 Squadron, whose account of Operation Calendar appears on these pages.

and called up for a homing. After a short pause a voice came up in good English and gave us a north-easterly heading to fly. Had we followed the instructions we should have been in trouble but, by a stroke of good luck, the cloud beneath us started to break up and we could see the sea again. Out to port was the Italian-held island of Pantelleria, which gave us a useful additional fix; it was clear that the homing instructions had come from an enemy station and we ignored them. Bisdee led us in a turn to the south-east, to regain our proper track.

Just as we were passing Pantelleria I nearly had my own personal disaster. Without warning my engine suddenly cut out. I thought 'Oh God, this is it!' and decided that if I could not get it restarted I would glide over to the island and bale out. I jettisoned the drop tank to clean up the aircraft for the glide, then it occurred to me that perhaps the tank had run dry. So I switched over to my almost full main tank and to my relief the engine restarted without any difficulty. I opened the throttle and regained my place in the formation.

After Pantelleria the skies cleared up completely. My first sight of Malta was the cloud of dust towering over the island after the morning visit by the Luftwaffe. Now my great worry was that after three hours in our cramped cockpits,

stiff and with sore backsides, we should not be in good shape if we had to fight our way in. Fortunately for us however, the Germans had gone home by the time we got there and we had no trouble getting down. Our squadron, No. 601, landed at Luqa and No. 603, coming up behind, landed at Takali a few miles to the west.

After landing I was directed to one of the many blast pens scattered round the airfield, I taxied in and shut down my engine and almost immediately the ground crew began the slow process of refuelling the Spitfire using twenty-one 4gal petrol tins. Of the forty-seven Spitfires which had taken off from *Wasp*, forty-six landed safely in Malta; the remaining aircraft flown by a sergeant pilot of No. 603 Squadron was listed as missing.

The Germans had watched our arrival on radar and that afternoon all hell broke loose over the Maltese airfields. In spite of strenuous efforts by the fighters and the anti-aircraft gun defences, the Ju 87 and Ju 88 dive bombers and the strafing Messerschmitts managed to damage and destroy several of our newly delivered Spitfires on the ground. The blast pens were made of local stone or stacks of petrol tins filled with sand and they provided useful protection against cannon shells and anything apart from a direct hit. They had no roof, however, and several aircraft received damage when rocks blown high into the air by exploding bombs fell on them from above.

Every single-engined fighter delivered to Malta for over a year had been flown in, so there was no shortage of pilots for the few Spitfires available for operations at any one time. As a result, I did not make my first operational sortie from the island until 24 April, four days after my arrival. Led by Flight Lieutenant 'Laddie' Lucas, three of us were scrambled and told to climb to 20,000ft to engage an incoming formation of Ju 87s escorted by Messerschmitt 109s. Almost from the beginning things began to go wrong. Lucas had engine trouble and had to turn back. Then the controller took us up too high with the result that when we dived to attack we came in much too fast and two of us overshot the dive bombers. The third pilot managed to get in a good burst at a Ju 87, but then the hoard of escorting Messerschmitts got on to us and we were lucky to escape with our lives.

By the end of April the enemy attacks on our airfields had destroyed so many aircraft that there were only about half a dozen serviceable fighters on the island. Things got so bad that when enemy formations were reported coming in, those fighters which were flyable but unfit for action (for example with unserviceable guns or radios) would be ordered to scramble and orbit to the south of Malta until the raiders had gone.

There were a lot of anti-aircraft guns positioned to cover the airfields and Valletta harbour, but ammunition was short and usually the gunners were rationed to a few rounds for each engagement. At irregular intervals however, the restriction was lifted and the gunners were allowed to put up a brave display to show the German dive-bomber pilots that the defences were still in business.

I did not get my second operational sortie until 9 May, when we learned that a further large reinforcement of Spitfires was on its way in. One of the problems when I

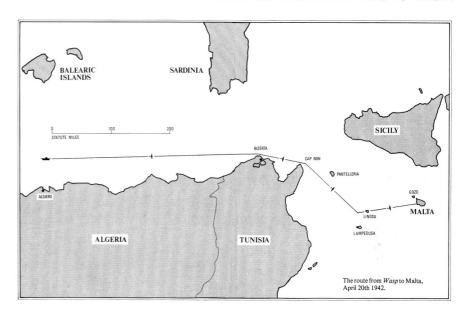

The route from *Wasp* to Malta, April 20th 1942.

Map of the Spitfires' route to Malta.

arrived was that the operation had been kept so secret that too few people had been told that we were coming. The incoming Spitfires had not been refuelled and rearmed quickly enough, with the result that they could not take off to meet the attacks and several were knocked out on the ground. This time we were much better organised.

As each Spitfire came in it was picked up at the end of the runway by a resident RAF pilot, who sat on the wing and guided the aircraft to its blast pen. At each pen were waiting RAF ground crew and some soldiers to help with the refuelling. I guided one Spitfire in and, even before I had shut down, men were clambering on to the wings to load the cannon with their full complement of ammunition and the soldiers had started a human chain to pass up the petrol tins. The pilot pulled off his helmet and shouted to me, 'That's jolly good. Where's the war?' I told him, 'The war hasn't started yet for you mate, Get out and be quick about it!' Within fifteen minutes of landing the Spitfire was ready to fight. Shortly afterwards I received the order to scramble.

Operating with No. 126 Squadron I took part in the interception of a formation of Italian CANT bombers escorted by Macchi 202 fighters: three of the latter and two of the former were shot down.

The arrival of the Spitfires on 9 May, sixty of them from the carriers HMS *Eagle* and USS *Wasp*, marked a major turning point in the Battle of Malta. Before then, the fighter force had been hard-pressed to merely survive in the face of the almost incessant enemy attacks. After that date the fighter squadrons were able to hit back hard, and they never looked back.

Once there was an adequate fighter defence for the Maltese airfields, the bombers and torpedo bombers could return to the island. The whole point of hanging on to Malta was to provide a base so that these aircraft could strike at the German and Italian ships carrying supplies to their armies in North Africa.

The Spitfires delivered during March and April had all been painted in brown and yellow desert camouflage. That was fine when flying over land in that part of the world, but Malta was so small that we spent most of our time over the sea. In those colours the Spitfires showed up beautifully. As a result there were a lot of locally improvised paint schemes to make the aircraft less conspicuous; later reinforcement Spitfires would arrive wearing the grey and green sea camouflage.

The Spitfires which had been launched from USS *Wasp* and HMS *Eagle* during April and May were all Mark VC versions, fitted with four 20mm cannon instead of the more usual two cannon and four machine guns. When operating from Malta, however, that heavier armament was unnecessary. Even against the Junkers 88, the toughest bomber we had to deal with, two Hispano guns were quite enough. The weight of the two extra cannon imposed a performance penalty, especially in the climb. The extra two cannon were soon removed from the aircraft. On the island there was a perennial shortage of 20mm ammunition, so cannon tests were prohibited; those weapons were to be fired only at the enemy.

After the arrival of the additional Spitfires on 9 May, I was on operations or stand-by almost every day. We remained at readiness from dawn to dusk waiting for the enemy to come to us; if they did not come we stayed on the ground and it was the luck of the draw whether we had three scrambles a day or none at all. If one received the order to scramble, getting off the ground was always a bit of an adventure. If further sections had also to scramble, things got complicated. At each blast pen someone had to be watching the control tower the whole time, because if a

Very light was missed one could get in a muddle and either take off at the wrong time or not at all. After the start-up there was always a long run from one's dispersed blast pen, along the taxi way, to the end of the runway. This was made with an airman sitting on the wing, whose job it was to guide the pilot round any new bomb craters that had appeared. Immediately one reached the runway one took off; it was always much safer to be in the air. After take-off the fighters would orbit the airfield until the section or squadron had formed up. Once we were airborne we could get our orders from the ground controller. He usually told us to go to the south and climb to a given altitude, then he would bring us in to engage the enemy.

Reinforcements of Spitfires continued to arrive on the island from aircraft carriers. Seventeen arrived on the 18th, twenty-seven on 3 June and thirty-two on 9 June. By the middle of June things were a lot quieter over Malta, but things were going badly in Libya. The German armour had outflanked the Gazala line and on 21 June Tobruk fell. At that time there was only one full Spitfire squadron, No. 145, in the Western Desert and the Messerschmitt 109Fs were having an easy time against the slower Hurricane and Kittyhawk fighters. So on 23 June I flew one of eight Spitfires of No. 601 Squadron to a landing ground near to Mersa Matruh in Egypt. For the flight the Spitfires were fitted with 90gal drop tanks. The formation was accompanied by a Beaufighter, whose navigator looked that side of things on the four-and-a-half -hour flight that covered about 800 miles.

With that flight my part in the Battle of Malta ended. After we arrived in the Western Desert, we pilots who had taken part in the defence of the island tended to stick together. I can imagine we got on a lot of peoples' nerves going on all the time about the desperate conditions during the siege. We proudly wore on our battledress little Maltese crosses, carved out of shilling coins until a very senior officer ordered us to remove them. Looking back, the thing that strikes me is the tremendous spirit that existed amongst the fighter pilots during the siege of Malta. It simply never occurred to us that the island might fall.

As the summer wore on, the British forces were pushed back further and further into Egypt. Mersa Matruh fell and no more Spitfires could be 'exported' from Malta during 1942. In

July and August there were four further resupply operations during which a total of 125 Spitfires reached the island. These would be sufficient to enable the Malta fighter squadrons to go over to the offensive and begin mounting sweeps over Sicily.

On the day after Operation Baritone, the reinforcement operation on 17 August, the Air Ministry in London sent the following signal to the air commanders at Gibraltar and Air Vice-Marshal Keith Park, the new air commander in Malta:

Now that Baritone is completed it is intended to dispense with further carrier operations for these reinforcements and to make deliveries of Spitfires from Gibraltar to Malta by air carrying 170gal jettisonable tanks. Still-air range is 1,389 land miles and therefore you will have to restrict dispatches to days of favourable winds on the route or at worst to days of average still air…

Some previous delivery flights by Spitfires over the Mediterranean had been impressive enough, but the new reinforcement method called for flights appreciably longer: the flight from Gibraltar to Malta would take the Spitfires over a distance about equal to that from London to St Petersburg.

By Malta standards, September and the early part of October 1942 had been relatively quiet. Following a run of successes by the island's anti-shipping units, however, the Luftwaffe returned in force. During a series of hard-fought actions there were losses on both sides. Still the first Spitfires were not ready to make the direct flight from Gibraltar to Malta, however. To make good the losses one further carrier reinforcement operation was mounted: Operation Train, on 24 October, delivered a further twenty-nine Spitfires to the island from HMS *Furious*. This brought the Spitfire strength on Malta to 123 aircraft, of which eighty were serviceable. However, even before the additional fighters arrived, the final large-scale bombardment of the island by the Luftwaffe had petered out.

On the day after Operation Train, 25 October, the first two Spitfire fighters arrived in Malta after flying direct from Gibraltar. The Air Ministry in London was informed:

First 2 Spitfires with 170gal tanks reached Malta after 5¼ hours flying. On landing both had 13gal oil and 43gal and 47gal petrol respectively. Long-range tanks were not jettisoned and have been returned with extra oil tanks by Liberator. 5 more Spitfires awaiting favourable weather for dispatch. Briefing of these regarding engine control only required slight modification as result of experience gained in first flight. Take-off presented no difficulty and run was under 800yd.

During November and the first week in December fifteen Spitfires took off from Gibraltar bound for Malta; all except one arrived safely. The flights could have continued but there was no longer any urgency to supply fighters for the defence of the island. The victory at El Alamein and the subsequent German retreat meant that the siege of the island could be lifted. Never again would Malta face any serious threat from the enemy.

Spitfires Flown to Malta from Aircraft Carriers, 1942

Date	Operation	Carrier	Launched	Arrived
7 March	Spotter	*Eagle*	15	15
21 March	Picket I	*Eagle*	9	9
27 March	Picket II	*Eagle*	7	7
20 April	Calendar	*Wasp*	47	46
9 May	Bowery	*Wasp*	64	60
18 May	L.B.	*Eagle*	17	17
3 June	Style	*Eagle*	31	27
9 June	Salient	*Eagle*	32	32
16 July	Pinpoint	*Eagle*	32	31
21 July	Insect	*Eagle*	30	28
11 August	Bellows	*Furious*	38	37
17 August	Baritone	*Furious*	32	29
24 October	Train	*Furious*	31	29
Totals			**385**	**367**

MALTA SPITFIRE ACE

Reade Tilley, a US citizen, volunteered to join the RAF before his country entered the war. After completing his flying training he served with No. 121 US Eagle Squadron. He then moved to No. 601 Squadron and took off from the deck of USS *Wasp* as part of Operation Calendar. He fought in the desperate air battles over Malta in the spring and summer of 1942, in which he was credited with the destruction of seven enemy aircraft. At the end of 1942 he transferred to the US Army Air Force with the rank of captain, and was sent to a fighter training school to pass on his hard-won experience. While in that post he wrote an important tactical treatise on how to get the best out of the Spitfire in combat, excerpts of which are set down below. Tilley opened his treatise with some do's and don'ts for the take-off and climb away from base.

When fighters are scrambled to intercept an approaching enemy, every minute wasted in getting off the ground and forming up means 3,000ft of altitude you won't have when you need it most. Thus an elaborate cockpit check is out. It is sufficient to see that you are in fine pitch and the motor is running properly before opening the throttle. Don't do a Training School circuit before joining up. As you roll down the runway take a quick look up for the man off ahead of you, when you have sufficient indicated air speed give him about six rings of deflection [of the gun sight] and you will be alongside in a flash. Don't jam open the throttle and follow along behind as it takes three times as long to catch up that way. If you are leading, circle the aerodrome close in, throttled well back, waggling your wings like hell.

The instant you are in formation get the cockpit in 'fighting shape': trimmed for the climb, oxygen right, check engine instruments, gun button to fire. Now you are ready for action. If something is wrong, now is the time to go back. Waggle your wings then slide gently out of the formation, or if following break sharply down and go home. Never wait until you are in the vicinity of enemy aircraft then make a break for it on a last-minute decision. There are several reasons:

A. The leader may be depending on you.
B. The rest of the formation may think you are diving on the enemy. This has happened plenty of times and it plays hell with everything.
C. The enemy may spot you and take advantage of your solitude.

Tilley set great store by the 'fours line abreast' formation, a variation of the four plane 'Schwarm' used by the Luftwaffe. Although the aircraft are shown in exact line abreast here, there was a tendency for the leader to be slightly in front of the others. Woe betide any fighter pilot who edged in front of his formation leader!

The formation that has proved its worth in both offensive and defensive fighter operations is the 'fours line abreast'. The diagram explains it – the squadron is divided into three sections, aircraft flying 200 to 250yd apart. Red Section leads, with the squadron commander at Red 1. Red 3, the second in command, flies next to the squadron commander on his left; he will take over the lead in case the squadron commander's radio fails or he has to leave the squadron because his aircraft is unserviceable. On the signal Red 3 will open up and forge ahead meaning he understands and has taken over...

White and Blue Sections fly 500 to 800yd behind, to one side and slightly above the Red Section. The individual aircraft fly 5 to 7 spans [60 to 85yd] apart. When the leader turns, White and Blue Sections will cross over at full throttle...

Squadron commanders must bear in mind that the squadron must be intact to do maximum damage to the enemy in combat; to this end throttle back and even turn towards straggling sections while climbing to meet the enemy. There is no better feeling than to arrive at 25,000ft with the full squadron properly deployed and then start hunting.

In section 'fours line abreast' each aircraft watches the other's tails, above and below; and in doing so all four cover each other. The arrows indicate the direction in which the pilots keep watch. When everyone does his job it is impossible for enemy aircraft to get into a firing position without being seen by at least three out of the four pilots. On a larger scale the sections cover each other. Any one section that is being attacked will be covered by the next section; and the pay-off is that the enemy frequently sees only one or two sections, and in attacking or manoeuvring lay themselves wide open to the attentions of the third section.

One further advantage of this formation is that if one man is attacked, the man next to him is at the exact distance where he can throttle back and fire at the attacker from the beam. Moreover, the sections are at the exact distance apart so that they are in effective range of any aircraft which is within range astern of one of the others.

For the sort of co-ordinated fighter operations Tilley described, good radio communications were essential. Without a radio a fighter pilot was deaf and dumb, a liability to himself and his comrades. Moreover, in Tilley's view, one of a fighter pilot's worst sins was to use his radio wantonly or thoughtlessly.

Forget all the fancy pleasantries you learned to put before and after the message in voice radio procedure. In your business there is no time for it and the message is the important thing. The squadron leader is the only man who uses the R/T for transmission when the squadron is in pursuit of the German. There is no need for you to say anything, just keep your mouth shut and reflect on the ground controller's messages to the leader. You will learn all you need to know: how many of the enemy to expect, at what altitude and from what direction they are approaching. The leader acknowledges messages from the ground controller with a sharp 'OK'. That is all that is necessary unless several squadrons or sections are operating independently, in which case `Red Leader OK` or 'Blue Leader answering OK' is sufficient. The latter message takes two and a half seconds; until the enemy is sighted no transmission should be longer.

Flying Officer Reade Tilley, a US citizen, joined the RAF before his country entered the war. The tactical treatise he wrote on air fighting, describing the lessons learned during the heavy air fighting over Malta, was a classic of its type.

If a four- or five-second transmission about nothing in particular is in progress, when everyone suddenly realises that the wingman is being fired at by a Focke Wulf, then no one can warn him till the message is completed and he probably won't be interested by then. It's amazing how many holes can be punched in an airplane in four or five seconds...

So keep your eyes open and your mouth shut until you spot the enemy, then your moment has come. If they are far ahead, or off to one side or below and far away from you, there is plenty of time. Don't get excited, just sit there and look them over – it doesn't help much if you report Spitfires as 109s. Try to count them or make a rapid estimate (for your log book). If you recognise them give their identity; if not, report them as 'aircraft'.

The procedure: make your voice purposely calm, slow and unexcited: 'Hello Red Leader; 109s at 4 o'clock above' or 'Red 3 to Red Leader, aircraft at 9 o'clock our level'. Red Leader sees the aircraft and acknowledges 'OK'. Now above all leave the R/T clear, for the next words will be your leader's instruction. If these are jammed it may queer the whole set-up.

Sometimes enemy aircraft are not seen until they are actually attacking. Then the message must be instantaneous and precise. If it is incoherent or garbled because you are excited the man being attacked may get a cannon shell instead – and first. The proper procedure: '109s attacking Red Section' or if you see one man being fired at 'Look out Red 4' or 'Red 4 break'; any one of these messages spoken clearly is perfect. Just be sure you designate the man being attacked correctly. It doesn't help much if you tell Red 4 to break (which he does) while Red 2, who is being fired at, looks on admiringly.

The one sure way to lose friends and help the enemy is to give a panic message over the R/T at the critical moment. 'Look out, there's a 109 on your tail', said in a screech, is usually sufficient to send every Spitfire within a radius of 50 miles into a series of wild manoeuvres. There is no call sign used so every pilot in every squadron responds automatically. Far better to say nothing at all and let one pilot be shot down, than to break up several formations for Jerry to pick off at his leisure. In fighter flying a panic message is the greatest of all crimes. Practise on the ground the exact words you will use to cover any situation in the air, say them over and over again until they become automatic.

If your R/T packs up near base, go back; if near the enemy, stay with the squadron. A fighter pilot without R/T is a liability to himself and his squadron. Never take off with a faulty R/T.

For the fighter pilot, the sun could be either a powerful ally or a deadly foe. Which one depended on how well the pilot used its protection and guarded the sector in which it lay.

Always note the bearing of the sun before taking off; then, if you get in a scrap miles out at sea or over the desert and a cannon shell prangs your compass, you may be able to save yourself a lot of unnecessary walking or paddling.

Never climb down sun. If it is necessary to fly down sun, do so in a series of 45-degree tacks. If circumstances permit, always climb up sun. If a German is hiding in it, he can make only one head-on pass at you, then you can turn smartly and jump him out of the sun thus foxing him at his own game.

If you are patrolling an objective, split your force into two sections and patrol across sun. The sections will fly more or less line abreast, but with the up-sun section out in front just a bit. Vary the length of the legs you cover and gain and lose altitude all the while. If the Germans spot you first, this will make it more difficult for them to time an attack to get you on the turn; and always make the turns into sun...

Cloud, also, could prove to be either a friend or a foe depending on how well it was used.

Cloud is greatly overrated as cover for offensive fighter operations. It is of most use to a fighter pilot who is in trouble. If you are shot up or the odds are impossible, it is great stuff to hide in. Layer cloud is most useful as you can pop in or dive out below to take a look. Remember that it is not healthy to maintain a straight course when there are gaps in the cloud. If you are being pursued turn 90 degrees in every cloud you pop into. If it seems in order, a quick 180 about may put you in a position to offer some head-on discouragement to the pursuer along the way.

Never fly directly on top of layer cloud, as you stand out like a sore thumb to an unfriendly element, even those as far as 10 miles away, if they are slightly above you. It is no use to play hide and seek in amongst the clouds when you are hunting for 109s. You get a tremendously safe feeling in amongst the white stuff and expect an enemy to pop out directly in your sights at any moment. Actually it is very dangerous, because you are silhouetted in all directions and he will see you first, then take mean advantage of your cover and your posterior.

On days when there is very high layer cloud, fly halfway between it and the ground in order to spot fighters above you. High layer cloud is perfect for defensive fighter work, because you can see the enemy formations and distinguish between fighter and bomber long before they can see you.

Next, Tilley discussed the raison d'être for the fighter: combat. Usually it was short and sharp, and fraught with perils for the unwary.

German top cover is usually at 28,000ft, though it may be as high as 32,000ft. When you attain maximum altitude, you will have an even break with the small number of enemy aircraft usually employed as top cover. If they are sighted it is better to detach an equal number to deal with them; then you can tackle the main force, more or less confident that you will have no unwelcome attentions from above. Remember, regardless of where or when you go in to attack an enemy formation, if at all possible leave two or four aircraft to cover you from above. Enemy aircraft do not fly alone; they fly in pairs or fours. If you can see just one, have a damn good look round for his pal before you go in to attack … and remember, look out behind.

When you attack, a series of two- or three-second bursts with new aim and angle of deflection each time is most effective. Don't cease attacking just because the enemy aircraft is beginning to smoke or a few pieces fall off; then is the time to skid out for a good look behind, before closing in to point blank range and really giving it to him.

When actually firing at the enemy aircraft you are most vulnerable to attack. When you break away from an attack, always break with a violent skid just as though you were being fired at from behind – because maybe you are!

It would seem reasonable to suppose that the straggler in a fighter formation would be the last man to get home; but he rarely is! Play hard to get, don't straggle, and look out behind, always!

The first action after combat is not to shake hands with yourself but to look at the engine instruments. Dropping oil pressure and rising engine and oil temperatures mean trouble. If you have been hit in the radiator or in the glycol pipes, white smoke starts to flow immediately. This is usually visible from the cockpit. If you have had bad luck the main glycol feed pipe running alongside the cockpit may be ruptured, in which case the cockpit will be filled with hot glycol and dense white vapour which causes choking and blindness. There is no hope to save an aircraft so hit. If, however, the glycol smoke is outside, open the hood, turn the oxygen on to emergency and land at the nearest aerodrome. If you have a long way to go to reach your lines or coast, throttle well back in coarse pitch and prepare to get out or crash-land should the engine quit.

A hit through the oil piping or motor block is not so obvious, though it will show on your oil pressure and engine instruments immediately. Often it is possible to cover a good many miles well throttled back in coarse pitch, before the engine seizes. When your aircraft starts trailing heavy smoke it may catch fire at any moment, so watch for the first sign of flame; if it appears, bale out immediately as an explosion may follow without further warning.

The only way you can't get out of a Spitfire is to climb out. The best method, if you have time, is to roll over on your back, trim her a bit tail heavy then pull the pin (holding together the seat harness) and fall clear. If you are in a hurry (and sometimes this is the case), just pull the pin and jam the stick forward; your last sensation will be your fingers leaving the stick. This works with the aircraft in any position. If the hood is jammed shut and you can't open it (sometimes a bullet or a shell may foul the track) lower the seat to the bottom, pull the pin, stiffen the neck and back muscles, then give the stick one hell of a shove forward. You won't even notice the hood…

Look out behind, then all of this won't be necessary.

28

BESIEGED ON MALTA

George Hows volunteered for the RAF in 1940 and trained as an engine fitter. In August 1942 he was posted to Malta, which was then nearing a critical period of its long siege. He was one of the overworked men who sweated to maintain in an airworthy state the small force of Spitfires on which the island's survival depended.

We flew in by night in a Dakota and, after holding off for about an hour because an air raid was in progress, we were unceremoniously dumped at Luqa and the aircraft made a hasty getaway. No sooner had we set foot on the island than the sirens sounded again. With the other new arrivals I was hustled away from the runway and into a cave which was being used as a shelter

The following day I was assigned to No. 1435 Flight which operated Spitfire Vs. To the east of Luqa airfield was a patch of wasteland known as the Safi strip, where the flight and other units were dispersed. The aircraft were parked in improvised blast pens, made out of 4gal petrol cans filled with sand and erected to a height of 12–14ft. Working under a corporal, my task was to carry out 25-hour and other inspections on the Spitfires as they became due. Also we did repairs on engines that were beyond the fitters assigned to the aircraft. All our work had to be done in the open, in the blast pens. As well as this routine work, we patched up the Spitfires which had been damaged in battle, to keep as many as possible flying. Sometimes the pressure was such that we had to cut corners; bullet holes in the aircraft were often patched over with bits of cloth, even pieces of paper, doped in place. Later we were able to do a smarter job – if the Spitfire survived that long.

That summer we were desperately short of spare parts and ground equipment. Any aircraft which crash-landed and was damaged beyond repair was a Godsend, providing us with virtually our only source of spares. Everything, apart from the simplest of tools, was in short supply. I remember there was only one Rolls-Royce Merlin tool kit for the whole of the Safi dispersal area. The only crane we had was a home-made affair, made of pieces of scrap angle-iron bolted on the chassis of an old lorry and incorporating a hand-operated cable winch. Necessity was indeed the mother of invention.

Compounding the problems of those trying to keep Malta's dwindling force of Spitfires serviceable were the frequent attacks on the airfields by German and Italian aircraft. The worst of our tormentors were the low-flying Messerschmitt 109s, which came in unannounced during the day to bomb and strafe us. Like everyone else, after about ten days I became used to them. We learned to ignore the sirens and took cover in the slit trenches only when the red flag was hoisted to indicate an imminent danger of attack to Safi itself. As things got hotter, the flag stayed up for so long that we could get hardly any work done, so we ignored that too.

At the beginning I was terribly scared by the almost continual air attacks on our aircraft dispersal areas. But fortunately we had plenty of slit trenches and caves; all of our offices and workshops were in caves.

The worst parts of the siege were the almost continual bombing and the shortage of food. By November 1942 things were getting very bad, the heavy anti-aircraft guns were limited to a few rounds each day; it must have been terrible for the gunners to have to sit under cover for the rest of the day after they had fired their allocation of rounds, but there was no alternative. During the siege we always seemed to have enough fuel and ammunition for our Spitfires, but everything else was in short supply. Motor fuel was so short that bus services on the island had to be suspended. I remember seeing Lord Gort, the governor of Malta, coming to visit Luqa on his bicycle – that was a great morale booster for those who saw him.

The deep cave shelters which had been blasted out of the solid rock gave considerable protection, and surprisingly few people were injured during these attacks. I have been in caves when they suffered direct hits from bombs, and all we felt was a slight shudder. The main problem in the caves was from the damp, which created health problems when people slept in them for months on end.

Frequently the runway at Luqa was cratered. Standing by ready to fill in the holes would be a gang of soldiers from the Lancashire Fusiliers with a lorry kept filled with rubble – of which there was never any shortage. An old Valentine tank was used to drag away any aircraft that was wrecked on the runway. It also made a pretty good roller, to compact the rubble in the crater and level it off. Our runway repair teams had the whole thing down to a fine art. It was a rough-and-ready process, but the runway had to be repaired quickly if our aircraft were to be able to land. After a period of such treatment the runway got very rough and pitted, and this caused a lot of wear to the Spitfires' tyres. But, such was the loss rate in the summer of 1942, that few Spitfires outlived their tyres. One problem after each raid was that there would be numerous splinters from bombs and shells lying all over the runway. So early each morning a detail of about forty men known as the 'Shrapnel Party' would walk shoulder to shoulder down the length of the runway, to pick up metal pieces of aircraft, bombs or AA shells.

In the squadron there was a tremendous esprit de corps. If one of our Spitfires brought down an enemy, every man felt he had a share in it, be he the cook, copper or technical ground staff. Everyone was part of a team with a common cause, to beat the enemy and get home. Discipline was self-imposed; nobody wanted to let the side down. We never knew what it was to have somebody put on a charge, there weren't such things.

During the siege uniform dress simply ceased to exist, it was a question of what one could get hold of. Hardly two people were dressed the same. Often one would see an airman wearing an RAF tunic and Army trousers, and that would be his 'best' uniform.

Towards the end of August 1942 the siege really began to bite, following the near-destruction of a long-awaited supply convoy. Our rations, which had been small enough when I arrived, were cut first to one half and then to one third of normal British Army rations. Breakfast would be a slice of bread and lunch was a ladleful of watery bully-beef soup. The main meal of the day, supper, would usually be a thin slice of bread with some bully beef and a small portion of potatoes with sometimes – if we were lucky – some dried vegetables,

but seldom enough to allay one's hunger. At Safi village, just off the airfield, an old woman ran a black market eating house. We had to pay five shillings for a rather foul pancake made out of flour and water, fried in Spitfire hydraulic oil which we had to bring ourselves; and we had to queue for the privilege.

▲ ▲ ▲

At about the time George Hows arrived, No. 1435 Flight was expanded and redesignated No. 1435 Squadron, under the command of Squadron Leader Tony Lovell. One of the most successful pilots on the unit was Flight Lieutenant Henry McLeod, a Canadian who that summer was credited with six and a half enemy aircraft destroyed or probably destroyed, and one damaged.

Very little mail got through to the island and news from home was sparse and spasmodic. Things became a little easier after a convoy got through in September. With the arrival of another convoy in December we knew the worst of the siege was over. From then on the air defences of the island became progressively stronger, while the enemy air attacks tailed off to the point where the sounding of a siren became something of an event. The long siege was over.

Spitfire Vs of No. 126 Squadron parked in line in the open at Luqa, during the spring of 1942. The lack of security precautions indicates that the shot was taken at a time of relative quiet in the aerial combat.

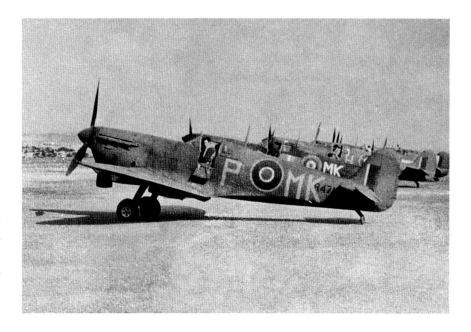

29

THE BALANCE RESTORED

The supremacy of the Focke Wulf 190 in the West ran from September 1941 until July 1942, before No. 64 Squadron went into action with an early production batch of Spitfires Mk IXs. As this Air Fighting Development Unit report shows, the performance of these two fighter types was about as close as they could possibly be, considering they were quite different aircraft.

The Fw 190's clear edge in performance over the Spitfire lasted until July 1942, when the Spitfire IX appeared on the scene. The Mark IX used the airframe of the Mark V with a minimum of modification, but was fitted with the Merlin 61 engine which employed a two-stage supercharger using two centrifugal impellors in series. The new engine gave a substantial improvement in high-altitude performance over the Merlin 46 which powered the Spitfire Mark V: at 30,000ft the Merlin 46 developed 720hp, whereas the Merlin 61 developed 1,020hp – an improvement of more than 40 per cent. That extra power was sufficient to close the gap in performance between the Spitfires and the Fw 190. The Spitfire IX at most heights was slightly superior in speed to the Fw 190, the approximate differences in speeds at various heights are as follows:

SPEED
At 2,000ft the Fw 190 is 7–8mph faster than the Spitfire IX.
At 5,000ft the Fw 190 and the Spitfire IX are approximately the same.
At 8,000ft the Spitfire IX is 8mph faster than the Fw 190.
At 15,000ft the Spitfire IX is 5mph faster than the Fw 190.
At 18,000ft the Fw 190 is 3mph faster than the Spitfire IX.
At 21,000ft the Fw 190 and the Spitfire IX are approximately the same.
At 25,000ft the Spitfire IX is 5–7mph faster than the Fw 190.

CLIMB
During comparative climbs at various heights up to 23,000ft,

with both aircraft flying under maximum continuous climbing conditions, little difference was found between the two aircraft, although on the whole the Spitfire IX was slightly better. Above 22,000ft the climb of the Fw 190 is falling off rapidly, whereas the climb of the Spitfire IX is increasing. When both aircraft were flying at high cruising speed and were pulled up into a climb from level flight, the Fw 190 had a slight advantage in the initial stages of the climb due to its better acceleration. This superiority was slightly increased when both aircraft were pulled up into the climb from a dive.

It must be appreciated that the differences between the two aircraft are only slight and that in actual combat the advantage in climb will be with the aircraft that has the initiative.

DIVE
The Fw 190 is faster than the Spitfire IX in a dive, particularly during the initial stage. This superiority is not as marked as with the Spitfire VB.

The Fw 190 is more manoeuvrable than the Spitfire IX except in turning circles, when it is out-turned without difficulty.

The superior rate of roll of the Fw 190 enabled it to avoid the Spitfire IX if attacked when in a turn, by flicking over into a diving turn in the opposite direction and, as with the Spitfire VB, the Spitfire IX had great difficulty in following this manoeuvre. It would have been easier for the Spitfire IX to follow the Fw 190 in the diving turn if its engine had been fitted with a negative 'G' carburettor, as this type of engine with the ordinary carburettor cuts very easily.

The Spitfire IX's worst heights for fighting the Fw 190 were between 18,000 and 22,000ft and below 3,000ft. At these heights the Fw 190 is a little faster.

Both aircraft 'bounced' one another in order to ascertain the best evasive tactics to adopt. The Spitfire IX could not be

Spitfire IX of No. 402 (Canadian) Squadron. Apart from slightly lengthened nose contours, compared with the Spitfire Mark V, the Mark IX had no clear identification pointers that could be used by enemy pilots in combat. Since the two could not be told apart, the only safe solution for enemy pilot was to treat both variants as Mark IXs, and respect them accordingly.

caught when 'bounced' if it was cruising at high speed and saw the Fw 190 when well out of range. When the Spitfire IX was cruising at low speed its inferiority in acceleration gave the Fw 190 a reasonable chance of catching it up and the same is applied if the position was reversed and the Fw 190 was 'bounced' by the Spitfire IX, except that the overtaking took a little longer.

The initial acceleration of the Fw 190 is better than the Spitfire IX under all conditions of flight, except in level flight at such altitudes where the Spitfire has a speed advantage and then, provided the Spitfire is cruising at high speed, there is little to choose between the acceleration of the two aircraft.

The general impression gained by the pilots taking part in the trials is that the Spitfire IX compares favourably with the Fw 190 and that, provided the Spitfire has the initiative, it undoubtedly has a good chance of shooting down the Fw 190.

30

DUEL IN THE STRATOSPHERE

In August 1942 a Luftwaffe unit formed at Beauvais in northern France, in readiness to launch a new series of bombing attacks on England: the Hohenkampfkommando (High Altitude Bomber Detachment). With German cities coming under increasingly heavy attack from the Royal Air Force, the nation's leaders judged that it was vitally important to deliver some form of retaliation, if only for propaganda purposes. Conventional bomber attacks by day or night suffered heavy losses from the steadily improving defences. So now the Lufftwaffe was to try a new type of attack – from ultra-high altitude.

The Hoehenkampfkommando was equipped with two Junkers 86Rs, aircraft designed and built specially for operations above 40,000ft. The power was from two Jumo 207 compression-ignition diesel engines, fitted with turbo-superchargers and with a system of nitrous oxide injection to boost power at high altitude. The two-man crew was ensconced in a fully pressurised cabin, enabling them to work effectively for long periods at ultra-high altitude. With a long narrow wing spanning just over 15ft, the Ju 86R had exceeded 45,000ft during test flights and its maximum speed was just over 200mph. Given the sheer technical cleverness of the Ju 86R the aircraft could, however, only carry one 550lb bomb to such a high altitude. Nevertheless, the main consideration in mounting these attacks was to derive the maximum possible propaganda value from daylight attacks against which the defenders had no answer.

The new bombers delivered their first attacks on 24 August. Both Ju 86Rs took part, one bombed Camberley and the other bombed Southampton. Fighter Command scrambled fifteen Spitfires, all Mk Vs, to engage the intruders, but none of them reached to a firing position.

That evening the German propaganda ministry jubilantly announced the Hoehenkampfkommando had opened with the first of a new series of daylight revenge attacks. All aircraft had returned safely. There was no mention of the fact that only two aircraft were involved, or that they each had dropped only one small bomb.

On the following day one of the bombers was over England again. This time, more confident of their immunity to interception, the German crew flew a meandering course that took them over Southampton and north of London. They deposited their bomb near Stanstead, then flew down the east side of London and left the coast at Shoreham. This time nine Spitfires were scrambled, again Mk Vs, and again they failed to get anywhere near the intruder.

During the next two and a half weeks the Ju 86Rs flew nine more sorties over England. On 29 August a couple of Spitfire Mk VIs of No. 124 Squadron were among the fighters that attempted to intercept the high-flying bomber, but again with no success.

Meanwhile, the nature of the new threat had become clear and Fighter Command was developing its own response.

Below: Oberfeldwebel Horst Goetz piloted the Ju 86R during the 15 September action.

Below left: Leutnant Erich Sommer was navigator aboard the Ju 86R.

At Northolt a new unit, the Special Service Flight, was formed with specially-modified Spitfire Mk IXs to counter the new menace. Pilot Officer Prince Emanuel Galitzine, a Russian emigre who had come to England as a child in 1919, was one of the pilots who volunteered to join the new unit.

Early in September the first of the modified Spitfire Mk IXs arrived at the unit. Galitzine described the aircraft:

The aircraft had been lightened in almost every way possible. A lighter wooden propeller had been substituted for the normal metal one; all of the armour had been removed, as had the four machine guns and their ammunition, leaving an armament of only the two 20mm Hispano cannons. The aircraft was painted in a lightweight finish, which gave it a colour rather like Cambridge blue. All equipment not strictly necessary for high-altitude fighting was removed. It had the normal, not the extended span, wing tips. A pressure cabin would of have been nice, but the Spitfire VII, which was in effect a Mk IX with a pressure cabin, was not yet ready for operations.

Galitzine recalled:

On 10 September I made my first flight in the modified Spitfire IX. I found it absolutely delightful to handle. During the war I flew eleven different versions of the Spitfire and this was far and away the best. The 450lb weight reduction was immediately noticeable once one was airborne, and with the Merlin 61 she had plenty of power and was very lively. I made a second flight that day to test the cannons, during which I took her up to 43,400ft.

Two days later Galitzine was again airborne in the modified Mk IX, this time in earnest. At 0927hrs he was scrambled to intercept an aircraft detected on radar climbing to high altitude over northern France. This was the standard tactic used by the Junkers 86Rs, to get to high altitude before they crossed the south coast of England.

Galitzine spiralled up to 15,000ft over Northolt, before the ground controller informed him that the intruder was midway across the Channel heading for the Portsmouth area. The Spitfire turned to the south-west and continued its climb. As he approached the Solent at 40,000ft, Galitzine caught sight of the enemy plane slightly higher and to his starboard.

I continued my climb and headed after him, closing in until I could make out the outline of a Junkers 86; by then I was about half a mile away from him and we were both at 42,000ft to the north of Southampton. The German crew had obviously seen me, because I saw the Junkers release a bomb, put up its nose to gain altitude and turn round

The unarmed Junkers 86R, with a pressurised cabin and heavily supercharged diesel engines, was designed to attack targets from ultra-high altitudes around 45,000ft.

Flying Officer Emanuel Galitzine piloted the modified Spitfire Mark IX during the action.

for home. My Spitfire had plenty of performance in hand, however. I jettisoned my 30gal slipper tank which was now empty, and had little difficulty in following him in the climb and getting about 200ft above the bomber.

Oberfeldwebel Horst Goetz, the pilot of the German bomber, now gives us his side of the story:

Suddenly Erich [Leutnant Erich Sommer], sitting on my right, said that there was a fighter closing in from his side. I thought there was nothing remarkable about that – almost every time we had been over England in the Ju 86R, fighters had tried to intercept us. Then he said the fighter was

climbing very fast and was nearly at our altitude. The next thing, it was above us. I thought Erich's eyes must be playing tricks on him, so I leaned over to his side of the cabin to see for myself. To my horror I saw the Spitfire, a little above us and still climbing.

Goetz immediately jettisoned the bomb, switched on the nitrous oxide injection system and de-pressurised the cabin to reduce the risk of an explosion decompression if it was punctured. He then pushed open the throttles to try to out-climb his would-be assailant.

To the Spitfire pilot, the German bomber seemed enormous, and the long curling condensation trail behind it looked like the wake from a large liner ploughing through a calm sea at speed. Galitzine continued:

> I positioned myself for an attack and dived to about 200yd astern of him, where I opened up with a three-second burst. At the end of the burst my port cannon jammed and the Spitfire slewed round to starboard, then, as I passed through the bomber's slipstream, my canopy misted over. The canopy took about a minute to clear, during which time I climbed back into position for the next attack. When I next saw the Junkers it was heading southwards, trying to escape out to sea. I knew I had to get in close behind him if I was to stand any chance of scoring hits, because it would be difficult to hold the Spitfire straight when the starboard cannon fired and she went into a yaw. Again I dived to attack but when I was about 100yd away the bomber went into a surprisingly tight turn to starboard. I opened fire but the Spitfire went into a yaw and fell out of the sky; I broke off the attack, turned outside him and climbed back to 44,000ft.

Horst Goetz managed to avoid two further attacks, then he made good his escape in a patch of mist. Galitzine broke off the action and, short of fuel, he landed at Tangmere. Goetz put the Junkers 86R down at Caen and the crew made a careful examination of the aircraft to check it for damage. They found that it had been hit by just one round, which entered the top of the port wing and exited through the leading edge. The two men had indeed been fortunate to escape, and it was clear that the high-flying bombers' immunity from fighter attack was an illusion. Less then three weeks after they started, the operations of the Hoehenkampfkommando were brought to a precipitate end.

While conducting interviews in Germany, the author met Horst Goetz and Erich Sommer, and was able to bring them together with Emanuel Galitzine. The three men became firm friends. After their meeting Goetz commented, tongue firmly in cheek: 'Emanuel and I have talked about our battle in great detail and now we understand each other's problems. The next time we fly against each other, we shall be able to do things much better!'

Above: Exit hole of Galitzine's 20mm round, after it passed through the port wing of the Ju 86R.

Left: Horst Goetz (left) and Emanuel Galitzine at the author's home, reliving the details of their first meeting.

115

31

EAGLE SQUADRON, EIGHTH AIR FORCE

Ervin Miller, a citizen of the then-neutral USA, volunteered for service as a pilot in the Royal Air Force in 1940. He had fallen in love with flying and his job, working for the US government, served merely as a way of raising money to pay for his time airborne.

By the middle of 1940 I had amassed about 400 flying hours in light aircraft. In volunteering for the RAF I must admit I had no noble motives like helping defeat Nazism, or defending freedom, or anything like that. All I wanted was to get my hands on a really high-performance aircraft. At that time, entry as a pilot into the US Army Air Corps was very restricted; if one did not have a degree – and I did not – it was almost impossible.

Initially things moved very slowly and it was mid-1941 before I began my advanced flying course at a private flying school at Tulsa, Oklahoma, paid for by the British government. Towards the end of the year I received a commission as a pilot officer in the RAF, and came to Britain for further training which culminated at the Spitfire Operational Training Unit at Llandow in the spring of 1942.

The following May I joined No. 133 'Eagle' Squadron at Biggin Hill, which was operating Spitfire Vs; the commander, Squadron Leader 'Tommy' Thomas, and the ground crewmen were British; the rest of the pilots were American. After a period of familiarisation I began flying on operations in June, but not until the end of July did I see (or rather, take part in) an air combat. On the 28th we were operating as one of the support wings for a sweep over France when Focke Wulfs and Messerschmitts 'bounced' us. I was flying as No. 2 to Flight Lieutenant Don Blakeslee, my flight commander, and before take-off he had said to me, 'If we get bounced, for Christ's sake don't lose me.' Well, we were 'bounced' – and I didn't lose him. I just hung on like a leech and all I recall of my first dogfight was the sight of his tailwheel. I don't think I even noticed a Jerry!

I flew on a few more operations, then, in August, the squadron received some exciting news: we were to re-equip with the new Spitfire Mk IXs. I made my first flight in one on the 26th; she was a beauty. While the old Mark V became 'mushy' above 20,000ft as the engine power began to fall away, the Mark IX, with her powerful Merlin 61 with a two-stage supercharger, just seemed to go on and on. Conversion presented no problems; as soon as we had sufficient Mark IXs we were declared operational on type.

⊼ ⊼ ⊼

In the meantime, even more fundamental changes were in the wind. It had been decided at high level that the three RAF 'Eagle' Squadrons, Nos 71, 121 and 133, were to transfer to the US Army Air Force where they would become respectively the 334th, 335th and 336th Squadrons of the 4th Fighter Group to be based at Debden. A few pilots elected to stay in the RAF, but Miller was one of those who made the switch.

Just before the hand-over ceremony, however, disaster struck No. 133 Squadron. On 26 September we were ordered to send twelve Spitfires, plus two spares, to the airfield at Bolt Head in Devonshire. The airfield would serve as a forward operating base for a routine covering patrol for B-17 Fortresses attacking a German airfield near Brest. Only twelve of the Spitfires were required for the operation and as I was about to walk out with the others my flight commander, Flight Lieutenant Marion Jackson, called over, 'You stay behind this time, Dusty.' The drop-out from the other Flight, Don Gentile, and I had both been itching to have a go at the Focke Wulfs with our new Spitfires and we begged not to be left behind, but the flight commanders were adamant: we would stay at Bolt Head.

Don and I did not realise it, but our respective guardian angels were watching over us that day. The squadron started up and took off, then formed up and disappeared into the layer of cloud. On the ground Don and I kicked our heels until their planned time of return, but there was no sign of them. Then the Spitfire Vs of a Canadian squadron engaged in the same operation returned late, on the very last of their fuel. When our squadron's Spitfires' limit of endurance time came and went, with still no sign of them, we knew that something dreadful had happened. Then we heard that one of our pilots, Bob Beaty, had crash-landed a few miles up the coast; he had run out of fuel, but managed to glide back the last few miles and had reached land.

Later we were able to piece together the story of what had happened to the others. The squadron had set out over 10/10th cloud cover which concealed the ground features and, unknown to them, at their altitude there was a north-easterly jet-stream with winds of over 100mph. The Spitfires were blown far into the Bay of Biscay before, on ETA [Estimated Time of Arrival] and having sighted nothing the leader, Flight Lieutenant Dick Brettell, turned round for home. He called one of the ground direction-finding stations for a steer and the one he received placed him about where he expected to be – a single direction-finder could not, of course, provide a fix. Again on ETA the formation closed up and let down through the layer of cloud. When they emerged out the bottom they found themselves over land, which they took to be Cornwall. After a fruitless search for their airfield the eleven Spitfires found a large town, which they flew over at low level in an attempt to get a fix.

By that time the aircraft were getting low on fuel. Suddenly all hell broke loose: the town was the port of Brest, one of the most heavily defended German positions in France. Several Spitfires were shot down immediately by flak or fighters; my good friend Gene Neville, who was occupying my usual position as No. 2 to the flight commander, suffered a direct hit from flak and was killed instantly. And those Spitfires which were not shot down simply ran out of fuel and crashed. Beaty had managed to get back only because his engine was running roughly and he had left the formation to return early. For him, Don Gentile and me, it had been a very narrow escape.

Afterwards there was a court of inquiry. I understand that the existence of the strong tail wind had been known, but this vital information had not been passed to the fighter squadrons. I heard later that as a result some of the sector controllers received hasty postings to insalubrious destinations in the Far East.

The formal ceremony to hand the 'Eagle' squadrons over to the USAAF took place at Debden on 29 September, three days after the Brest disaster, and it was a sadly depleted No. 133 Squadron which took part. Moreover we had had to leave our shiny new Mark IX Spitfires at Biggin Hill, and at Debden there were only the old Mark Vs. We were soon brought up to strength again with replacement pilots, however, and operations continued much as before.

From time to time we provided support for the daylight bomber attacks into occupied Europe, but the Spitfire was so restricted in range that we could not go where the action was. Of course the Germans knew this and again and again we saw them closing in on the bombers as shortage of fuel forced us to turn back.

In January 1943 General Hunter, the commander of the 8th Fighter Command, came to visit us at Debden. He said he had a 'surprise' for us – we were soon to re-equip with the very latest American fighter, the P-47 Thunderbolt. As he spoke we heard an unusual engine note outside and one of the new fighters landed and taxied up beside one of our Spitfires. We went outside to look it over. It was huge: the wing tip of the P-47 came higher than the cockpit of the Spitfire. When we strapped into a Spitfire we felt snug and part of the aircraft; the Thunderbolt cockpit, on the other hand, was so large that we felt that if we slipped off the Goddamned seat we would break a leg! We were horrified at the thought of going to war in such a machine: we had had enough trouble with the Focke Wulfs in our nimble Spitfire Vs; now this lumbering 7-ton monster seemed infinitely worse, a true 'air inferiority fighter'.

Initial mock dogfights between Thunderbolts and Spitfires seemed to confirm these feelings. We lost four Thunderbolt pilots in rapid succession, spinning in from low level while trying to match Spitfires in turns. In the end our headquarters issued an order banning mock dogfighting in Thunderbolts below 8,000ft.

Spitfire V belonging to the 31st Fighter Group based at Membury, England, early in 1943. In total the US Army Air Force took delivery of just short of a thousand Spitfires, comprising Marks V, VIII, IX, and XIs.

Gradually, however, we learnt how to fight in the Thunderbolt. At high altitude she was a 'hot ship' and very fast in the dive. The technique was not to 'mix it' with the enemy but to pounce on him from above, make one quick pass and get back up to altitude; if anyone tried to escape from a Thunderbolt by diving, we had him cold. Even more important, at last we had a fighter with the range to penetrate deeply into enemy territory – where the action was. So, reluctantly, we had to give up our beautiful little Spitfires and convert to the new juggernauts. The war was moving on and we had to move with it.

The change to the Thunderbolt might have been necessary militarily, but my heart remained with the Spitfire. Even now, many years after I flew them on operations, the mere sound or sight of a Spitfire brings me a deep feeling of nostalgia and many pleasant memories. She was such a gentle little aeroplane, without a trace of viciousness. She was a dream to handle in the air. I feel genuinely sorry for the modern fighter pilot who has never had the chance to get his hands on a Spitfire; he will never know what real flying was like.

32

ENTER THE SEAFIRE

Throughout the early years of the Second World War, the Royal Navy suffered from its lack of a high-performance, carrier-based fighter. Following successful deck operating trials with Hurricanes during 1941, it was only to be expected that the Spitfire would also be considered for that role. A key to the Spitfire's success as a fighter was the mating of the most powerful engine available with a cleverly designed lightweight airframe. That made for an excellent land-based fighter, but it also produced one that was not really robust enough to withstand the rough-and-tumble of carrier deck operations. The service career of the naval variant of the fighter, the Seafire, would be dogged by that fundamental problem.

The initial trials to test the suitability of the Spitfire for deck operations took place in December 1941. Commander Peter Bramwell made a series of landings on HMS *Illustrious* in a Spitfire V fitted with an A-frame hook under the fuselage. The carrier was available for only a short time and the trials were not comprehensive, though they did show that the idea was worth pursuing. As a result, the Royal Navy initiated a programme to modify a batch of Mark V Spitfires for carrier operations.

The first naval fighter variant was designated the Seafire IB. It was an existing Spitfire VB aircraft with a minimum of modification for its new role. In addition to the arrester hook, the naval variant was fitted with slinging points for hoisting it on and off decks. It also carried specialised naval radio equipment in the shape of a high-frequency R/T set, a homing beacon receiver and naval IFF equipment. For training purposes another batch of Spitfire VBs was modified to a lower standard, with the arrester hook, navy R/T set and IFF equipment, but without the slinging points or beacon receiver. To differentiate these aircraft from those fully equipped for carrier operations, they were known as 'hooked Spitfires'.

Meanwhile, work advanced rapidly on a batch of new-build Seafires, Mark IICs. This variant was based on the Spitfire VC, which had a redesigned and rather more robust wing structure. As well as the naval modifications applied to the Seafire IB, it

had catapult spools and some strengthening of the fuselage to accommodate the stresses of a deck landing. Again, the 'C' referred to the type of wing fitted and there was no Seafire IIA or IIB. At the same time, Supermarine engineers began working on the design of a suitable folding wing mechanism for the Seafire. Although this refinement was highly desirable for carrier operations, it was not indispensable. In order not to delay the entry of the Seafire into frontline service, both the initial variants lacked folding wings. The first Seafire IBs and IICs were taken on Royal Navy charge in June 1942 and, in the weeks to follow, five fighter squadrons re-equipped with the Seafires and began working up.

In Action During Operation Torch

Five squadrons of Seafires, with a total of fifty-four Seafires, embarked on carriers taking part in Operation Torch – the invasion of Morocco and Algeria. Nos 801 and 807 Squadrons embarked in HMS *Furious*, No. 880 in *Argus*, No. 884 in *Victorious*, and No. 885 Squadron in *Formidable*.

The Seafire first went into action on 27 October 1942, when Lieutenant S. Hall of No. 800 Squadron claimed hits on a Junkers 88 that had been shadowing the force. On 8 November, the first day of the landings, all Seafire units flew in support of British troops going ashore in Algeria. In addition to the fifty-four Seafires, the Royal Navy fighter force in the area comprised some eighty Sea Hurricanes and Martlets. The main Vichy French air threat to the landings in Algeria comprised seventy-five Dewoitine 520 fighters and fifty-four LeO 451 and Douglas DB-7 bombers. In addition there were thirteen Latécoère 298 torpedo bombers.

The Seafire IICs of No. 807 Squadron, operating from *Furious*, were particularly active. Early that morning the unit sent ten aircraft to strafe the airfield at Tafaraoui, causing the destruction of four LeO 451 bombers. On their way back to their carrier they passed La Senia airfield, then under attack from Albacores and Sea Hurricanes, and the Seafires joined

Early type arrester hook, as fitted to the Seafire Marks I, II and III.

in. French D.520s then appeared on the scene and after a brief fight Sub Lieutenant G. Baldwin shot down one of them to gain the Seafire's first confirmed aerial victory.

After the first day, French resistance in the air virtually came to an end. As invading troops seized airfields ashore and land-based fighter units flew in from Gibraltar, the previous dependence on the aircraft carriers to provide fighter cover waned. At dusk on the 9th, *Furious* and two escort carriers made their programmed withdrawals, and the last of the Seafires departed from the area in *Victorious* and *Formidable* on 13 November.

During Operation Torch the Seafires destroyed three enemy aircraft and damaged three more in the air, and destroyed four on the ground in strafing attacks. During the operation twenty-one Seafires were destroyed; three fell to enemy action and nine were wrecked in deck landing accidents. Of the rest, most ditched or made forced landings ashore after running out of fuel. Two pilots were killed.

It would be misleading to judge the Seafire's performance during 'Torch' solely on its kill-to-loss ratio, however. The Vichy French combat units in the area possessed sufficient modern aircraft to cause serious losses to the troops coming ashore. Only fighters could prevent this and, initially, those supporting the landing could come only from the supporting carriers. In flying conditions that were far from ideal, the Royal Navy pilots ensured that the landings went ahead with no interference from the air.

In Action During Operation Avalanche

The next major action involving the Seafire was Operation Avalanche – the landings at Salerno near Naples in Italy in September 1943. The beachhead was some about 230 miles from the newly captured airfields in Sicily, which placed it close to the limit of effective action for Allied land-based fighters. At that distance the Spitfire could spend only twenty minutes on patrol, while the twin-engined P-38 Lightning could spend forty minutes there. On the other hand, Seafires operating from carriers close to the beachhead could spend sixty minutes on patrol.

The Royal Navy force assigned to provide fighter cover the landings comprised five escort carriers: *Attacker*, *Battler*, *Hunter*, *Stalker* and *Unicorn* with a total of 106 Seafire LIICs. From dawn on the first day of the landings, 8 September, until dawn on the 14th, the Seafires flew a total of 713 combat sorties from carriers and a further fifty-six from airstrips established ashore. Enemy bombers and fighter-bombers made several attempts to hit targets ashore, but most of their attacks were broken up or turned away and no serious damage was inflicted. Seafires shot down two enemy aircraft and inflicted damage on four others, and no Seafire was lost to enemy action.

Those were the positive aspects of the Seafire's performance over Salerno. On the negative side, no fewer than eighty-three of these fighters were wrecked or damaged beyond immediate repair in accidents during that period. On an average sortie involving a deck landing, one in every nine resulted in the loss of, or serious damage to, a Seafire. Seven pilots were killed and three injured. Thirty-two Seafires were wrecked in catastrophic deck-landing accidents, an average of one in every twenty-two sorties. The primary cause of the crashes was the light winds present in the area throughout the operation. When landing on the slow and small escort carriers, the fighters approached the deck at a greater relative speed than normal. The limited deck-landing experience of many of the pilots compounded the problem. In the resultant heavy landings, many Seafires suffered damaged undercarriages or wrinkling of the skin of the rear fuselage, both of which would put a fighter out of action until it could be overhauled ashore.

33

THE SECOND GREATEST THRILL

By Frank Hercliffe

Landing any sort of fixed-winged aircraft on the deck of a ship requires flying skill of a high order. But to land a Seafire on the short flight deck of a relatively slow-moving escort carrier was particularly difficult, for there was so little margin for error.

Having completed almost 100 hours' flying time in the Seafire and having made scores of aerodrome dummy deck landings at the Naval Air Station at Henstridge in Somerset, as a young sub-lieutenant I was judged to be ready for my first landing on a carrier at sea. Accordingly I took off from the Naval Air Station at Ayr one fine summer's day and made off north-eastwards at 3,000ft towards the training carrier HMS *Ravager*, which was cruising off the Isle of Arran. A few minutes after take-off I caught sight of her – or rather her wake – as she pushed herself through the water at about 20 knots (kts). From the air she looked ridiculously small. Could I really land on that?

Over the radio I received clearance to join the carrier's circuit, and once I was down at 500ft she did look a little bigger – though still too small for my liking. Quickly I ran through my pre-landing checks: wheels, flaps and hook down, mixture rich and propeller in fine pitch. Then I pulled my harness tight, pulled down my goggles, and slid back the hood. The view over the nose of the Seafire was notoriously bad and the only way to put one down on the deck was to fly a curved approach to enable one to keep the carrier in sight throughout. I began my run in from a position about half a mile off *Ravager's* port quarter, with my head out the port side of the cockpit watching the antics of the batsman on the port side of the carrier.

During the final approach I knew I had to follow the batsman's instructions implicitly; since my own head was outside the cockpit I had no idea what my instruments were reading and I had to rely on him to bring me in. But the batsmen were all very experienced deck-landing pilots themselves and they knew their business; merely by observing the attitude of the Seafire, they could judge her speed to within 2 or 3kts.

That final approach took well under a minute, but at the time it felt like a lifetime: nose well up, plenty of power on and the deck getting progressively larger and larger. The batsman's signals told me I was doing all right: down a bit ... down a bit ... OK ... OK... Suddenly his left forearm went horizontally across his chest: cut! I yanked back the throttle and for an instant everything seemed to go quiet. Then the hook caught the No. 2 wire, my Seafire was plucked from the sky and the wheels hit the deck with a thump. Firmly I was drawn to a halt and, thanks to my tightened straps, I had no feeling of violent deceleration. I was down!

Almost at once people seemed to emerge from holes all round the deck. The deck control officer (DCO) ran out to a position in front of my starboard wing, two seamen ran out clutching chocks and made for my wheels, and through the corner of my eye I could see others struggling to clear my hook from the wire and lock it in the 'up' position under the fuselage. The next thing I knew, the DCO was waving his flag above his head: the signal for me to rev up the engine for an immediate take-off. I was much too busy for any self-congratulations, which was probably just as well.

The take-off from a carrier was straightforward, though it involved a bit of juggling immediately afterwards. Because of the risk of the aircraft ditching, we always launched with our canopies open and the door catches on half-cock so that we could get them open quickly if we had to make a hurried exit. For the take-off we held the stick in the right hand and the throttle in the left. Then, as soon as we were airborne, we had to change hands and take the stick in the left, so that we could retract the undercarriage with the lever on our right. That done we had to change hands again, controlling the

The moment of truth: the Batsman gives the 'Cut!' signal to close the throttle, as the Seafire takes an arrester wire.

Seafire with the right hand while closing fully the door with our left. Then we changed hands yet again, holding the stick in the left hand while sliding forward the canopy with our right. After that a final change of hands, to enable us to press the throttle-mounted transmit button and announce to the world that I was safely airborne.

That first day I did eight landings, with a break for coffee in the middle; my third was a bit hairy, when I took No. 7 out of the eight wires – had I taken the eighth, I should also have hit the barrier. So it was that I had my initiation into the realities of landing a Seafire on the deck of a small and relatively slow escort carrier – the second greatest thrill a man can have.

34

REPORT ON SEAFIRE DECK LANDING

The Seafire entered service with No. 897 Squadron in June 1942 and first saw action over the Mediterranean the following autumn. It soon became clear that the naval derivative of the Spitfire was not really strong enough for the rough-and-tumble of deck operations; this, combined with problems of control near the stall and a landing speed higher than previous aircraft operated by the Royal Navy, resulted in numerous deck-landing accidents. The Seafire gained a reputation as a bad naval fighter, but with no other British aircraft available with a comparable performance the Royal Navy had little choice but to use the type.

Jeffrey Quill, the chief test pilot at Supermarine Aviation Ltd, was seconded to the Fleet Air Arm with the rank of lieutenant commander to investigate the problems encountered with Seafire deck operations. In February 1944 he submitted his analysis of the problem as 'Report on Spitfire Deck Landing', excerpts of which are given below.

It is thought that there are four main factors which contribute to the success and practicability of deck landing on ships under conditions as they exist today. These are:

(1) The method of approach.
(2) The view from the aeroplane.
(3) The 'Speed controllability' of the aeroplane.
(4) The robustness of the aeroplane to withstand the degree of rough usage which may be expected on the deck under sea-going conditions.

No (1) is entirely up to the pilots and DLCOs [Deck Landing Control Officers – the 'batsmen' who guided aircraft in to land]; the remainder depend on the suitability of the design of the aeroplane.

It is proposed in this report to deal with the above four factors in so far as Seafire aircraft are concerned, with an additional section at the end dealing with some miscellaneous points which directly or indirectly affect the issue.

SECTION 1: THE APPROACH

The success of a deck landing in any aircraft depends very largely on a suitable method of approach being employed. This is particularly the case in Seafire aircraft in which, to get the best results, a fairly high degree of accuracy on the part of the pilots and DLCOs is necessary.

Broadly speaking, there are three separate methods of making an approach in a Seafire, which are as follows:

- Firstly, the straight approach for some distance dead astern.
- Secondly, the 'crab' type of approach which follows a flight path dead astern of the ship, but provides an improved view by pushing the nose of the aircraft away to starboard.
- Thirdly, the approach made from a steady left-hand turn arriving from the port quarter, straightening up to the deck only for the last few yards of the approach.

The first two methods are, in the opinion of the writer, both unsatisfactory. The dead straight approach brings the aircraft straight through a Seafire blind area, which lies some distance astern of the ship. That is to say, when the Seafire is in that area and pointing straight for the ship, the pilot is completely blinded. The result of getting into this blind area is in nearly every case the same: the pilot, finding himself suddenly unable to see either the deck or the DLCO, allows his aircraft to wander off towards the starboard quarter in order that he may regain his view of the deck over the port side of his aircraft, and, by the time he has done this, he is getting very close to the ship and must at the last minute make a sort of 'S' turn in order to arrive at the deck at all. The result is always the same, and may frequently be witnessed when watching pilots carrying out their initial deck-landing training. The aircraft arrives on the deck from the starboard side, following a line of direction across the deck towards the port side, frequently also with drift to port, and thereby putting a severe side load on the tyres and

This Seafire of No. 807 Squadron came to grief when landing aboard HMS *Hunter* in the Indian Ocean, in light wind conditions. The aircraft came in too fast, bounced over all the arrester wires, and then leapt over the crash barrier. In the process it tore off both main wheel legs and the tail wheel. It came to a halt on its nose for a few seconds, and then the law of gravity took command.

undercarriage, and the back structure as well. Furthermore, should he fail to pick up a wire or break his undercarriage, the chances are that he will go over the port side. Any question of teaching or encouraging Seafire pilots to make approaches from dead astern should be ruled out absolutely.

The 'crab' approach is merely a modification of the straight approach, the idea being that when the pilot finds himself in the blind area he gets round the difficulty by bringing his aircraft on in what is virtually a left-hand side slip, which enables him to see the deck and the DLCO over the port side of his cockpit. This is all very well for skilled and experienced pilots, but it must be realised that at the best of times a deck-landing approach is made at a speed which, in normal conditions, would be regarded as being dangerously close to the stall. The Seafire has very good control characteristics and lateral stability right down to the stall, provided the flight path is straight, but to introduce an element of yaw at speeds close to the stall is a highly dangerous procedure unless the pilot is very sure of himself in the matter of accurate speed control. The accepted way of putting an aeroplane into a spin is to stall it and then apply yaw. Therefore, to ask comparatively inexperienced pilots to fly their Seafire at a speed within a few knots of the stalling speed and then deliberately to apply yaw, is simply asking for trouble.

It is therefore very strongly the opinion of the writer that the best way to avoid the blind area and provide the pilot with a comfortable view of the deck throughout his entire approach is to teach him to bring his aircraft in from the port quarter in a gentle left-hand turn, which is maintained down to a distance very close to the round-down, thereby successfully getting in ahead of the Seafire blind area which lies astern of the ship and which can cause so much trouble. It must not be thought that the degree of the left-hand turn necessary to achieve the desired result is very high. The final line of approach may be described as being from 'fine leg' and the turn automatically resolves itself into straight flight at the last minute, due to the relative speed of the ship to the aircraft.

Achieving the correct line of approach is, of course, entirely a matter of judgement, and can only be achieved by first explaining thoroughly to pupils and pilots exactly what is required and then giving them practice in carrying it out. It depends on the pilot making his turn-in from the downwind leg at precisely the right moment, which in itself will vary with the wind speed over the deck and the distance abeam of the ship at which the pilot has made his circuit. The pitfall is trailing; that is to say, the pilot, while endeavouring to come in off a gentle turn, misjudges his approach, arrives lined up with the deck too far astern, thus getting into the blind area, whereupon he wanders off to the starboard quarter, and the result is the same as it would have been if he had made a straight approach all the way. The only way to practice pilots in this is to work them up during their ADDL [Aerodrome Dummy Deck Landing] training to a point where their ultimate distance of straight approach on to the runway is getting down to an absolute minimum. At the end of his ADDL training, a pupil should be capable of judging his approach to the runway off a steady left-hand turn, which he should be able to correct accurately at the very last moment. If he becomes used to making the last 300 or 400yd of his runway approach from a dead straight line, he will inevitably have difficulty when he goes to land on a ship.

Apart from the foregoing remarks, there is another powerful argument in favour of this type of approach which cuts the straight way down to a minimum, and this is that when ships are working in company, aircraft which trail astern of their own carrier are using up too much sea room and too much time. A landing circuit which trails astern is a menace to itself and to any ships which may be operating astern of it and, for that reason, even if the view from a Seafire was so good that it was a practical proposition to make a dead straight approach, such an approach would still be bad carrier technique.

The following are considered to be reasonable rough rules for Seafire deck landing:

(1) Circuit height – 300/400ft.
(2) Fly ahead of the ship for ten to fifteen seconds according to the wind speed before commencing circuit.
(3) Keep circuit small.
(4) Lower hook, undercarriage and flaps during circuit before getting abeam of the ship on the downwind leg.
(5) While still ahead of the beam, slow down to 80kts and watch for moment to commence turn-in, which can only be a matter of judgement, but it will be easier to judge it when you have nothing else to concentrate on.
(6) When on the port quarter during your turn, settle down to your correct speed (70 to 75kts with a [Seafire] IIC); keep

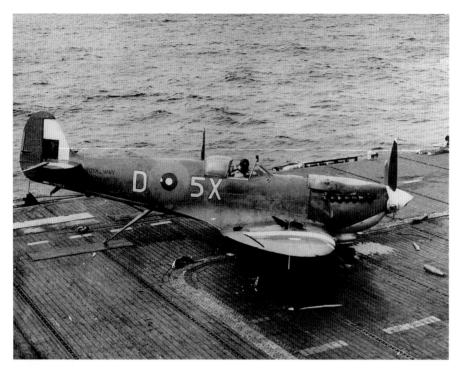

The tail of the aircraft in the previous image fell heavily on to the deck inflicting further damage, as shown above. The aircraft was pronounced to be 'damaged beyond repair'. After everything useful had been removed, the remains were 'Tested for buoyancy' (Navy-speak for pushing the remains over the side).

ejector type with fish-tail flame dampers is very bad indeed, and frequently obscures the pilot's view of the batsman. The triple ejector type without flame dampers is better, but the multi ejector type is the only really satisfactory type. It is appreciated that this fact is realised by the authorities, but at the same time there are still a very large number of the unsatisfactory manifolds in use in the squadrons.

However, in general it can be said that the deck-landing view of a Seafire is not as bad as it has sometimes been made out to be, but it can be bad if a wrong approach is made.

It is not thought to be a major factor contributing towards deck-landing difficulty; other defects in the aircraft, which are dealt with hereafter being, in the writer's opinion, far more important.

SECTION 3: SPEED CONTROLLABILITY

This is the quality in an aeroplane which is dependent on the features of its design which renders it either easy or difficult to fly at a steady and accurate speed under conditions of a deck-landing approach. Factors in the design which go towards providing either good or bad speed controllability are, firstly, a good degree of fore and aft stability at low speeds and, secondly, the provision of plenty of drag when in the flaps and undercarriage down condition, or, more simply, a low lift/drag ratio.

Now it is in the above respects that I feel bound to report that the Seafire is decidedly lacking. The fore and aft stability is decidedly lacking. The fore and aft stability during the approach at low speed is very poor, with the result that the aeroplane tends to vary its speed considerably if the pilot allows his attention to wander for a moment. Also, when in the flaps and undercarriage down condition, the machine is still far too clean aerodynamically, and generally lively; if you are going a little too fast you cannot stop, and if you are going a little too slowly and put on a slight burst of engine, the response is so immediate that before you know where you are you are liable to be going too fast again.

Therefore, to maintain that steady speed, steady altitude and steady rate of descent which are so essential in deck landing, the pilot has to exercise a considerable nicety of touch on both the stick and the throttle. In fact, a degree of skill is required which, while being perfectly well within the capacity of most pilots, is regrettably not to be relied on altogether.

steady rate of descent; watch the DLCO and your speed and make up your mind that you are going to arrive from the port quarter and NOT the starboard quarter.

(7) If you have difficulty in seeing the batsman, put your head out of the port side of the cockpit.

SECTION 2: PILOT'S VIEW

The method of approach outlined in the previous section is designed specifically to provide the pilot with an adequate view of the deck during his approach and landing. The conclusion to be reached is therefore that the pilot's view from a Seafire is not adequate to permit a straight approach to the deck.

If, however, a correct turning approach is made, the view is not too bad. During the latter part of the approach, it is considered advisable that the pilot should put his head out of the side of the cockpit to look round the left-hand side of the windscreen. Furthermore, pilots doing ADDLs ashore should be trained to do their ADDLs with their heads out of the cockpit in order to accustom them to landing in this manner.

A detail which has considerable bearing on the question of view is the type of exhaust manifold fitted. The triple

It is the opinion of the writer that the poor speed controllability of the Seafire is the chief cause of trouble with such pilots who do have trouble with Seafires. As an example, the American Hellcats and Corsairs, although they are very much heavier aircraft and approach the deck very much faster, are, in fact, generally considered easier to land and it is my opinion that their good speed controllability contributes towards this easiness of deck landing more than anything else.

In view of the suggestions made above, i.e. that the Seafire is inclined to be difficult to control at a steady speed and yet, owing to its lack of drag, must be controlled very accurately, it is thought that slow flying practice, apart from ADDLs, should form a fairly large part of the Seafire pilot's deck-landing training ashore.

Needless to say, the remarks on the subject of stability and drag have been communicated to the designers, who are fully aware of the situation.

SECTION 4: ROBUSTNESS OF THE AEROPLANE

By comparison with the types of ship-borne aircraft produced in America, the Seafire would appear to be a somewhat delicate structure which is very easily prone to minor damage on landings which would not have damaged an American fighter. This is to a very large degree true, but it must be borne in mind that everything to do with an aircraft is a compromise and there is no question of something for nothing. One of the main principles which has governed development of the Spitfire aircraft is the reduction of weight right down to the lowest practicable limit, and it is only by adhering to this principle that the rate of climb of the aeroplane has been kept superior to the enemies' (and the Americans') contemporary development. What the correct compromise is, between strength to withstand excessively rough treatment on ships and maintenance of good performance in the air, is very difficult to decide. It would appear that in so far as the Fleet Air Arm is concerned, slightly too much strength has been sacrificed in the Seafire in order to maintain a first-rate performance, and that in the case of the American fighters too much performance had been sacrificed in order to provide the tremendous robustness which they seem to achieve for deck work. For example, if you cut down the load of petrol on a Hellcat or a Corsair to give it the same fighting range as the Seafire IIC, the performance in climb of those two aircraft is still vastly inferior to that of the Seafire LIIC, indicating that their structure weights and power loadings are far too high to be able to cope satisfactorily with opposition from shore-based enemy fighters.

It may be quite rightly argued that the American fighters are required for long-range escort work, which will probably not involve them with shore-based opposition, and that, therefore, is in the interests of the other advantages. However, in the case of Seafires, which are short- or medium-range interceptor fighters and assault force fighters, it is felt that it is not reasonable to expect the same degree of robustness and general resistance to rough handling, as the performance requirements are necessarily so much more severe in order to be able to deal with the best that the enemy can put up in the way of fighter opposition from land. Therefore, if the Navy have a requirement for an aeroplane which is to equal the best of contemporary RAF development, they must inevitably have a higher rate of damage and unserviceability when operating from ships.

This, however, is not in any way intended to infer that the Seafire cannot be greatly improved on in its resistance to bad deck landings etc., by making use of knowledge and experience which has been gained up to date. It is evident, for example, both from statistics and from trials that have been carried out, that the present type of splined undercarriage leg does not absorb sufficient energy to prevent damage to the other parts of the structure and that although the new type torsion link leg is an improvement, there is still room for further improvement, which no doubt can be achieved without paying too much in weight. It is held that there is at the moment far too much damage resulting to Seafire undercarriages as a result of what may be termed 'reasonable landings', and that the whole question of developing suitable undercarriage legs, from whatever source, should be tackled energetically.

A lot of minor damage to arrester hooks and to the frames round the snap-up gear, and to the snap-up gear itself, is experienced in service. It can be established from Cine films that the hook snaps up after hooking a wire in less than 1/24th of a second; furthermore, accidents occur at present due to the hook bouncing on contact with the deck and not picking up wires while it has the chance. This was pointed out to Messrs Supermarines, who designed a hydraulic damper to attach between the hook arm and the fuselage. This was fitted to aircraft and flown by me on HMS *Pretoria Castle*. It had the effect of reducing the force with which the hook snapped up and should, if adopted in service, alleviate the damage to snap-up gears and surrounding frames. As regards the anti-bounce question, this device was tried out by building a ramp across the deck about 18in abaft No. 1 wire, which was intended to cause the hook to bounce over the wire. In every case where the hook struck the ramp when the damper was fitted, it rode over the ramp without bouncing and still picked up No. 1 wire. This is merely mentioned as an indication of what can be achieved in the way of reducing minor damage without necessarily resorting to large increases in weight. It is felt that with regard to all further Fleet Air Arm development the provision of a sting type hook, as fitted to most American aircraft, should be obligatory. These hooks are better in every way; in most cases they avoid too much lift of the tail when the wire is picked up but, primarily, they hang down from what is the lowest part of the aircraft and, therefore, their tendency is to pick up an earlier wire than the normal type hook, even if the aircraft is held too high.

MISCELLANEOUS POINTS

DLCOs [Deck Landing Control Officers]

The importance of making a correct type of approach has been mentioned before, and it applies perhaps more to Seafires than to some other aircraft, but yet is still of the utmost importance to all types.

This brings up the question of the DLCO's contribution towards achieving these two things. The importance of correct and consistent batting cannot be overestimated. A good deck landing is made by the combined efforts of the pilot and the DLCO; if either makes a mistake a bad landing is likely to result. But here there is one thing that is important to remember, that it is comparatively easy for the DLCO to correct a pilot's error, but it may be impossible for the pilot to correct a DLCO's error.

There must be very few pilots indeed who would care to try and land a modern type of aircraft on the deck of a carrier without the aid of a DLCO. The landing, therefore, must be regarded as a joint effort, and it is essential that the DLCOs should be as competent and as carefully trained as the pilots themselves. Pilots who are carefully trained to obey the bats reach a stage where they obey them so quickly and instinctively that if the bats make a serious mistake the pilot is very liable indeed to crash. The writer himself in carrying out landings for the purpose of giving practice to a pupil DLCO experienced the fact that the reaction to obey the bats was quicker than the reaction to query the signal, with the result that he allowed himself to be batted into the rundown, thereby damaging the hook. It might almost be said, therefore, that the bats can hypnotise the pilot into committing suicide and are consequently a most potent weapon in the hands of an untrained or unskilled officer. The following points are therefore submitted for consideration:

(1) Careful selection of Pilots for Training as DLCOs
Squadron cast-offs due to incompetence, nerves, etc., will not do. Batting is hard work, frequently dangerous, and requiring long periods of concentration and expenditure of energy. A batsman is quite useless unless he holds the confidence of the pilots in his ship and, therefore, his past flying record should be such as to learn their respect and not their amusement.

(2) Standardised and Thorough Training
This goes without saying and it is realised that Easthaven [the training school for DLCOs] have this matter in hand. At the same time it is felt that not enough DLCOs are passing through Easthaven and that there are too many 'quacks'.

(3) Limited Periods of Service as DLCOs
If the best type of pilot is to be attracted towards the job of DLCO, there must be an assurance that the job is of limited duration and that it forms a definite step in his progress as a squadron officer and that it will not constitute an indefinite delay in achieving what should be his ambition, namely, to command a squadron.

At the moment the average young pilot regards, and with some justification, batting as a dead-end or backwater for tired and finished pilots. He would be horrified at the idea of being sent on a batting course because he would regard it as having put paid to his flying career for an indefinite period, possibly for ever. This impression must be removed if the best type of pilot is to be attracted towards a period of service as DLCO. The ability to be a batsman must come to be regarded as an extra qualification which assists in the career, rather than as a 'stooge' job.

RECONNAISSANCE TO BERLIN

Reginald Mitchell and his team had originally designed the Spitfire as a short-range interceptor fighter. Yet such was the versatility of his design that it was also to prove one of the most effective photographic reconnaissance aircraft of the Second World War.

Operating at extreme altitudes, reconnaissance Spitfires ranged far and wide over German-occupied territory, bringing back thousands of valuable photographs. A few Spitfire PR XIs were supplied to the US 8th Air Force and equipped the 14th Photo Squadron, 7th Photographic Reconnaissance Group, based at Mount Farm, near Oxford.

In this account Walt Weitner, who as a major commanded the unit, describes the mission on 6 March 1944 when, flying in his Spitfire 'High Lady', he conducted the post-attack reconnaissance following the first full-scale US daylight attack on Berlin.

This mission to Berlin would take the Spitfire PR XI close to the limit of its effective radius of action. So, beforehand, Walt Weitner flew 'High Lady' to the Royal Air Force airfield at Bradwell Bay, near Clacton, where the aircraft's tanks were filled to capacity: 84gal in the two main tanks in front of the cockpit, 132gal in the integral tanks built into the leading edge of each wing, and 90gal in the 'slipper' drop tank under the fuselage. This gave a total fuel load of 306gal, more than four times the capacity of the tanks of the prototype Spitfire when she made her maiden flight almost exactly eight years earlier.

Once the refuelling was complete Weitner, wearing several layers of thick clothing to keep out the cold at high altitude, climbed into 'High Lady' and strapped in. At 1330hrs, as briefed, he took off.

With a full load of fuel and that narrow undercarriage, the Spit would 'lean' disconcertingly during turns when one taxied. But once you got off the ground and got a little speed she really perked up, she would leap away. Once the gear was up and you pulled up the nose, boy would she climb!

I took the direct route for Berlin, heading out on 86 degrees over the North Sea towards Holland. Thirty-nine minutes after take-off I passed my first checkpoint, The Hague, at 39,000ft. There was 5/10ths cloud cover below, through which I could make out the Zuider Zee.

The Spitfire was easy to handle at very high altitude. This one was well trimmed and stayed pretty level. One had always to have hold of the stick, but it needed hardly any pressure. In the reconnaissance business you do not fly straight and level for long, you are continually banking to search the sky all around for enemy fighters and check the navigation.

With all the extra clothing, the parachute, dinghy, life jacket, and oxygen mask, the narrow cockpit of a Spitfire was no place for the claustrophobic! The heavy flying clothing kept me pretty warm, though my extremes did begin to get cold. The temperature outside was about minus 60 degrees F, and from time to time I would stamp my feet to get the circulation going.

Throughout the flight at high altitude my Spitfire left a long condensation trail. I could have avoided it by descending below 22,000ft, but I did not think that was the thing to do on a deep penetration like this. I thought the best bet was to cruise near to the ceiling of a Messerschmitt 109; then, if I had to go up, I had a little margin of altitude I could use. The Germans must have known I was up there but nobody was paying any attention to me. I thought that if enemy fighters did come after me they would have to leave trails too, and I would get plenty of warning.

As I passed over Hannover the skies were clear and I decided to make a photo run over the city. The intelligence people could always use such photos. There were trails ahead at about my level, but they were moving on an easterly heading and obviously not aware of my presence.

Spitfire XI of 14th Photo Squadron, 7th Photo Reconnaissance Group.

The reason for the Germans' lack of interest in the lone Spitfire is not hard to fathom: almost every available Luftwaffe fighter in the area was in action against the force of more than 600 Flying Fortresses and Liberators and their escorts now battling their way westwards back to England, after the attack on Berlin. Over the VHF, Weitner could hear snippets of conversations from combats: 'Three Me's at 12 o'clock, 2,000ft above us. Let's go! Good show! He's smoking now! One lone bomber down there, shall I escort him home?'

As the Spitfire neared Berlin, however, the Luftwaffe finally took notice of the intruder high over the Fatherland. Glancing in one of the mirrors in the side-blisters of his canopy, Weitner suddenly realised he was no longer alone: 'I saw three black forms, also trailing, following an uncomfortable 1,500yd behind, their altitude just below my own.' The discovery came at a bad time for the American pilot. He was running his engine on the drop tank and from his calculations he knew it was almost empty, but since it had no fuel gauge the only indication when it was dry would be when the engine started to sputter – which might leave him without power at a critical time. He thought of switching to one of the wing tanks and dropping the slipper tank, but the mission required all the fuel the aircraft could carry; if he released the tank it would mess up his fuel calculations and might force him to abandon the mission short of the target. Nor would it solve the problem of when to switch the engine over to one of the wing tanks, so for the time being he left the slipper tank in place because the latter contained insufficient fuel for him to be sure it would resume feeding if he re-selected it. Weitner decided to try to outrun the enemy fighters, using the last of the fuel in the drop tank, and see what happened.

I pushed the throttle forward as far as it would go without selecting emergency power, eased up the nose and began to climb. The whole time I nervously held the tank selector valve, ready to switch to one of the internal wing tanks the moment the engine faltered. As I climbed through 40,000ft I could see that the German fighters behind me had split: one went on my right and two on my left, to try to box me in. And at that moment the engine coughed. I immediately selected internal fuel and the engine caught right away.

At 41,500ft I levelled off and my indicated airspeed increased to 178mph [a true airspeed of about 360mph]. After what seemed forever, but was probably only two to three minutes, the German fighters began to fall back and slid out of sight. Had they come any closer I should have gone to emergency boost, but it never got that desperate.

Almost certainly the enemy fighters were Messerschmitt 109s belonging to one of the special high-altitude interception units fitted with the nitrous oxide power boosting to enhance their high-altitude performance. From German records there is evidence that the aircraft which attempted to intercept Weitner belonged to I/JG 3, based at Burg, just to the south of the Spitfire's track.

Still keeping a wary eye on the enemy, Weitner checked his navigation and prepared for the first photographic run on the target.

By now the target was only a few minutes away. I could see the huge Lake Mueritz, some 50 miles north-north-west of Berlin, away to the north. But I could not yet see the city itself because of the smoke and industrial haze. I looked around and noted with relief that the enemy aircraft appeared to have abandoned the chase.

Major Walt Weitner flew the post-strike reconnaissance mission following the first major daylight attack on Berlin.

As the Spitfire lacked a pressurised cabin Weitner had no wish to remain at maximum altitude longer than necessary, so he eased the aircraft down to 38,000ft before suddenly catching sight of the enemy capital laid out beneath him. The time was 1530hrs, exactly two hours since he had taken off from Bradwell Bay.

There was quite a lot of haze, but I could see the sun glinting off the red brick and tile houses. If the German fighters reappeared I might be able to make only one photographic run, so I planned to make the first from almost due north, down wind, to get a good line of photos without drifting off the target. I rolled the Spitfire on its side to line up the string of lakes I was using as checkpoints, levelled out using the artificial horizon and switched on the cameras.

In the rear fuselage of the Spitfire the two vertically mounted F.52 cameras, each with a 36in telephoto lens, clicked at five-second intervals to photograph a 3-mile-wide strip of ground beneath the aircraft. During the photography accurate flying was essential: even a small amount of bank could cause gaps in the cover, and 10 degrees would be sufficient to miss a target altogether. Any correction to the aircraft's flight path had to be made in the five-second intervals between photographs.

My orders were to photograph the bombers' targets and I had been given aerial photos of the city taken previously by the RAF, with the targets marked on them. But I could see smoke rising from places other than my assigned targets so I decided to photograph the sources of the smoke also. The whole time I kept checking the sky behind my tail, as I expected further interference from the enemy fighters, but none came. There was some flak, I could see the smoke bursts mushrooming, but none of it was close.

I spent about twenty-five minutes over Berlin, during which I made runs from different directions and took about seventy photographs. Then a solid layer of cloud began moving over the city from the east, and as fuel was beginning to run low I set a course of 297 degrees for home.

On the return flight Weitner had another drama with his fuel system. The order of using the Spitfire XI's fuel was: first the pilot used the drop tank; next he used the fuel in the wing leading edge tanks, alternating between the two at fifteen-minute intervals so that the aircraft did not get out of trim; then he was to switch to the lower main tank and finally to the upper main tank. As the last of the fuel in the wing tanks was consumed, the Merlin coughed briefly. Weitner switched to the lower main tank and the engine's even roar resumed. How long it would continue to do so was a moot point, however, for the American pilot was disconcerted to see the needle of the fuel gauge hard against the zero mark. Could there have been a fuel leak, leaving the aircraft with insufficient to regain friendly territory? Or might it be simply that the gauge had frozen up?

I discovered why I had toiled over maths for so long without learning its true value! Some rapid calculations proved the main tanks had to be full. During these reveries nothing of a threatening nature showed itself except a few far-off trails to the east. Soon the cloud covering the English coast was within gliding distance, and all was well again. Over the North Sea I descended to 30,000ft and called 'Gangplank' [Bradwell Bay] on the VHF for a homing. Over the coast of East Anglia the gas gauge suddenly came to life showing about 20gal. At my altitude I knew I had enough fuel to reach Mount Farm without having to land at the coast to take on more.

Walt Weitner descended to Mount Farm with the engine throttled back and made a low pass over the airfield. He then pulled the aircraft round hard into position, lowered his flaps and undercarriage, and landed. 'High Lady' had been airborne for four hours and eighteen minutes.

On entering the dispersal area the fuel and the maths ran out simultaneously, leaving a dead engine on my hands just a few safe feet short of 'according to plan' …

36

SPITFIRE MOST SUCCESSFUL

Few national air forces record the detailed combat successes of individual combat aircraft, and the Royal Air Force is not one of them. However, from surviving records it appears most probable the EN398, a Mk IX, was the most successful Spitfire of them all in action.

She was assembled at Chattis Hill, near Andover, and came off the production line early in February 1943. She made her maiden flight on the 13th. Five days later she was delivered to RAF Kenley, the home of four Canadian Spitfire units: Nos 403 and 416 Squadrons with Mk IXs, and Nos 411 and 421 Squadrons with Mk Vs.

The Spitfire was in the hangar undergoing acceptance checks when Wing Commander 'Johnnie' Johnson arrived at Kenley to assume command the Canadian fighter wing. At that time, Johnson's personal victory score stood at seven enemy aircraft destroyed, plus two shared, four probably destroyed and five damaged. In his autobiography *Wing Leader*, he describes his first encounter with EN398:

I found the engineer officer, and together we had a look at her, gleaming bright in a new coat of camouflage paint. Later I took her up for a few aerobatics to get the feel of her, for this was the first time I had flown a [Spitfire Mk] IX. She seemed very fast, the engine was sweet and she responded to the controls as only a thoroughbred can. I never had occasion to regret the choice.

Thus the careers of 'Johnnie' Johnson and Spitfire EN398 became entwined. Having selected his personal mount, Johnson exercised his wing leader's prerogative to have his initials, JEJ, painted on the fuselage in place of the usual squadron code letters. He also had the fighter's weapons re-harmonised to his taste. Before delivery to units, Spitfires had their cannon and machine guns harmonised to a standard pattern that spread the rounds over a circle a few yards across.

That gave a pilot of average ability the best chance to score hits. Johnson's shooting skills were far above the average, however, and he ordered that his weapons be set for the rounds to converge on a single point ahead of the aircraft, to inflict maximum destruction at that point.

As Johnson became familiar with his new mount, he discovered that she had a small but unusual idiosyncrasy. He commented to the author:

The aeroplane always flew with the turn needle of the turn-and-bank indicator a little bit to one side, even when flying straight and level and on an absolutely even keel. That was disconcerting sometimes when you were flying on instruments, because if you corrected for it you would swing off to one side. Changing the turn-and-bank did not cure it – it must have been something to do with the aeroplane. I even took the aeroplane to Eastleigh and had Jeffrey Quill fly it. I asked if he could have it put right. I left it at the works for a few days but they couldn't cure the problem.

Since the Spitfire handled so beautifully in every other respect, the fighter ace decided to live with the small failing.

During the latter part of March, Johnson led his Wing on four separate operations over northern France, flying EN398 each time, although on each occasion the Spitfire returned without having fired her guns in anger.

It was different on Johnson's next mission, on 3 April. During the afternoon his two Mk IX squadrons provided top cover for Typhoons delivering a dive-bomber attack on Abbeville airfield. The raid drew a vigorous German fighter reaction and Johnson was able to manoeuvre his squadrons into a position above and behind a similar number of Focke Wulf 190s. In the 'bounce' that followed, the Spitfires achieved total surprise. Johnson hauled EN398 into a firing position behind one German fighter:

Probably the most successful Spitfire of them all, Mark IX EN398. Flown by fighter ace Wing Commander 'Johnnie' Johnson and bearing his initials 'JEJ'.

I missed the 190 with my first short burst and steadied the gun platform with coarse stick and rudder. I fired again and hit him on the wing root and just behind the cockpit. The spot harmonisation paid off and the cannon shells thudded into him in a deadly concentration of winking explosions. He started to burn, but before he fell on his back I gave him another long burst. Then I broke away in a steep climbing turn and searched the sky behind. Still nothing there.

During the action the Spitfires claimed five Fw 190s shot down, one probably destroyed and one damaged, for the loss of one of their number.

By the end of June, Johnson had added a further eleven victories and two shared victories to his score and that of EN398. He was also awarded the Distinguished Service Order, in recognition of his own rising score and that of the Wing he led so effectively into action.

EN398 was now established as Johnson's personal aircraft. Only he flew her, unless he was absent from the unit for some reason and the Wing needed her to make up the numbers for an operation. That occurred on 20 June when Squadron Leader Robert McNair, commanding No. 421 Squadron, flew EN398 in action and was credited with the destruction of a single Fw 190.

After a spell of well-earned leave, Johnson resumed operations on 15 July, when he led the Wing on a fighter sweep and added a Me 109 to his score. His run of success in EN398 continued with a Me 109 destroyed on the 25th, one damaged on the 29th, a share in the destruction of one more on the 30th, a further share in a Me 109 destroyed, and another of these aircraft damaged on 12 August.

On 17 August the Canadian Wing escorted B-17 Flying Fortresses during the initial part of their penetration to attack the important ball-bearing factories at Schweinfurt. The Spitfires then returned to Kenley to refuel and took off again to escort the badly mauled raiding force during its withdrawal. The Canadian Wing arrived in time to break up an attack on part of the bomber formation, and Johnson and three other pilots shared in the destruction of a Messerschmitt Bf 110. Five days later, Johnson shot down another Me 109.

Since he had made EN398 his personal Spitfire back in March, Johnson had flown the fighter to the exclusion of all others. Near the end of August she needed to go to Air Service Training at Hamble, to receive a replacement engine. While she was there, Johnson flew a borrowed Spitfire on the 26th, and again on 4 September when he shot down two more Fw 190s.

On 5 September Johnson was again in action in EN398, and was credited with one Messerschmitt Bf 109 damaged. He flew her on operations on the 6th and twice on the 8th, but had no further contact with enemy planes. A few days later, he relinquished command of the Wing and was posted to No. 11 Group Headquarters.

During his six-month operational tour, Johnson had been flying EN398 when he shot down twelve enemy aircraft, shared in the destruction of five more and inflicted damage on a further seven enemy aircraft. In addition, Squadron Leader Robert McNair had flown her on 20 June, when he shot down an Fw 190. Thus adding up the half shares in victories, EN398 can be credited with the destruction of fifteen enemy aircraft and causing damage to seven more. She never had to return early from a mission due to mechanical failure, and in Johnson's skilled hands she never received so much as a scratch in combat.

Having achieved so much, the reader might think that EN398 deserved an honourable retirement in an air museum somewhere. Alas, people did not think that way four years into a hard-fought conflict. As Johnson moved away and took up his staff appointment, life went rapidly downhill for his once-pampered Spitfire.

For a couple of weeks EN398 served with No. 421 Squadron, but then she suffered damage in an unexpected accident and went to Air Service Training Ltd at Hamble for repair. The next mention on her record card was in March 1944, when she arrived at No. 83 Group Support Unit at Redhill to await reallocation to a unit. By that stage of the war brand new Spitfires arrived at the unit faster than the operational units were asking for replacements. The newest Spitfires to arrive were the first to be allocated, so EN398 went progressively down the queue and she was still at the Support Unit when war in Europe ended.

In May 1945, EN398 was allocated to No. 80 Operational Training Unit (OTU) at Ouston in Northumberland, where French pilots were being taught to fly the large number of Spitfires bought by the French government. While she was at the training unit, EN398 undoubtedly suffered much harsh treatment from novice pilots ignorant of her distinguished past.

In March 1946, No. 80 OTU disbanded. EN398 made her last flight, to No. 29 Maintenance Unit at High Ercal, Shropshire, where she was placed in long-term storage. Her end came suddenly in October 1949 when, without ceremony, she was sold to H. Bath & Son Ltd for her scrap value.

37

EQUAL TO THE VERY BEST

The Mk XIV was the most potent version of the Spitfire to enter large-scale service before the end of the Second World War. In the spring of 1944 No. 610 Squadron became operational with the Mk XIV, eight years after the prototype Spitfire made her initial flight, and five and a half years after the first Mk Is entered service. How did the Spitfire XIV stand in 1944, in comparison with other modern fighters in the Royal Air Force, the US Army Air Force and the Luftwaffe? Fortunately we know in some detail, for early in 1944 the Air Fighting Development Unit ran a trial to compare her with the Tempest V, the Mustang III (P-51B), the Focke Wulf 190A and the Messerschmitt 109G. Had he lived to read the report, Reginald Mitchell would have had little reason to feel humble.

Tactical Comparison with the Tempest V

Range and Endurance: Rough comparisons have been made at the maximum cruising conditions of both aircraft. It is interesting that the indicated airspeed of each is about 280mph and the range of each is about identical; both with full fuel load (including long-range tanks) and without.

Maximum Speed From 0–10,000ft: The Tempest V is 20mph faster than the Spitfire XIV. There is then little to choose until 22,000ft, when the Spitfire XIV becomes 30–40mph faster, the Tempest's operational ceiling being about 30,000ft as opposed to the Spitfire XIV's 40,000ft.

Maximum Climb: The Tempest is not in the same class as the Spitfire XIV. The Tempest V, however, has a considerably better zoom climb, holding a higher speed throughout the manoeuvre. If the climb is prolonged until climbing speed is reached then, of course, the Spitfire XIV will begin to catch up and pull ahead.

Dive: The Tempest V gains on the Spitfire XIV.

Turning Circle: The Spitfire XIV easily out-turns the Tempest.

Rate of Roll: The Spitfire XIV rolls faster at speeds below 300mph, but definitely more slowly at speeds greater than 350mph.

Conclusions: The tactical attributes of the two aircraft being completely different, they require a separate handling technique in combat. For this reason, Typhoon squadrons should convert to Tempests and Spitfire squadrons to Spitfire XIVs, and definitely never vice-versa, or each aircraft's particular advantages would not be appreciated.

Regarding performance, if correctly handled the Tempest is better below about 20,000ft and the Spitfire XIV is better above that height.

Tactical Comparison with the Mustang III

Radius of Action: Without a long-range tank, the Spitfire XIV has no endurance compared with the Mustang. With a 90gal long-range tank it has about half the range of the Mustang III fitted with two 62½gal long-range tanks.

Maximum Speed: The maximum speeds are practically identical.

Maximum Climb: The Spitfire XIV is very much better.

Dive: The Mustang pulls away.

Turning Circle: The Spitfire XIV is the better.

Rate of Roll: The advantage tends to be with the Spitfire XIV.

Conclusion: With the exception of endurance, no conclusions should be drawn as these two aircraft should never be enemies. The choice is a matter of taste.

Combat Trial Against the Fw 190A

Maximum Speeds From 0–5,000ft and 15,000–20,000ft: The Spitfire XIV is only 20mph faster; at all other heights it is up to 60mph faster than the Fw 190A. It is estimated to have about the same maximum speed as the new Fw 190 (DB 603) at all heights*.

* This is a reference to the 'D' version of the Fw 190, fitted with the more powerful Daimler Benz 603 motor, whose appearance had long been predicted by Allied air intelligence. In fact, the

first Fw 190Ds were not encountered in combat until late in the summer of 1944.

Maximum Climb: The Spitfire XIV has a considerably greater rate of climb than the Fw 190A or (estimated) the new Fw 190 (DB 603) at all heights.

Dive: After the initial part of the dive, during which the Fw 190 gains slightly, the Spitfire XIV has a slight advantage.

Turning Circle: The Spitfire XIV can easily turn inside the Fw 190. Though in the case of a right-hand turn, this difference is not quite so pronounced.

Rate of Roll: The Fw 190 is very much better.

Conclusions: In defence, the Spitfire XIV should use its remarkable maximum climb and turning circle against any enemy aircraft. In the attack it can afford to 'mix it' but should beware the quick roll and dive. If this manoeuvre is used by an Fw 190 and the Spitfire XIV follows, it will probably not be able to close the range until the Fw 190 has pulled out of its dive.

Combat Trial Against the Me 109G

Maximum Speed: The Spitfire XIV is 40mph faster at all heights except near 16,000ft, where it is only 10mph faster.

Maximum Climb: The same result: at 16,000ft the two aircraft are identical, otherwise the Spitfire XIV out-climbs the Me 109G. The zoom climb is practically identical when the climb is made without opening the throttle. Climbing at full throttle, the Spitfire XIV draws away from the Me 109G quite easily.

Dive: During the initial part of the dive, the Me 109G pulls away slightly, but when a speed of 380mph is reached, the Spitfire XIV begins to gain on the Me 109G.

Turning Circle: The Spitfire XIV easily out-turns the Me 109G in either direction.

Rate of Roll: The Spitfire XIV rolls much more quickly.

Conclusion: The Spitfire XIV is superior to the Me 109G in every respect.

Combat Performance with 90gal Long-Range Tanks

As the Spitfire XIV has a very short range it has been assumed that when a long-range tank is to be carried, it is most likely to be the 90gal tank rather than the 30gal or 45gal. Pending further instructions, no drops or trials have been carried out with the 30gal or the 45gal tanks. The aircraft's performance with either can be estimated from the results given below of trials with the 90gal long-range tank.

Drops: The aircraft was fitted with assistor springs as for the Spitfire IX. Two drops were made with empty tanks at 50ft and 25,000ft, 250mph IAS, with no real trouble. Cine photographs were taken and show the tank dropping quite clear of the aircraft. Further trials would be necessary to check these results thoroughly.

Speeds: About 20mph is knocked off the maximum speed and correspondingly off the speed at intermediate throttle settings. The aircraft is then still faster than the Fw 190A and the Me 109G above 20,000ft.

Climb: Climb is most affected. With a half-full tank its maximum climb becomes identical with the Spitfire IX without the tank. Even with a full tank it can therefore climb as fast as the Fw 190A or the Me 109G. Its zoom climb is hardly affected.

Dive: So long as the tank is more than one-third full, the dive acceleration is similar.

Turning Circle: The Spitfire XIV now definitely has a wider turning circle than before, but it is still within those of the Fw 190A and the Me 109G.

Rate of Roll: Similar to that when no tank is fitted.

Conclusions: Even with a 90gal long-range tank, the Spitfire XIV can equal or outclass the Fw 190A and the Me 109G in every respect. Its main advantages remain the tight turn and the maximum climb.

38

SPITFIRE FLOATPLANE

During the campaign in Norway in April 1940 the RAF suffered from the lack of airfields on which to base its fighters. The Air Staff issued an urgent requirement for the construction of prototypes of floatplane versions of the Spitfire and Hurricane. A Spitfire Mk I, R6722, was passed to Folland Aircraft Ltd at Hamble for the fitting of a set of floats designed for the Blackburn Roc naval fighter.

Although the work progressed rapidly, in Norway events moved even faster. The campaign ended in defeat before the prototype Spitfire floatplane was ready to fly and ended the requirement for the floatplane fighter. So R6722 had her floats removed and she was returned to the landplane fighter configuration. After that the idea of the Spitfire floatplane lay dormant for a number of years.

In 1942 the idea of the floatplane fighter was revived and Folland Aircraft Ltd converted a Spitfire Mk V, W3760, to that configuration. The fighter was fitted with a pair of floats specially designed for her by Arthur Shirvall at Supermarine, who more than a decade earlier had designed the high-speed floats for the Schneider Trophy racing seaplanes. The new floatplane fighter was powered by a Merlin 45 engine driving a four-bladed propeller and had a fin extension below the rear fuselage to provide additional keel area to compensate for the directional instability caused by the floats. The floatplane carried a spin recovery parachute and a guard to prevent it snagging on the rudder horn balance. On 12 October 1942 Jeffrey Quill flew the Spitfire floatplane for the first time from Southampton Water.

The initial test flights of W3760 revealed that her directional stability was not good enough, so she was fitted with a revised fin giving increased area. Later she had her armament of two 20mm cannon and four .303 machine guns installed.

In January 1943 the floatplane went to the Marine Aircraft Experimental Establishment at Helensburgh, near Glasgow, for its service trials. Fully loaded, the floatplane version of the fighter weighed just over 1,100lb more than the equivalent landplane version. The maximum speed of the floatplane was 251mph at sea level, 285mph at 10,000ft and 324mph at 19,500ft. In each case, the speeds were about 40mph less than the equivalent landplane version and the rate of climb was about 400ft/min less throughout the altitude range. The recommended take-off speed was 115mph and the recommended alighting speed, with flaps down, was 71mph.

Test pilots reported that handling on the water during taxiing, take-off and alighting was generally good, although, due to the propeller torque, turns on the water to port were easier than turns to starboard. Similarly it was more difficult to taxi on a steady course at low speeds with the wind on the port side than on the starboard side. The aircraft was taxied without difficulty in crosswinds of up to 12mph, but if the crosswind exceeded 15mph it was advisable to shut down the engine and row the aircraft. Beaching and launching using the standard beaching gear presented no difficulties.

For the take-off the trials report advised the use of one-half rudder to correct the swing to port. It went on:

On opening the throttle the control column should be held central. The nose rises at first then falls as the speed increases. When on the step, the control column should be eased back to overcome a slight tendency to nose down further. This tendency is by no means pronounced and any correction made on the control column should be only slight because the elevator control is light and sensitive. A slight pull on the control column is required for take-off at a speed of 81–83 mph IAS [indicated airspeed] in moderate or calm sea conditions.

Once in the air, the Spitfire floatplane handled well, apart from developing an appreciable change of elevator trim during dives. For a floatplane, the aircraft was considered very manoeuvrable. She stalled at 69mph with

The first Spitfire floatplane to be completed was test-flown by Jeffrey Quill on 12 October 1942, from Southampton Water.

In a cloud of spray, a floatplane gets airborne.

The test pilots found the best speed for alighting was about 70mph, with the tail slightly down.

In the summer of 1943, the RAF began detailed planning for operations to exploit the Spitfire floatplane's unique capability. At that time, the German garrisons on the Dodecanese Islands in the eastern Mediterranean were dependent on supplies brought in by transport planes. An ambitious plan was hatched to operate Spitfire floatplanes from a concealed base beside an unoccupied island in the chain, to disrupt the important aerial traffic. A submarine would support the operation, carrying the necessary supplies and the ground crew. Between flights the Spitfire floatplanes would sit at their moorings under camouflage. It was the sort of operation that would succeed for only a few days, until the element of surprise was lost and enemy forces moved into the area to hunt for the perpetrators. But while they were in action the floatplane fighters might cause mayhem among the poorly armed transport planes.

Folland Aircraft Ltd received a contract to convert two further Spitfire Vs to the floatplane configuration. In August the work on these aircraft, EP751 and EP754, was completed, and after light testing the new floatplanes, together with W3670, were dismantled and crated. They were then loaded on a freighter and arrived at the port of Alexandria, Egypt at the end of October.

After offloading, the three floatplane fighters were transported to the seaplane base at Fanara on the Great Bitter Lake, near the Suez Canal, for reassembly. There it was discovered that W3760 had serious corrosion around the tail area and she was put to one side pending the arrival of a replacement tail unit from Folland. The assembly of the two other floatplanes went ahead rapidly and by the end of November both were ready for flight testing.

At the time, Flight Lieutenant Willie Lindsay was on a 'rest' tour at the Middle East Gunnery School at El Ballah in Egypt. Sitting in his tent one day he heard a Tannnoy announcement asking Spitfire pilots to call at the adjutant's office and give the number of hours flown on the type. That sounded as if it might produce something interesting, so Lindsay complied. The next thing he knew he was ordered to report to the station commander, Wing Commander Wilson MacDonald. The young pilot recalled:

flaps down and 82mph with flaps up. In both conditions the stall occurred with the control column almost central with the nose rather high and there was no increased load on the stick. At the stall there was a fluttering noise and the port wing dropped 20 or 30 degrees. Except for the nose-up attitude, there was no preliminary warning of the stall. Recovery was achieved by easing the control column forward. The floatplane was spun in either direction and the report noted that the spinning characteristics were similar to those on the landplane and were considered satisfactory.

On the approach to alighting on the water, it was recommended that the flaps be lowered at about 1,000ft at a speed not exceeding 140mph. When the flaps were lowered, the nose dropped sharply. The best speed for approach was 115mph, which gave a good forward view and enabled the pilot to judge his height better than when approaching at a slower speed with more engine.

The report then struck a cautious note:

Care should be exercised during an approach over hangars, trees etc., because the rate of descent with the engine throttled back is about 2,000ft/min, a fact which is not apparent at first since the gliding attitude of the aircraft is rather flat.

My answers to some prepared questions seemed to satisfy the CO, who then said 'Lindsay, at this stage I am unable to tell you much about the operation you have volunteered for, but it will involve flying seaplanes. Pack your shaving gear and a clean shirt and organise a Harvard for after lunch tomorrow when you will fly me to 107 Maintenance Unit at Kasfareet on the Great Bitter Lake'. I was not aware that I had volunteered for anything, but the prospect of something new and different sounded interesting, and seaplanes at that!

From Kasfareet we drove to the pre-war seaplane base at Fanata and there on the hard standing above the slipway stood two Mk V Spitfires fitted with floats. It was a wonderful moment. I can still feel the tingle of hairs standing up on the back of my neck. With their huge floats, they looked much larger than the normal Spitfire. Back came the thrilling childhood memories of the Schneider Trophy races, the names of Stainforth, Orlebar, Waghorn and others who flew those world-beating Supermarine seaplanes and here I was going to fly a descendant – powerful stuff for a twenty-two-year-old.

Moored beside the slipway was a Walrus biplane flying boat, on which the four selected Spitfire pilots were to learn the rudiments of operating from water. On 30 November, each pilot had a brief period of dual instructions on the Walrus, followed by a solo flight on the type. On 2 December the great day arrived for the pilots to begin conversion training on the Spitfire floatplane. In the meantime, Willie Lindsay had learned that he had been chosen to command the flight of Spitfire floatplanes, which meant he was first to take off in one from the Great Bitter Lake. He continued:

I will admit to being somewhat apprehensive at the pre-flight briefing. It was short and to the point. Standing in the launch and reading from a slip of paper, the CO stressed that I must be prepared for swing on take-off. Gliding and landing speeds were approximately the same but better to allow an extra 10mph or so just to be on the safe side. Lastly and very important, a three-point attitude when alighting so that the extreme end of the floats touched the water first. I recall the CO's words as I climbed onto the float: 'Off you go Lindsay, be a good lad and don't bend it!'

Once in the floatplane with the engine running, Lindsay opened the throttle halfway to get some idea of the swing he could expect during the take-off run. He found the swing was less than expected, though he was surprised at the long run needed for a take-off. Once airborne, he took the floatplane up to 5,000ft to test her handling. He throttled back and lowered the flaps and found that the plane reacted in the normal way, though with possibly a little more 'dip' than usual. Then, like the test pilots at Helensburgh, he discovered the floatplane's disconcertingly rapid rate of sink in that configuration.

Continuing to glide with the flaps down I lost 500ft rather faster than I expected or liked; mentally I added another 10mph to my approach speed. By this time, what breeze there had been at take-off had disappeared and the lake was like a mirror. Fortunately our very experienced Cox'n could see that there might be a problem for an inexperienced pilot judging the height above the surface of the water.

Both launches were dispatched to zigzag and roughen the surface, which was helpful. After levelling off there was some additional 'float' due to the increased speed at approach – however the touch-down was smooth. Speed reduced quickly on the water with some slight porpoising [bouncing] from the following wave, altogether a pleasant first alighting.

Not surprisingly I found the handling sluggish compared with the land version. On 6 December, before doing a cannon test, I took EP764 to 15,000ft to test handling at speed and to try some aerobatics. Starting a slow roll at around 240mph, the roll was more like a barrel roll and the 'barrel' was a big one; at least I was far enough away from critical eyes not to be embarrassed. The loop was better.

I judged it likely that at some stage I would be engaged by enemy fighters and did some further aerobatics and some very tight turns to get the feel of this unusual aircraft. However, I drew the line at test spinning. If I was unfortunate enough to get into that situation, then recovery would probably be via a quick prayer.

All four pilots practised take-offs and alightings, conducting the floatplane version of circuits and bumps. They found no

Flight Lieutenant Willie Lindsay leads a pair of floatplanes over the Great Bitter Lake.

In the event, the scheme to send the Spitfire floatplanes into action over the Greek islands came to nothing. In October 1943, while the floatplanes were still en route to Egypt, German forces with powerful Luftwaffe backing had re-entered the Dodecanese in strength and ejected British forces from the main islands of Kos and Leros. With German fighters now operating in the area in numbers, the plan to operate Spitfire floatplanes in that area was no longer feasible. On 13 December, Lindsay was informed that the operation had been cancelled and he and the other pilots were to return to their units. No other operational use was envisaged for the Mk V floatplanes and they went into storage.

That was not quite the end of the Spitfire floatplane story, however. In the spring of 1944, there were thoughts of using a floatplane version of the Spitfire IX for an operation planned for the Pacific theatre. MJ982 was selected as a prototype and underwent conversion in Folland's experimental workshop. The aircraft was then transported to the Saunders-Roe works at Beaumaris on Anglesey for reassembly. Jeffrey Quill took the new variant up for her maiden flight on 18 June 1944. Later he told this writer:

The Spitfire IX on floats was faster than the standard Hurricane. Its handling on the water was extremely good and its only unusual feature was a tendency to tramp from side to side on the floats, or to waddle a bit when at high speed in the plane.

Soon after the MJ892 began flying, the scheme to use these aircraft in action was dropped. The Mark IX floatplane also went into storage and eventually she and the three Mark V floatplanes were scrapped.

Altogether five Spitfires were converted to floatplanes and four of them flew. Although none of these aircraft saw action, it is yet another aspect of the story which illustrates again the enormous versatility of Reginald Mitchell's original design.

major problems, apart from difficulties in manoeuvring on the water when there was a crosswind.

Soon after his first flight in the floatplane, Lindsay learned the basic details of the operation for which he and the other pilots were preparing. During their flights from the Great Bitter Lake, the pilots found a couple of problems that might jeopardise such a venture. The first was that the Spitfire's floats suffered from small leaks. This did not matter during operations off the lake because after each day's flying the aircraft were hauled onto a hard standing and their floats were drained. At a concealed base in a war zone, however, the problem might have been more serious. Another difficulty concerned the difficulty of manoeuvring the floatplanes in crosswinds stronger than 15mph. During the flights off the lake, the solution had been to switch off the engine and have a launch tow the floatplane back to the slipway. Again, in a war zone, that might not have been so easy.

39

'ANYWAY, IT IS ONLY A SHORT SEA CROSSING'

One of the loneliest places on earth is a one-man dinghy out at sea when there appears to be no prospect of immediate rescue. On 15 June 1944 Squadron Leader John Saffery, commanding No. 541 Squadron, a photographic reconnaissance unit based at Benson, learned the truth of it after he was forced to bale out over the Straits of Dover. The quotations are from the report he wrote shortly after his rescue. The aircraft involved was RM633, a brand-new Spitfire PR XIX from the initial production batch.

On June 15 I was briefed for a target in the Ruhr. After I had got into my flying kit, I decided to wear a new pressure waistcoat which had been given to me to try out the day before. This waistcoat, which can be inflated and used as a Mae West in an emergency, is designed to assist the pilot to get sufficient oxygen into his lungs at great heights.

The initial batch of Spitfire PR XIXs did not have pressurised cabins; the waistcoat provided counter-pressure around the pilot's chest to assist him to exhale when breathing oxygen under pressure.

Among other gadgets, it has a small electric lamp attached to a skull cap that winks automatically for seventy-two hours. When I was strapped into the Spitfire I discovered that the new waistcoat had not been fitted with the quick-release attachment for the dinghy lead. As time was short I tied the dinghy lead on to the leg strap of the pressure waistcoat and remarked to the airman who helped me in, 'Anyway, it is only a short sea crossing'. These very nearly joined the list of famous last words.

I climbed to 30,000ft quickly as there was a trail wind of 120mph at that height, then levelled out and reduced to 2,100rpm. Towards the top of the climb I looked over the gauges out at North Foreland about twenty-five minutes after take-off. A few minutes later I saw that I was not getting quite the speed I had expected and at about the same time I had a feeling, twice in quick succession, of a sudden lack of traction, rather like slipping a car momentarily into 'neutral'. I looked round the cockpit and saw that my oil pressure was reading 5lb [the normal reading was about 80lb/sq in]. The oil and coolant temperatures were both reasonable so I thought perhaps it was just instrument failure. Nevertheless, I turned back for England and called Manston to say I was returning with engine trouble.

When I next looked at the instruments the oil pressure was nil and the temperature was rising, though not alarmingly. I moved the pitch lever to the fully coarse position and began to descend. At about 23,000ft the aircraft began to feel rather peculiar and on looking at the dashboard I found to my astonishment that the rev. counter was reading 4,000rpm.

This was the maximum reading the gauge would show – the normal maximum rpm for the Griffon was 2,750. Almost certainly there had been a failure of the control mechanism for the constant-speed propeller.

I hastily switched off and continued the descent in a glide at about 180 IAS [180mph, indicated airspeed]. I got another vector from Manston and could see the English coast but I began to doubt whether I could reach it as I was losing height very fast. At about 12,000ft I told Manston I could see them and asked whether they could see me. There were chalk cliffs on the coast, which meant that an undershoot would be disastrous, and as there was no future in ditching a Spitfire, I called up Manston and said that I was going to bale out. My height was 5,500ft.

I pushed back the hood, unplugged the radio and oxygen, took off my oxygen mask and undid the Sutton harness [the seat straps]. I saw that I was then doing 140 IAS, so I pushed the nose down until there was 200 on the clock, then rolled the aircraft over with the nose well above the horizon. I let the nose come down, eased the stick forward and dropped out at about 4,500ft.

I saw the [invasion] stripes on the fuselage slide past me and then looked for the handle of the ripcord. The parachute opened immediately. I saw the aircraft dive straight into the sea and burst into flames. This was reassuring as I thought that the column of smoke would be seen.

I went into the water drifting sideways, bobbed up again and got rid of the parachute. I then saw the dinghy pack floating beside me. It had burst open on impact and the dinghy was half out. I grabbed the bottle [containing compressed carbon-dioxide], pulled out the pin, shook the dinghy out of the pack and began to inflate it. When the dinghy was fully inflated I remembered that I had not blown up the Mae West part of the pressure waistcoat, so I inflated that too.

I climbed into the dinghy and lay on my face, puffing and blowing. I turned over to get into a sitting position and found myself back in the sea again. I got in a second time and turned over very cautiously. I then found that the dinghy pack cover had become detached from my harness and I could not find it anywhere. With it had gone the mast, sail, paddles, rations and, worst of all, the rockets and smoke-candles.

As I was rather exhausted, I sat back for a time and could see a big convoy about 3 or 4 miles west of me sailing northwards. Beyond it, about another 5 miles away, were the cliffs of England. It was about 0640hrs and the morning was warm and sunny with a fresh south-westerly breeze. There was a slight chop on the sea and quite a lot of water in the dinghy. I baled for a bit, threw the drogue over the side and fastened the weather apron about halfway up. I saw a buoy about a mile to the north and tried paddling towards it with my hands but soon gave it up as futile and exhausting. About half an hour after getting into the dinghy I saw a Spitfire go right overhead and guessed that he was looking for me. Soon after I saw two Thunderbolts and later an Avenger which also went overhead. This went on all day and was exasperating. I very much regretted the loss of my signal rockets because I was sure that I would have been spotted in the first hour if I could have made any kind of signal. I tried to use my goggles as a heliograph but without success. I think the search was probably made harder by the sun glinting off the choppy sea, which must have made one little 'K' Type dinghy very inconspicuous. I noticed that the drogue was always out to the port side and was pulling the dinghy broadside to the sea, so I pulled it in and found that the dinghy automatically kept head to sea very well indeed.

By noon I had drifted north-eastwards out of sight of the buoy, and I could only just see the coast of England when I rode on the top of a wave. The sea was getting higher so I baled 100 times with the baler, reducing the water in the dinghy to about 1½in in depth, and then fastened the weather apron right up. I did not put the weather cape over my head as I still had my helmet on and wanted to look about me. About every four hours I gave the dinghy ten puffs of the bellows pump. It was not really necessary but it gave me something to do.

The Avenger kept up the search right through the middle of the day and I saw him go past me out to sea on one side and then return the other side several times. I was spotted by a number of birds, particularly by a very pretty little tern with red legs and beak, who would have landed on my head if I had not upset his approach by moving. There was also a puffin who was greatly intrigued and swam around inspecting me from every angle. He eventually got to within about 3ft of me where he bobbed about for quite a time first on one side and then the other. Two porpoises also rolled past but did not come closer than about 20yd – to my relief. In the afternoon the sky clouded over and the swell got longer and higher but although the wind seemed to be freshening it was still quite warm. Some of the seas were breaking and I was periodically soaked, but rather to my surprise I did not suffer from cold. I was wearing ordinary blue battle dress, a woollen pullover, a big woollen sweater, long woollen stockings, flying boots, gauntlets, helmet and Mae West, and this outfit kept me very comfortable except for a rather chilly section around the thighs, which were only covered by the battle dress trousers. The search seemed to lower and intensify in the evening and I saw two Spitfires at about 500ft pass within a mile or two again and again. Sometimes they were even closer. It seemed to me that any aircraft in which the lookout could lie in the nose

Spitfire PR XIX of the initial production batch, similar to the aircraft John Saffery was forced to abandon on 15 June 1944.

and search straight ahead, would be a better search aircraft than a single-engined type. About this time I thought of opening my flying rations, but I was not really hungry and I feared that the eating might make me thirsty. I had no water and no prospect of getting water so I decided not to eat anything until the next morning. At about 1900hrs I saw a Walrus doing a careful search low down about 5 miles south of me. Then when he was about a mile away he headed straight for me and I thought he had seen me, but just about 400yd short he turned to port and returned the way he had come. As he was very close and only about 300ft up, I was very disappointed.

The Air Sea Rescue people put on a terrific search and kept it up all day. If I had not lost my signals they would have found me quite early, as they were always in roughly the right area.

By now dusk was falling, so Saffery pulled on the skull cap and switched on the small emergency lamp.

Everything was soaking wet and I did not really expect it to work. I then put the weather cape over my shoulders, held the weather apron up to my face and tried to get some sleep. About thirty minutes later I heard a terrific racket nearby, peeked out and saw an MTB (motor torpedo boat) about 30yd away. I was thrown a line and taken aboard.

The crew of the motor torpedo boat had seen the lamp winking on the pilot's helmet. Once on board the craft, Saffery was taken below decks and stripped of his wet clothing, rubbed down with towels, wrapped in blankets and filled with rum, then put to bed while the boat completed its patrol.

The incident shows well the difficulties of locating a dinghy from the air if there was any sort of sea running and the survivor had no smoke markers, flares or radio beacon. The problem persists to the present day. It was indeed fortunate for John Saffery that the naval patrol boat chanced upon him, had it not done so his chances of survival would have dropped markedly with each hour that passed.

40

D-DAY GUNFIRE SPOTTER

By Captain Dick Law, RN

Versatility was one of the most important assets possessed by the Spitfire, and during the Second World War she was employed on a range of tasks which probably went far beyond Reginald Mitchell's wildest dreams for his beautiful little fighter. One such task was that of spotting for the heavy naval guns which played such an important part during the invasion of Normandy.

In March 1944 I was a lieutenant serving as the senior pilot of No. 886 Squadron, equipped with the Seafire L III. It was then that we learned that our role in the forthcoming invasion was to be that of gunfire spotters for the bombarding battleships, cruisers and monitors. Our targets were to be the German coastal batteries with their large calibre guns set in massive concrete emplacements, positioned to cover all possible landing areas along the northern coast of France.

The importance of our spotting role was drilled into us from the beginning and there was no feeling that we, as fighter pilots, were to be misemployed during the great invasion. Only heavy naval gunfire, corrected from the air and sustained for a period of days if need be, could neutralise these powerful defensive positions during the critical period while our troops fought their way ashore: low-level bombing would have been too costly, high-level bombing would have been too inaccurate and neither type of bombing could have brought speedy retaliation against the new batteries the Germans were almost certain to bring up.

Gradually we learnt the mechanics of bringing heavy gunfire to bear on a target; first on a sand table, then with a troop of 25-pounders on an army gunnery range and finally with a cruiser firing off the coast of Scotland. Near the end of May we moved to our operational base for the invasion, at Lee-on-the-Solent; the great event, for which we had all trained so hard, was close at hand.

On the actual day of the invasion, 6 June, I was up very early and with my wingman I arrived over Normandy soon after 0600hrs to take control of the guns of the battleship HMS *Warspite*. I should mention that for gunfire spotting it was usual for our Seafires to fly in pairs, with one correcting the fire and the other standing off a couple of thousand feet above, keeping watch for any enemy fighters which might attempt to interfere.

The first target we were to engage was the battery at Villerville near Trouville, where there were six 155mm guns in a heavily concreted position. When I was ready, the carefully-rehearsed patter began. I called up *Warspite* on the VHF and told her: 'Target located, ready to open fire'. She gave me a call five seconds before opening fire, then as she fired she called 'Shot' followed by a figure, say '52', which gave the predicted time of flight of the shells – fifty-two seconds for the firing range of 15 miles. The battleship was a magnificent sight as she lay at anchor, loosing off four-gun salvoes with her main 15in guns. On the call 'Shot' I started my stopwatch and headed inland, so as to have the target in clear view when the shells impacted. As they burst I would radio back a correction to bring the fire directly on to the target, say 'Left 100, up 400', the distances being measured in yards. While the ship's gunners were reloading I would head back over the sea; there was no point in hanging around over enemy territory and risking being shot down and jeopardising the whole operation, for no useful purpose.

When *Warspite* indicated that she was ready to fire again, I would move into position to observe the target and the process would be repeated.

During one of the early salvoes I was a little over-enthusiastic in positioning myself to observe the fall of the shells, with the result that some thirty-five seconds after *Warspite* fired my Seafire suddenly shivered and I actually saw one of the giant shells, weighing almost a ton, go sizzling close past me on its way to the target. During subsequent salvoes, I made good and sure that I was well to the side of the line of fire!

From time to time the German batteries attempted to return *Warspite's* fire; when that happened we were treated to the spectacle of a giant-sized tennis match. During one of these exchanges a salvo straddled *Warspite*, but she received only slight damage.

After about forty minutes of spotting, my fuel was beginning to run low, and after being relieved by two more Seafires we returned to Lee. We spotted for *Warspite* during two further sorties that day.

On the second day of the invasion, 7 June, we were detailed to spot for American warships on the western flank of the bridgehead; accordingly, I found myself controlling the gunfire of the battleship USS *Nevada*. The shoot went according to plan and when the relieving Seafires arrived both my wingman and I had some fuel to spare; so we decided to seek out a 'target of opportunity' (anything on the ground that looked vaguely German) and shoot it up before going home.

That decision, casually made, nearly proved fatal. Looking back on that part of the sortie, I can see now that we were both grossly overconfident about the success of the invasion. We had been keyed-up for a ding-dong battle with the Luftwaffe over Normandy, but the enemy air force simply failed to show up. From our lofty viewpoint it appeared that the whole thing was becoming a walkover. Now we felt that we could hardly go home without having played some more direct part in the impending collapse of the Third Reich. Below us we saw an enemy gun position and we decided that we would wipe it off the face of the earth. It was not, however, a very professional attack; confident in our superiority we took our time turning in and lining up and the men on the ground could have had no doubts regarding our intentions. Unfortunately for us the guns were 37mm flak, manned by crews who certainly did not share our feelings regarding the hopelessness of their cause. As we ran in they were ready and their first few rounds of tracer were extremely accurate: I heard a rapid 'plunk plunk' as a couple

of the shells exploded against my aircraft. It was immediately apparent that they had hit my radiator, for almost at once my engine temperature gauge needle began to climb steadily until finally it was hard against the upper stop. Simultaneously I caught the unmistakable stench of vaporised glycol and the engine coughed to a stop.

I pointed the Seafire's nose towards the coast as I pulled up, but it soon became clear that I had insufficient height to reach the sea; I selected some flat land a little way inland and prepared to put her down there. The actual belly landing was a bit of an anti-climax: the Seafire slid gently to a halt on the soft marshland and there was no fire or drama of any sort.

As I clambered out of the aircraft I rapidly became aware of the appalling din of battle: there seemed to be guns of all calibres firing and shells exploding – the latter, fortunately, all some distance away. In the cockpit of my noisy aircraft far above, I had been quite oblivious to the intensity of the battle below.

Then the rushes in front of me parted, and there was a very tall American corporal who beckoned me over. Apparently, I had come down in an uncontested part of no-man's-land. When I reached him, his first gesture was to offer me a swig from his water bottle; I was not all that thirsty at the time but I thought it good manners to accept – and I was glad I did, for the bottle contained a very reasonable *vin rosé*. I later learned that he had been ashore only a few hours, so he must have been a pretty good organiser!

Gradually I worked my way back through the system to the beach, where I was taken out to a motor torpedo boat which took me back to England. I was soon able to rejoin my squadron and, after my salutary experience, contented myself with getting bigger guns than my Seafires to do the work of destruction.

The success of the Normandy landings and their effect on the course of the war, are now common knowledge. Without doubt the accuracy of the heavy naval gunfire played a major part in making this possible, and I am very happy that I was able to assist in this.

41

D-DAY TOP COVER SQUADRON

Having flown Spitfire Mk Vs in combat over Malta, Flight Officer Don Nicholson returned to England at the end of 1943 and joined No. 131 Squadron at Colerne in Wiltshire, operating the Mk IX. At the beginning of March 1944 the unit re-equipped with Spitfire VIIs, the specialised high-altitude version fitted with a pressurised cabin, an uprated Merlin and extended wing tips to enable it to operate above 40,000ft.

To provide sufficient fuel for a full-throttle climb to such an altitude, and a useful endurance when the fighter got there, the Mk VII was fitted with enlarged main tanks holding 96gal of fuel, and two 14gal tanks in the leading edge of the wings. The Mk VII thus had an internal fuel capacity of 124gal – 40 per cent more than other Merlin-engined fighter versions of the Spitfire operating from Britain (the Mk VIII had a similar tank arrangement, but all squadrons with this version were based overseas).

By the beginning of 1944 it was rare for German aircraft to attempt bombing or reconnaissance missions over England at extreme altitude, and No. 131 Squadron had no opportunity to use the Mk VII in its designed role as a high-altitude interceptor. The squadron, however, would be able to put the extended range capability which came with this little-known version of the Spitfire to good use.

It took the pilots of No. 131 Squadron only a few days to convert from the Spitfire Mk IX to the Mk VII. Don Nicholson remembered the new version with affection:

The Mk VII was designed for high-altitude operations and our planes wore high-altitude camouflage, light grey on top and blue-grey underneath. I liked the Mk VII, it was a good aeroplane. The highest I ever took one was to 39,000ft; it could have continued climbing, but I had no reason to go any higher.

On 18 March 1944 Nicholson flew his first mission in the new version, when the squadron put up eight Spitfire VIIs to escort a force of Mosquitoes attacking a target south of Dieppe. The raiders were engaged by flak, but no enemy fighters appeared and all planes returned safely.

At the beginning of March the squadron moved to Harrowbeer, near Plymouth, for a brief spell. There it got its first taste of the type of operation that would become its main task during the run up to the forthcoming invasion of Normandy: that of flying high-level patrols over ports along the south-west coast of England, where the ships were assembling for the operation. Nicholson continued:

Our job was to prevent German reconnaissance planes taking photographs of the ports. They made few attempts to send in reconnaissance planes; we chased them on one or two occasions but by the time we reached their level they had gone.

Later in May, No. 131 Squadron moved to Culmhead, near Taunton, where it joined No. 616 Squadron, also operating Spitfire VIIs. This airfield was to serve as a base for the Mk VII Wing during the invasion period. Events were now moving to a climax and Don Nicholson was treated to a grandstand view of the proceedings:

On 1, 2, 4, and three times on 5 June I took part in patrols to protect the invasion ships, flying up and down between Portland Bill and Star Point at 22,000ft. Below us, off Portland Bill and in Lyme Bay, were hundreds of ships of all sizes and types.

The term 'Top cover' was relative. If there was need for high cover, we would provide it. If there were other marks of Spitfire also flying over for the convoy, they would be at 10,000 or 15,000ft and we would be above them. But the

Germans were not coming in at high altitude and we were often used as an ordinary Spitfire squadron.

As if to emphasise No. 131 Squadron's 'ordinariness', on the morning of D-Day, 6 June, the unit was ordered to send eight Mk VIIs on a low-level armed reconnaissance of the Brest Peninsula. The Spitfires found and strafed three trains, two trucks and two cars, and returned without loss.

In the days following the invasion, the squadron settled down to a routine of patrols to cover the beach-head and shipping off the coast, punctuated with an offensive fighter sweep over northern France on most days. On 10 June, eight Spitfires on a sweep near Loudeac found a goods train with some twenty freight wagons covered with camouflage netting. Four of the fighters flew in line abreast to strafe the train from abeam, while the other four flew top cover. The attack left the locomotive enveloped in dense smoke and several wagons on fire.

On 12 June, Nos 131 and 616 Squadrons mounted a twenty-four-Spitfire 'Rodeo' operation against the German airfield at Le Mans. While No. 616 Squadron provided top cover, No. 131 Squadron strafed the airfield. Two enemy fighters were set on fire and others damaged. Intensive light flak greeted the attackers, and as he came off the airfield Flight Lieutenant Moody went into a steep climb and called on the radio to say he was baling out. Nothing more was heard from him. Two other Spitfires took hits but were able to continue with the operation. The squadrons reformed and flew to Laval airfield where the tactics were repeated, this time with No. 616 Squadron doing the strafing and No. 131 providing cover. Flight Officer Ken Parry spotted a Messerschmitt Bf 109 flying low to the west of the airfield, and he and his wingman pounced on it and shot it down.

Returning from Laval, Flight Officer 'Eddy' Edwards ran short of fuel, so he put down in the beach-head area at a small landing ground near St Mere Eglise. Used only by light spotting planes, the airfield had no supply of 100 octane petrol, so American soldiers helped Edwards siphon fuel from a fighter which had made a wheels-up landing nearby. Later that afternoon the Spitfire was able to take off and return to Culmhead.

Early on the morning of 15th, Don Nicholson set out from Culmhead for a mission that would prove all too exciting. With Flight Officer Edwards as wingman, he had been briefed to fly a low-level visual reconnaissance to St Peter Port, Guernsey, to follow up an intelligence report that a U-boat had arrived in the port:

We were tasked to have a look at St Peter Port to see if the sub was there. Trying to maintain the element of surprise we flew out at low level and went past the west of the island as if we were going to France. Then we cut back and came up the east side of the island on the deck. While my No. 2 stayed out to sea covering me, I roared over the harbour wall at about 50ft. And there sitting in the harbour was the U-boat, firing at me with everything he had!

Suddenly the plane juddered and I knew it had been hit; I saw a couple of bullet holes in the wings. And immediately afterwards it was clear I had lost my wireless and rudder trim. I jinked to throw the gunners off their aim and headed out to sea, keeping low and trying to make the most of the available cover.

As I came out my No. 2 closed on me. He could see I was damaged, he waggled his wings and led me home. It was a good thing he was with me, because by the time we reached the coast of England our airfield at Culmhead was fogged in and we had to divert to Harrowbeer. Apart from the lack of rudder trim, the Spit handled normally.

On the ground at Harrowbeer, Nicholson inspected the damage. A couple of rifle calibre bullets had passed through the starboard wing without hitting anything vital. More seriously, a 20mm round had exploded on the starboard side of the fuselage just aft of the cockpit. On detonating, the explosive shell had blown a hole the size of a man's fist and the blast sent splinters flying in all directions. Several went clean through the port side of the fuselage, others caused internal damage and wrecked the radio and severed the rudder trim cable. Following an engineering examination the Spitfire, MD172, was judged beyond economical repair and written off.

Later that afternoon the squadron put up a four-aircraft sweep of the area around Rennes, and claimed the destruction of ten supply trucks.

During the 17th, Flight Lieutenant Rudland and Flight Offcer Parry flew a comparative trial with two Spitfire VIIs, one with rounded wing tips and the other with the pointed tips fitted to the rest of the squadron's Spitfires. The trial established that the rounded tips were the better for operations at low and medium altitudes, and in the days that followed these were fitted to all aircraft. The pointed wing tips, which had been one of the main recognition features of the Mk VII, saw little further use.

At first light on 18 June the squadron sent eight aircraft on an armed shipping reconnaissance around the Channel Islands. South of Jersey the fighters found two large self-propelled barges, on which they carried out repeated strafing runs. Several hits were scored, and when the Spitfires left the scene both vessels were stopped and one was on fire.

During a mission over Northern France later that day, the Spitfires shot up four motor vehicles.

On the 19th Flight Officer Edwards was flying on a sweep with No. 616 Squadron near Mayenne when there was a rare encounter with German fighters. In the melee that followed, Edwards shot down a Messerschmitt Bf 109.

On 20 June the squadron sent ten Spitfires, each with 90gal slipper tank, for a fighter sweep operation over north-west France. They were supposed to have gone deeper, but south of Rennes a blanket of thick cloud covered the ground. The formation was forced to turn back without engaging ground targets.

On the 21st Warrant Officer Crayford and Flight Sergeant Tanner conducted a low-altitude shipping reconnaissance around Guernsey, and near St Peter Port they came under intense and accurate flak. Tanner's aircraft was hit, but he managed to get it across the Channel and made a wheels-up landing at Bolt Head airfield.

On the 22nd, the squadron put up twelve Spitfires to escort Lancasters attacking targets in the St Omer area; the mission was flown without incident.

For the rest of June and the first week of July, No. 131 Squadron continued with its routine of fighter sweeps over northern France, the occasional escort mission and frequent, if invariably uneventful, defensive patrols over the beach-head area.

On 8 July, No. 131 Squadron exploited its extended range capability for the first time. Each carrying a 90gal tank, the twelve Spitfires flew a sweep to Tours. The force strafed oil tanks, a truck and a couple of cars, but no enemy fighters were encountered and the fighters all landed at Culmhead after three hours and twenty minutes airborne.

On 12 July, Wing Commander Peter Brothers led the Spitfire VIIs of both Culmhead squadrons to Ford airfield in Sussex, where they refuelled and took off to escort Lancasters attacking the Vaires-sur-Marne marshalling yard east of Paris. The mission was uneventful.

During the next couple of weeks the squadron's operations were confined mainly to the shorter range sweeps. Then on 27 July the Spitfires went deep into western France, to the Poitiers area. The area was a hunting ground for fighter-bombers operating from airfields in the beach-head, however, and there was little to be found. Except for an attack on a single lorry near Tours, which was damaged, the mission was uneventful.

Early in August German fighters put in a few brief appearances over western France. During a long-range sweep to Tours by twelve Spitfires on the 6th, the squadron encountered a force of Fw 190s and claimed two shot down; on the following day, in the same area, there was another dogfight in which three more Fw 190s were claimed. No Spitfires were lost or damaged in either engagement.

On 11 August the squadron mounted what was to be its longest ranging operation of all, a round trip of 690 miles to escort Lancasters attacking the submarine pens at La Pallice. The Spitfires were airborne for three hours and fifty minutes, as Don Nicholson well remembers:

Three hours and fifty minutes – that's a long time to sit in a Spit, believe you me! It was very tiring, just sitting there. We went as high-level escort at about 25,000ft, way above the Lancs who were down at about 18,000ft. We flew throttled well back, we had to be careful with the fuel or we would run out. We didn't have enough fuel for a fight. Had there been a real shindig at the target, we would have been likely to run out of fuel on the way back. We just had to hope that nothing like that would happen.

Fortunately for the pilots of the escorting Spitfires, German fighters did not attempt to contest the incursion.

From the middle of August, as the Allied armies forced the Germans out of France, No. 131 Squadron shifted its main area of operations to the skies over Holland, Belgium and, finally, to Germany itself. The new phase began on the 15th, when the unit staged through Manston to escort Lancasters attacking Le Culot airfield near Brussels.

At the end of August, No. 131 Squadron moved to Friston in Sussex, to bring it closer to its new operating area. On

3 September its Spitfires escorted Lancasters attacking the airfield at Deelen in Holland. On the 6th the squadron staged through Coltishall for its first mission over Germany, to Emden in support of 160 Lancasters and Halifaxes attacking the port installations. On the 11th it supported bombers raiding Gelsenkirchen in the Ruhr Valley, and two days later the squadron penetrated still deeper into the enemy homeland when it escorted Lancasters to Osnabrück, in a mission lasting three hours and ten minutes.

On 17 September the Mk VIIs provided top cover for the Allied airborne landings at Grave, Nijmegen and Arnhem in Holland. On the 30th the unit escorted Marauders attacking a target near Arnhem and, as was the case on every deep penetration escort mission mounted by No. 131 Squadron, no enemy fighters were encountered. However, on the 30th the squadron suffered the rare loss of an aircraft, when Flight Officer Baxter had an engine failure and was forced to land in a ploughed field near Brussels. Unhurt, the pilot returned to the squadron a few days later.

The pace of operations continued throughout October, with the squadron providing escorts for bombers attacking targets at Arnhem, Nijmegen, Deventer and Walcheren Island in Holland, and Wanne-Eickel in Germany. On the last day of the month the unit was ordered to cease operations, pending transfer of its personnel to India where it was to reform with Spitfire VIIs. The re-equipment was not complete when the war ended in the Far East, however, and No. 131 Squadron saw no further action.

42

FOE WITHOUT MERCY

By 'Hank' Costain

In spite of the advances made in aviation, man is allowed to use the sky on sufferance, never as a right. As 'Hank' Costain tells us, the elements can regain control of their domain in the most brutal fashion.

During the summer of 1944 I was a flying officer with No. 615 Squadron, operating Spitfire VIIIs. During the battle to repel the attempted Japanese invasion of India, we had been flying from Palel on the Imphal Plain, but the time came for us to pull back out of the frontline for a brief rest. Accordingly on 10 August our sixteen aircraft took off from Palel with the CO in the lead, for a nice easy trip back to Baigachi near Calcutta; for a quarter of the pilots, however, the flight would be their last.

'Hank' Costain.

For much of the route we had underneath us puffs of thin fair-weather cumulus, and as we neared our destination we let down through them. Soon afterwards the cloud cover above us became complete, but as we had good contact with the ground everything seemed all right. Indeed it was, until straddling our path we found a thick brown storm cloud extending right down to the ground. Clearly we could not go forwards through it and, because we had passed our point of no return, we could not go back to Palel either. So the CO decided to take us back a little way, then we could climb up through the layer of cumulus and once above it we could

search for a way through the storm. But it never happened that way.

Soon after re-entering cloud there was a sudden bang, and everything seemed to happen at once: the sky turned black as pitch, my Spitfire reared up and the stick seemed to go wild in its attempts to wrench itself out of my grasp. Somehow we had slid into that dreadfully turbulent monsoon storm cloud. Within seconds I was completely out of control and with the artificial horizon toppled I had not the faintest idea which was way 'up'. Outside it was so dark that I could not even see my wing tips and the pounding of the walnut-sized hailstones on the fuselage drowned even the noise of the engine. In my earphones I heard the frenzied chatter of the other pilots as they tried to fight their way free from the storm's clutches.

Of my flight instruments only the altimeter seemed to be reading correctly, and from its spinning needles I learned that I was in a violent up-current. After going up rapidly through near 10,000ft, during which my stick seemed to have no effect at all, the Spitfire bucked and entered an equally-vicious down-draft and we were plunging earthwards just as fast. I was terrified. Again, nothing I did with my controls seemed to make the slightest difference. As the altimeter reading neared 1,000ft it became clear that this was no place for Mrs Costain's young lad. I had to bale out.

First I had to get rid of the hood, so I yanked hard on the jettison ball above my head; but the tropical heat had perished the rubber and it came away in my hand. Charming! Since the hood would not jettison I slid it fully back on its runners, then trimmed the nose fully down and undid my seat harness. Finally I let go of the stick and, as the Spitfire bunted forwards, up I went like a cork out of a bottle. At least I would have done,

'Hank' Costain's Spitfire VIII in readiness at Palel in India in June 1944.

but my parachute pack caught on the overhanging lip of the hood. The next thing I knew I was tumbling head-over-heels along the fuselage before ramming hard into the tailplane and shattering my leg. As the tail disappeared into the gloom I grabbed at the parachute 'D' ring and pulled it, then I glanced down to see the ground rushing up to meet me.

The canopy developed just in time, but even so the landing on my fractured leg was excruciatingly painful. As I lay in a sodden heap in that flooded Indian paddy field and began to collect my wits, my first thoughts were for the perfectly good Spitfire I had just abandoned. 'Good God', I remember thinking, 'What on earth am I going to tell the CO?' Luckily I was picked up by some of the locals soon afterwards and they took me to a doctor.

In less than five minutes, No. 615 Squadron had lost its commander and three other pilots killed and three more including myself injured; we had written off half of our aircraft, eight of the most modern fighters in the theatre. And it had all happened without there being a Jap within a hundred miles. When it is angry, the sky is a foe without mercy.

43

AN AERODYNAMICIST'S VIEW

By Sir Morien Morgan

From the time of her first flight, to well after the end of the Second World War, the Spitfire was continually modified to improve her fighting ability. In this section Sir Morien Morgan summarises these changes and throws a new light on the basic reason for the Spitfire's long and successful service career.

In 1935 I joined the Aerodynamics Flight at the Royal Aircraft Establishment at Farnborough and from the start specialised in aircraft stability and handling. At that time there were several new monoplanes being built – including the Spitfire – which flew faster, climbed faster, and landed much faster than the biplanes that preceded them. I remember that there was a terrific rush to develop these new aeroplanes and learn their foibles, to telescope the whole business of background research, design, pilot training and the rest of it. Looking back, I am amazed that everyone did as well as they did – the designers, the research people and, of course, the pilots.

Let me give an example of the sort of mistaken ideas that got around early in the life of the Spitfire. We at Farnborough worked closely with the Aeroplane and Armament Experimental Establishment at Martlesham Heath, where they did the preliminary trials on the Spitfire and the other new military aircraft. I remember being there one day and talking to a very experienced RAF aerobatic pilot who had been involved with the tied together formation aerobatic displays at Hendon. He had just landed after his first flight in the Spitfire prototype, utterly convinced that the days of close formation flying in fighters were numbered; he had handled his throttle in the same way as he did in a biplane and the much cleaner Spitfire had taken so long to lose speed that he thought close formation flying in such an aeroplane would be impossible. I was a young man at the time and what he said made a great impression on me; what effect would this have on future aerial combat? Later, when Martlesham had two or three Spitfires, they tried flying them in formation and there was no real

problem. I think the lesson here is that it is important for the pilots to get their hands on a new aircraft; when they do, it is surprising how fast they are able to adapt themselves to new conditions.

Looking back, I think that the greatest problem at the end of the 1930s was that it was extremely difficult to visualise what combat would be like in the new monoplane fighters; the only air fighting experts we had were from the First World War and that had been twenty years earlier. I think we all paid too much attention to the behaviour of an aeroplane flying on a calm sunny day and harmonising the controls so that they could do nice aerobatic displays; we seemed to miss the importance of handling at speeds around the maximum permissible, in fast dives. Before the war, I remember, people thought that it was rather an academic exercise to scream downhill at one's maximum permissible speed.

The war soon brought us face to face with reality: once our fighter pilots started to mix it with the enemy they found that their main adversary, the Messerschmitt 109, which was less manoeuvrable than the Spitfire, simply refused to dogfight in the manner expected; any German pilot who tried it did not live very long. Frequently the fight would develop into a diving race, either trying to 'bounce' the other fellow from out of the sun, or else trying to get away after being 'bounced'. And with the early Spitfires, as one neared 400mph the ailerons became heavier and heavier, until at 430mph the pilot needed all the strength of both hands to get about one tenth aileron movement. In an air combat this was a crippling defect: if one was diving on an enemy the idea was to fire at him on the way down, and the poor aileron control made this very difficult. At the time there was a terrific flap about it and my Handling Research Team at Farnborough had the job of helping to track down the cause. Luckily the reason was found quite quickly: at high speeds the fabric covering of the ailerons ballooned out, so that the trailing edge became much thicker. Now the amount of stick force required to move a control surface is critically dependant upon the sharpness of the angle of the trailing edge of the surface and just a small increase in the angle can make a considerable difference to the force needed. The answer was to replace the fabric on the ailerons with light alloy, which did not balloon at high speeds. Vickers hastily knocked out a set of metal-covered ailerons and when these were fitted to the Spitfire there was a dramatic improvement in its high-speed handling characteristics. During 1941 there was a large-scale retrospective modification programme to fit all the Spitfires with the new ailerons.

In war nothing stands still; the Germans and the Japanese improved their aircraft and so did we. They key to higher performance was a more powerful engine and Rolls-Royce began to get more and more power, first out of the Merlin and then out of the Griffon. The Spitfire began to carry progressively larger propellers, with four and later five blades, to absorb this extra power. Aerodynamically, such a propeller produced an effect on stability similar to that one would expect from a large cruciform fin on the nose, while the slipstream rotation tried to screw the machine into a roll; the rotating propeller would twist the air behind it so that it hit the fin and tailplane at an angle. These factors combined to produce unpleasant handling characteristics during the climb at full power: a great deal of twist and airflow on the side of the fin, trying to make the aircraft roll and yaw simultaneously, at a time when there was insufficient airspeed over the rudder for it to 'bite' properly. These effects tended to become more and more serious as the Spitfire progressed through its various marks, and had to be corrected by adding more area to the fin and rudder. For the most part, the story of the aerodynamic development of the Spitfire was one of piling on more and more power transmitted through larger and larger propellers, and the airframe designer having to tailor the rear end to compensate for this. Some of the very late versions of the Spitfire were fitted with the contra-rotating propeller, which was the only real solution to the problem, but these did not go

into service until well after the end of the war and then only in small numbers.

I have mentioned some of the problems we had with the Spitfire, but with her thin wing she was able to cope with the greater engine powers and the higher speeds better than any other fighter of her vintage. The thickness-chord ration at the wing root of the Spitfire was only about 13 per cent, compared with 14.8 per cent for the Messerschmitt 109 and 16 per cent for the Hurricane; even the later Mustang, hailed as a very clean aeroplane, had a 16 per cent wing. After the first year of war there was a steady pressure on designers to increase the maximum permissible diving speed of the new fighters entering service, because this was one of the things the pilots really wanted for combat. As a result we soon found ourselves on the brink of the subsonic region, with shock waves beginning to form on the wing. Now on a fattish wing the shock waves begin to form quite early, at about 0.7 Mach (roughly 500mph at 20,000ft, depending on temperature). As the aircraft neared the speed of sound the shock waves got stronger and on those wartime aircraft they would begin to upset the airflow over the wing, affect fore and aft stability, and cause all sorts of unpleasant effects. One way to postpone the Mach effects is to use a swept-back wing, but another is to have a thinner wing and that is why we at Farnborough selected the Spitfire as one of the aircraft for the exploratory work on high-speed dives. This series of trials began in May 1943, and during its course Squadron Leader 'Matty' Martindale managed to get a Spitfire XI diving at about 0.9 Mach*. This was a most remarkable effort for an aircraft designed in 1935 and I think I am right in saying that this speed was not exceeded until the Americans began their trials with the rocket-powered Bell X-I in 1948; certainly the RAF had nothing able to out-dive the Spitfire until the swept-wing F-86 Sabre came into service in 1951. It was during one of these high-speed dives, in April 1944, while he was coming down at more than 600mph, that 'Marty' suffered a loss of oil pressure to the airscrew constant speed unit; the propeller simply went round faster and faster, taking the protesting engine with it, until the blades fractured and the engine shook itself to pieces. In masterly fashion he regained control and after a glide of some 20 miles he landed safely at Farnborough in his strained aircraft. The following month he was flying a replacement Spitfire in a further trial in the series, and again at a high Mach number he suffered a burst supercharger. This time the weather was bad and he eventually crash-landed in a wood not far from the airfield; he managed to scramble clear of his burning aircraft on the ground then, in spite of spinal injuries, he returned to the wreck and retrieved the vital recording camera. For this he received a well-earned AFC.

* It must be stressed that to achieve such a high Mach number the Spitfire had to be taken straight down in a 45-degree dive, from 40,000ft to about 20,000ft. Thus the ability to reach such a high Mach number was unlikely to occur during a fighter-versus-fighter combat, though reconnaissance Spitfires were sometimes to use high-speed dives to escape from enemy jet fighters.

Why was the Spitfire so good? I think it was because it had such a thin wing. Of course, Mitchell had been meticulous in his attention to detail in the design of the Spitfire, but basically the reason for her ability to remain in the forefront of the technological race for so long was the fact that she had a wing thinner than that of any of her contemporaries. Considering that he could have had little knowledge of Mach effects, Mitchell's decision to use such a thin wing was not only bold but inspired. We now know that it was a close run thing: had he made the wing just a little thinner it would probably have been too weak, and aileron reversal would have been encountered lower down the speed scale. And if that had happened, the Spitfire would have been just one more of those aircraft that did not quite make the grade.

44

SPITFIRE VERSUS V2 ROCKET

By Raymond Baxter

Known to millions of television viewers for his popular science programme 'Tomorrow's World', Raymond Baxter spent most of the Second World War flying Spitfires. This section deals with his operational career during the final phase of the conflict.

In the autumn of 1944 I was a flight lieutenant commanding 'A' Flight of No. 602 Squadron, with Squadron Leader Max Sutherland as my 'boss'. Prior to that I had flown Spitfires on operations almost continuously since the middle of 1941: in Britain with No. 65 Squadron, then in the Mediterranean area with No. 93, and after that with No. 602 Squadron during the Battle of Normandy. So by October 1944, when the squadron re-equipped with the Spitfire XVI and began retraining for the dive-bomber role, I was a fairly experienced operator.

In September 1944 the Germans began firing V2 rockets at London and the south-east from launching sites in Holland. Together with the similarly equipped Nos 229, 453 and 603 Squadrons, we on No. 602 were given the task of maintaining vigorous patrol activity over the areas from which the rockets were coming, mainly round The Hague. If we saw any V2 activity on the ground we were, of course, to go in and sort it out. But the Germans were good at camouflage and it was unlike them to leave anything out in the open. So, to keep up the pressure, we were given a pretty wide-ranging brief. Since we knew that the Germans were very short of petrol at that stage, it was a safe assumption that any motor vehicle seen moving on the Dutch roads was doing something to assist the German war effort – it might even be associated with the V2 bombardment. Accordingly, we were given a free hand to 'shoot at anything that moved' – though naturally we went to great pains to avoid causing casualties to the Dutch civilian population.

In addition to our offensive patrols and interdiction sorties, we often carried out pre-planned dive-bombing attacks on suspected rocket storage areas and launching sites (the Dutch resistance organisation was particularly helpful in providing intelligence on these). Sometimes such a target would appear, from the air, as no more than a ring of wheel tracks on some scrubby heath land; even a careful study of aerial reconnaissance photographs often failed to reveal more.

The usual force to attack these small targets was four or six Spitfires, each loaded with either one 500lb and two 250lb bombs, or two 250lb bombs and a long-range fuel tank. From our base at Coltishall, or its satellites at Ludham or Matlaske, we would head out across the North Sea climbing to about 8,000ft. Once we made our landfall at the Dutch coast navigation was rarely a problem, because we quickly came to know our 'parish' like the backs of our hands. As we crossed into enemy territory we were liable to be engaged with predicted fire from heavy 88mm guns, but in a Spitfire this was no great danger, provided one continually changed one's direction and altitude in a series of long climbing or diving turns; if one did it right there was the immense satisfaction of seeing the black puffs of the shells going off where one would have been.

Generally the V2 targets were defended with light flak, so when we reached the target area our approach tactics would vary. Sometimes we would go straight in and attack; other times we would dodge from cloud to cloud until we were in a favourable position, then go in; other times still we would overfly the target, then nip back from out of the sun to take the defenders by surprise. We were pretty wily birds!

Once we were committed to the dive-bombing attack, the procedure was usually standard. Running in at between 6,000 and 8,000ft we would throttle back to just below 200mph, and aim to place the target so that it passed under the wing just inboard of the roundel. As it emerged from under the trailing edge we would roll over and pull the aircraft into a 70-degree dive – which felt vertical. At this stage one concentrated entirely on bringing the graticule of the gyro gunsight on to the target, ignoring the cockpit instruments and trying to ignore the flak. Accurate bombing was dependant upon accurate flying during the dive and once the target was in the sight it was important to avoid side-slipping, skidding or turning for these would have induced errors. The Spitfires would go down in loose line astern, with 30 to 40yd between aircraft and each pilot aiming and bombing individually. In a dive the speed would build up quite rapidly to a maximum of about 360mph before the release. When he judged the altitude to be about 3,000ft each pilot let go of his bombs in a salvo, then do a 5G pull-up to bring the nose up to the horizontal; by the time we had levelled out we were pretty low and the drill was to make a high-speed getaway using the ground for cover. The great temptation was to pull up after attacking, to see how well one had done, but that could be fatal if the Germans were alert – and they usually were. We believed in going in tight, hitting hard, and getting the hell out of it; there was no place for false heroics. The bombs we dropped were often fitted with delayed action fuses, some of them set to explode after as long as six hours; the object of the exercise was to make life difficult for the enemy for as long as possible.

During one of our attacks on a launching site we must have caught the V2 firing crew well into their countdown. After we had released our bombs and were going back for a low-level 'strafe' with our cannon, one of the great flame-belching monsters began to climb slowly out from a clump of trees. Flight Sergeant 'Cupid' Love, one of my pilots, actually fired a long burst at it with his cannon – which must have been the first ever attempt to bring down a ballistic missile in flight!

Sometimes we would mount set-piece attacks with other squadrons, if some particularly important target had been found. On 18 March 1944, for example, No. 453 Squadron provided a diversion while we put in a six-aircraft strike at zero feet on the Baatasher-Mex office building in the middle of The Hague; we had had information that the missile firing experts were housed there. It was a very 'twitchy op', because we had to attack in close line abreast. All went well, however, and we wrecked the place. Max Sutherland received a bar to his DFC for that one – and had half of his starboard elevator shot away by flak.

Often we flew two or even three sorties during a single day, with a landing at an airfield in Belgium between each to refuel and rearm. On 18 March I flew three sorties: the first was a skip-bombing attack on a road bridge north of Gouda; the second was the raid on the Baatasher-Mex building; and the third was a low-level interdiction sortie against the railway between Delft and Rotterdam.

All things considered, our losses during these attacks were light, and not all of them were due to enemy action; on at least one occasion a Spitfire shed its wings after the bombs had hung up at the end of the dive, and the pilot pulled up too hard. By this stage of the war, there was virtually nothing to be seen of the Luftwaffe.

Just how much our efforts contributed to the gradual run-down in the rate of firing V2s at England, I never did discover. But certainly it was all damned good fun for an unmarried twenty-two-year-old.

What did I think of the Spitfire? Every single one was different, with her own characteristics and foibles; if your own was unserviceable and you took somebody else's, you could feel the difference at once. During the war I never wanted to operate in any other type of aircraft; the Spitfire was a darling little aeroplane.

Opposite: Flight Lieutenant Raymond Baxter pictured briefing pilots of No. 602 Squadron before an attack on a V2 target in Holland.

EXOTIC OPPONENT

For much of the war the unarmed photograph reconnaissance Spitfires had been able to go about their task without serious interference from the enemy. Flying fast, high and alone, they frequently came and went without any attempt being made to intercept them. During the closing months of the Second World War, however, there were ominous signs that the day of the uneventful reconnaissance sortie deep into German territory was fast drawing to a close. The new jet fighters entering large-scale service in the Luftwaffe, the Messerschmitt 163 and the Messerschmitt 262, had the speed and the altitude performance to enable them to hack down the wide-ranging Spitfires. Typical of the brushes that resulted is this one which took place on 7 March 1945; the pilot, Flight Lieutenant Raby, was flying a Spitfire XI of No. 542 Squadron.

On the morning of 7 March, I was briefed to photograph the Bohlen Synthetic Oil Plant, the Molbis Termat Power Station and the Oil Storage Depot at Rositz, all being to the south of Leipzig. A damage assessment was also required of Chemnitz which the RAF had attacked two days before.

At 0930hrs I took off carrying split 36in cameras with full magazines and all tanks full including a 90gal drop tank. I was soon well above cloud and heading over the North Sea, eventually setting course at 35,000ft. 10/10ths cloud lay well below and continued to within ten minutes of the target area. The trip was uneventful except for the disconcerting factor of the thick 100yd non-persistent contrail I was trailing behind.

At 1125hrs I arrived in the area, Leipzig was clearly visible to the north and all my targets, including Chemnitz, in full view to the south-east. Chemnitz lay under a thick pall of smoke which was drifting slowly to the south, otherwise little or no cloud was visible in the sky. I felt very visible to those on the ground; however, I had no interference over Bohlen and Molbis, the first two targets.

It was during the first run over Rositz that, in looking behind towards Leipzig, I saw two large trails at approximately 20,000ft and 10,000ft respectively coming from Leipzig/Mochau airfield. Their speed was phenomenal, rate of climb about 10,000ft per minute at an angle of about 60 degrees. It was not long before two tiny Me 163 rocket-propelled aircraft became visible.

The first enemy aircraft drew up to my altitude and about a mile distant, passing on up to about 40,000ft before turning off his rocket and becoming very difficult to see. This happened in what seemed to be a second; meanwhile the other Me 163 was already drawing very close and it was obvious that I would stand no chance of seeing both aircraft when they were gliding above endeavouring to position themselves. On the other hand, with the contrail flowing behind me, I was a very conspicuous target.

My first impulse was to get out of the contrail zone; I rolled over on my back, opened up to full boost and revs and dived to about 18,000ft where my airspeed was in the region of 500mph, then I levelled out and swinging on a violent 90-degree turn to port I looked back up my descending trail. One Me 163 was already diving parallel to my trail and when I saw him he was only 5–6,000ft above and rapidly closing. I swung round in a sharp 180-degree turn as he made his pass, thereby causing us to be heading in opposite directions and drawing apart so rapidly that he was soon only a tiny speck. I again altered course and descended rapidly. The enemy came back to the area but was well above me. Realising I was not seen I descended to 6,000ft in a southerly direction; I tried to see the second Me 163, but was unable to do so.

The engagement lasted only five minutes and as I had obviously lost the enemy I decided to fly east. I climbed to just below trail height in order to photograph Chemnitz which was now about 50 miles to the north-west. No further sign of the enemy was seen and I had no difficulty in completing my photography. At 1345hrs I landed at Bradwell Bay with ten minutes' fuel left.

The inability of the enemy to position himself owing to his high speed and lack of manoeuvrability was, I thought, the most outstanding feature of this short engagement.

SPITFIRES OVER THE BALKANS

David Green was founder and first president of The Spitfire Society. In 1945 he was a Flight Officer posted as 'A' Flight commander to No. 73 Squadron whose main base was at Biferno in Italy. The unit was flying Spitfire IXs in the fighter-bomber role, in support of partisan forces in Yugoslavia. In this account he gives his impressions of operations in this theatre, and how the end of the war came suddenly.

Although its main base was at Biferno, by this stage of the war No. 73 Squadron was one of several Balkan Air Force units which used the airstrip at Prkos, near Zara, as a forward operating base.

There was a unique little war going on in Yugoslavia, it was the first time partisan operations had been employed on such a large scale. Although there were no regular forces defending Prkos and there were German troops all over the area, we did not feel particularly threatened. There was a row of mountains between us and the enemy forces and we figured we would have plenty of warning if they tried to advance in our direction.

Other units using Prkos at that time were Nos 253 and 352 Squadrons with Spitfires, Nos 6 and 251 Squadrons with rocket-firing Hurricanes and No. 249 Squadron with Mustangs. Normally the Spitfires of No. 73 Squadron would take off from Biferno in the morning, land at Prkos to refuel, fly two or more sorties from the forward base, landing there to refuel and rearm between each, then return to Biferno in the evening. David Green flew his first missions in this way on 22 March in PV852 (aircraft letter 'B'). He flew to Prkos, refuelled, then took off to attack the German headquarters at Gospic, about 30 miles north of the airstrip. Afterwards he returned to Prkos, took on more bombs and attacked Gospic again. After these raids he noted in his log book 'bags of accurate flak'. Later in

the day he flew two road reconnaissance sorties from Prkos, then returned to Biferno.

David Green explained the dive-bombing tactics employed by No. 73 Squadron during these operations.

Carrying two 250lb bombs the Spitfire made a very fine dive bomber. It could attack accurately and didn't need a fighter escort because as soon as the bombs had been released it was a fighter. The briefing beforehand had to be good

David Green. founder and first president of The Spitfire Society.

David Green, in the aircraft nearest the camera, leading a section of four Spitfire IXs of No. 73 Squadron at the forward operating base at Prkos, Yugoslavia, in the spring of 1945.

enough for us to be able to fly right up to the target even if we had never been there before, identify it and bomb it – because the flak was often accurate we didn't want to spend time circling in the target area before we went down to attack.

We normally operated in sections of four, and would fly to the target at 10,000ft in finger-four battle formation. We would make for an 'Initial Point' (IP) decided at the briefing, a distinctive point on the ground in the target area with, ideally, a linear feature like a road, a river or a railway line

leading to the target itself. By the time it reached the IP the formation would have increased speed to 260mph IAS [about 305mph] and we would by flying in loose echelon to starboard, ready to begin the dive. As the target came into view I would position it so that it appeared to be running down the line of my port cannon. As the target disappeared under the wing I would hold my heading, and when the target emerged from under the trailing edge I would pull the aircraft up to kill the forward speed, roll it over on its back and let the nose drop until the target was lined up in the gunsight graticule. That way one got the Spitfire to go down in the correct angle of dive of 60 degrees. It is a pretty steep dive; it felt as if one was going down vertically. The other aircraft in the section, Nos 2, 3 and 4, would be following me down still in echelon. It was important to trim the aircraft nose-down, otherwise the pressure on the stick would become enormous as the speed built up and the Spitfire tried to pull itself out of the dive. During the dive the speed built up rapidly and it was important to keep an eye on one's height, because the altimeter lag was considerable. When the altimeter read 5,000ft above the target altitude, indicated, that meant the true altitude above the target was about 4,000ft. I would let go my bombs and call 'Bombs gone!' and the other chaps in the section would then release theirs. At the time of release the aircraft would be going about 420mph IAS [about 450mph].

If there had been little or no flak the desire to see the results of the bombing was usually so great that I would pull hard on the stick to bring the aircraft out of the dive and into a slight climb so that I could look over my shoulder to see where the bombs had done. But if we were being fired at, we would use our high forward speed to get us down to ground level where there was cover.

David Green flew a series of similar attacks on 22 March. On the 24th and 25th he flew to Prkos to refuel, then escorted Dakota transports flying into landing strips deep in German-occupied Yugoslavia. On each occasion the Spitfire escorts would orbit while the Dakotas landed, off-loaded their cargo and took on wounded, then took off again. During his mission on the 25th, David Green was airborne for two hours and twenty-five minutes. On the 28th he bombed a German position near Otoka, on the 30th flew two attacks on Ostrazac, and on the 31st flew three missions to attack enemy positions at Gospic, Krupa and Ostrazac.

David Green spent most of April on a detachment to the Italian Air Force and returned to his squadron early in May. By then aircraft were staying overnight at Prkos. On the 3rd he flew a bombing and strafing mission against Lipke, with similar missions against enemy positions at Ljubljana and Zelchi on the 4th.

We were never worried by enemy fighters. People did see them on the odd occasion, but it was very rare. By this time one felt that most of the fighting was going on in the hinterland. Zagreb, for example, was hotly defended by flak and our chaps did see the odd fighter there. But they never made any attempt to interfere with our aircraft.

Operations continued in this way until the evening of 6 May, when David Green and other pilots in the Officers' Mess tent at Prkos heard on the BBC News that the war in Europe was over and the German High Command had ordered all of its forces to surrender to the Allies the following morning.

We had been slotted for the dawn mission the next day, so I called the operations tent on the field telephone and said, 'It's all over, isn't it? You won't want us to fly tomorrow.' Back came the answer, 'Yes we do, we've got an armed recce for you.' I said, 'The war's over, they have just said so on the radio.' And back came the reply, 'It isn't necessarily over for us. We don't know if the German forces here know the war is over. We want you to go and find out.'

The next morning I was briefed for a reconnaissance quite different from any I had ever flown. With my section I was to search roads and railway lines in northern Yugoslavia leading out of the country, to see what, if anything, the enemy forces were doing. Our people wanted to know, first, if the German troops in Yugoslavia were indeed surrendering. And if they were, whom were they trying to surrender to? Were they going to stay where they were and surrender to the Yugoslavs or the Russians? Or were they trying to move north and surrender to British and American forces moving into Austria?

To me it seemed unlikely we would see anything – up till then we had seen very little of the German troops from the air. If they moved it was usually in small numbers, they were very good at camouflage and difficult to spot. Normally we didn't see any activity on the ground until we began an attack and they started to fire at us. For the reconnaissance our aircraft were to carry the normal armament including bombs, but we were not to engage in offensive action unless we were fired at first or threatened.

With my section I took off from Prkos at first light. I remember thinking this was a funny sort of a mission: nobody could tell me what a surrendering army would look like. We couldn't shout out the cockpit to ask! The only way

I could think of to discover whether they were surrendering was to show ourselves and see if they opened fire.

Initially we headed due east into the brightening sky, past Kazanci and the Makljen Pass as far as Sarajevo. Then we turned north-west and flew along the road past Zenica and towards Banja Luka. With my wingman I flew low up the road between 150 and 500ft, weaving back and forth with the other pair giving us top cover. There was hardly any activity on the ground and no light flak. It was a clear day, with good visibility and the sun just climbing over the mountains. Below us was the usual lovely Yugoslavian countryside, a bit like South Wales with its moderate hills and valleys and rolling countryside.

We had just looked at one valley, and pulled up over a line of hills to look at the next. And suddenly, there in front of us, was this enormous convoy of German vehicles extending along the road as far as the eye could see – what in modern parlance we would call a 'ten-mile tailback'. Some of the vehicles were horse-drawn, they were all heading north at a walking pace.

As soon as I saw them I told the pilots to increase speed, fuse the bombs and set guns to 'fire' in case we ran into trouble. Under normal conditions we would have climbed to height for a dive-bombing attack, but now my job was to find out whether they were surrendering.

We thundered up the road at 100ft at about 300mph, snaking back and forth. It must have looked fairly threatening to the German troops as we ran in. As soon as they saw us a white Very light arced away from one of the vehicles, leaving a trail of white smoke in the still morning air. Men ran away from the slowly moving convoy, waving their empty hands above their hands while others waved white towels and sheets. The trucks and carts were piled with kit and had men sprawled on top riding wherever they could. Not a shot was fired or a weapon raised, and it was clear these people knew the war was over and had no wish to continue fighting. We flew up the convoy for about 8 miles without reaching the head, with similar signals of surrender all the way. I did not see a single hostile act anywhere. I got the impression that there was a gang of chaps who could not wait to get home. We pulled up and circled the vehicles, and the white flags continued to wave.

For us there was a lot of curiosity value – it was the first time we had seen Germans that we hadn't attacked. For the whole of my adult life, since 1938, I had grown up convinced that all Germans were dangerous; and for the previous six years we had been killing each other. And now all of that had come to an end. Suddenly I wondered, 'What are we going to do tomorrow?'

The other pair of Spitfires had been giving top cover, but when it was clear there was going to be no fighting I called them down to have a look too. And they did, we just trailed in line astern past the convoy. When I had seen enough, I led the formation into the climb and radioed back to base the position of the convoy and the fact it was not hostile.

We formed up in a box and climbed quietly and undramatically away from the enemy of yesterday. Their task was to surrender to the West and keep out of the hands of the Reds. Ours was to return to base – and then see what the future held for us all. There was one small job to be done first. Our bombs were fused and had to go. Leading the formation round in a wide sweep to port we coasted out south of Rijeka, past the low-lying islands of Cres, Losinj and the oddly named Krk, and out over the clear, clean sea. I put the formation into a shallow 30-degree dive, then we let go our bombs in a salvo.

I looked back over my shoulder as we climbed away, opening the canopy for the view and some fresh air. The water was already settling where the eight bombs had fallen. We had made what was perhaps the last modest bang of the war in Europe. It was time to go home.

THE SPITEFUL, A SPITFIRE TOO FAR

Patrick Shea-Simonds – Shea to his friends – learned to fly at the Reading Aero Club in 1934, and gained a commission in the Fleet Air Arm in 1940. Early in 1942 he was appointed workshop test pilot at RNAS Halston where he qualified as an engineer officer and was also able to fly every type of aircraft operated by the Royal Navy. In June 1943 he joined No. 1 Course at the Empire Test Pilots' School, Boscombe Down, which he completed in February 1944, and was then posted to 'C' Flight at Boscombe, engaged in performance testing. Early in September 1944 Frank Furlong, the deputy chief test pilot at the Supermarine company, was killed while flying the prototype Spiteful and Shea accepted an offer to take his place. In this account Shea tells of his experiences flying the new fighter, and why it was not accepted into service.

⋏ ⋏ ⋏

The prototype Spiteful, NN660, had in fact been a hybrid aircraft with a Spitfire XIV fuselage and tail married to a completely redesigned wing of the laminar flow type. Shea arrived at High Post, the Supermarine test airfield, five days after Furlong's death and while the accident was a matter of some controversy:

> Frank had been coming back to High Post in NN660 when he met up with one of the production test pilots flying a Spitfire XIV, and the two amused themselves with a mock dogfight. Suddenly Frank's aircraft rolled on its back and went straight into the ground. Afterwards the inevitable happened: the pilot wasn't alive to answer back, so the accident was put down to 'pilot error'. There was a lot of bad feeling about this amongst the firm's test pilots, it was felt that Frank was not the sort of chap who would have pulled too much 'G' and lost control of the aircraft. I had known Frank earlier and I felt the same, but of course I was in no position to comment on the accident because I had not seen it, nor had I flown the Spiteful. So, for a time, the matter had to rest there.

Following the crash of the prototype the Spiteful test programme had come to an abrupt halt, but there was plenty of work for the pilots testing late-mark Spitfires and Seafires. The first task for Shea was to complete the maker's trials of the Seafire XV, before the aircraft went to Boscombe Down for service trials.

In January 1945 NN664, the second prototype Spiteful, was ready for testing. This aircraft was the first 'real' Spiteful, with the redesigned fuselage as well as wings. Jeffrey Quill carried out the initial trials with the second prototype, in the course of which he encountered a problem with the aircraft's controls which seemed to explain Furlong's crash.

The Spiteful had aileron control rods (instead of the cables on the Spitfire), and these should have given more positive control, but during a test flight in the second prototype, while Jeffrey was doing a tight turn to the left and pulling 'G', he suddenly found his stick locked hard over. He gave the stick a bash with the palm of his hand which freed it, and after that everything was all right. However, had he been at low altitude, as Frank had been, it could have been very nasty. Jeffrey felt that this could well have been the cause of Frank's accident, and was able to get the court of inquiry to reverse its initial finding that the cause of the accident was 'pilot error'. Later, Frank was awarded a posthumous King's Commendation for Valuable Service in the Air for his work

Patrick Shea-Simonds.

The Supermarine Spiteful tips a wing to show the redesigned laminar flow wing fitted to the new fighter.

There were obvious similarities with the Spitfire, but there were also many differences. The cockpit layout of the Spiteful was quite different, and it was no longer a 'Spitfire cockpit'. The most obvious change was the seating position, which was more reclined. Sitting in the seat, one's feet on the rudder pedals felt as if they were 'up in the air'. Several of the shorter pilots did not like the new seating position. But being 6ft 6in tall, sitting in a Spitfire even with the seat fully down I always felt rather squashed in. I found the Spiteful cockpit much roomier and the view over the nose was definitely better than in the Spitfire.

The next noticeable thing was that the wide track undercarriage of the Spiteful made the feel of the aircraft on the ground – during taxiing, take-off or after landing – very different from that of the Spitfire. A lot of people grizzled on about the Spitfire's narrow track undercarriage, and it certainly wasn't ideal for deck operations. But it did have a curious sort of 'bicycle stability' and once the aircraft was rolling it tended to go straight in the direction in which it was pointing. The Spiteful was different, during taxiing and landing runs it tended to wander off course and one had to rely on differential braking to keep the aircraft going straight.

Normally the Spiteful's lack of directional stability on the ground was only a minor irritation, but during a test flight in the new fighter Shea suffered a hydraulic failure while airborne and found himself in a potentially embarrassing position.

The undercarriage, brakes and flaps were all hydraulically operated in the Spiteful (on the Spitfire the undercarriage was hydraulically operated, but the brakes and flaps were pneumatically operated). I knew I could get the undercarriage down with the carbon dioxide emergency system, but I would have no brakes or flaps. Since I had to make a flapless landing I decided to go to Boscombe Down, where the runway was much longer than the one at High Post. I got the aircraft on the ground all right and was trundling down the runway, but as the speed fell away the rudder became less and less effective and the aircraft started to wander to one side. With no brakes, the only thing I could do was give a quick burst of engine to put a bit of slipstream over the rudder and get the aircraft going straight again. I ran on down the runway with a series of ever-decreasing

as a test pilot. After that the control rods of all Spitefuls were very thoroughly checked for freedom of movement, and there was never a recurrence of the problem.

Shea made his first flight in NN664 on 9 April 1945 and from then on became heavily committed to the Spiteful test programme.

The Spiteful shows off
its redesigned fuselage.

'blips' of the engine, gradually getting slower and slower. The Spiteful ran off the end of the runway going at a walking pace, and came to rest without damage on the grass.

As I got used to the Spiteful I found it not unpleasant to fly. It took off all right and its high speed performance was quite good. To be frank I never liked the 'feel' of it as much as I liked the Spitfire, but by then I had a lot of hours on Spitfires and Seafires and they were such beautiful aircraft

to fly that it would have been difficult to find anything else that felt as nice. But the main snag with the Spiteful was its low-speed handling. The Spitfire had 'washout' along the wing [i.e. the angle of incidence was greatest at the wing root, and decreased progressively toward the tip]; if you held a Spitfire straight and level, then throttled back and eased back on the stick, the stall started at the wing root and worked its way out toward the tips. If you continued to hold the aircraft straight, it could be made to sink in a stalled glide with even a measure of lateral control.

The approach to the stall in the Spiteful was quite different. With the laminar flow wing there was no 'washout', and in fact the stall seemed to begin at the tips and work its way in. You didn't get a violent wing drop, but you did get a wing drop and there was pronounced 'kicking' of the ailerons. As a warning of an incipient straight stall it was reasonable enough, but it felt nothing like as pleasant as the Spitfire. Approaching a stall, the Spiteful felt as if it was about to do something nasty. On the flare-out before landing, for example, it felt as if it was balanced on a pin and might tilt one way or the other at any moment. In fact the aircraft didn't finally do anything unpleasant, but it felt as if it might and that was disconcerting until one got used to it.

Oddly enough, the spinning characteristics of the Spiteful were surprisingly good – it was practically impossible to keep the aircraft in a sustained spin. It would go into a violent flick with the nose right up in the air, rather in the same way as the Spitfire, but would often flick itself right out of the incipient spin. You didn't have to worry about taking full recovery action, if you just let go of the controls it would usually come out on its own. Even if you held the controls in a spin-inducing position, the Spiteful would be trying to recover by itself.

Because of the low-speed handling characteristics encountered with the Spiteful we spent a lot of time trying to improve matters on the second prototype and early production aircraft. In due course these aircraft were all fitted with new wings having slightly blunted leading edges, and enlarged tails. We also tried out root spoilers and modifications to the ailerons. The various modifications finally adopted did improve the aircraft's low-speed handling, which became noticeably pleasanter. But these improvements were all made at the expense of all-out level speed, with the result that the performance of the Spiteful ended up little better than that of the Spitfire 21.

One reason why the high-speed performance of the Spiteful showed no great improvement over that of the late-model Spitfires was that the redesigned wing fitted to the Spitfire 21 and later marks proved to have greater strength and better high-speed characteristics than had originally been expected.

Initially it had been thought that the wing would run into aileron reversal problems at airspeeds below 500mph and that a new stronger wing of laminar flow profile would be needed if Spitefuls were to be able to exceed this speed safely.

The idea of the laminar flow wing was very fashionable during the mid-war period as a means of achieving low drag at high speeds. But when it was tested on the Spiteful, the new wing did not give much improvement in performance over the later-type Spitfires. The theory of the laminar flow was all right, but only so long as the wing profile had been manufactured to very fine tolerances and the whole thing was kept free of dirt or minor dents. It needed only a squashed mosquito on the leading edge, and the airflow over that part of the wing went for a burton!

With the end of the war in Europe the Royal Air Force lost interest in the piston-engined interceptor; the new jet fighters promised to be considerably more effective and the order for 150 Spitefuls was cancelled. However, nobody had yet landed a jet aircraft on an aircraft carrier, and the poor throttle response of the early jet engines threatened to make a missed approach hazardous. With the war in the Pacific likely to continue well into 1946 the Royal Navy had a clear requirement for a piston-engined fighter with the performance of the Spiteful. Less than a week after the Royal Air Force cancelled its order the Admiralty signed a contract for a similar number of its navalised version, the Seafang.

At the time the war against Japan seemed likely to go on a lot longer, and the Seafang would probably have been a better naval fighter than the Seafire. With the improved forward view over the nose deck landings would have been a lot easier. And it had a very much more robust wide-track undercarriage – during an arrested landing the tendency of the aircraft to 'wander' after touchdown would not have mattered. Even with the modifications made to the wing and the tail to improve low-speed handling, the performance at high speed would have been comparable with or slightly better than that of the latest-model Seafires.

During a flight on 28 September 1945 Shea experienced a near-catastrophic engine failure in RB515, the first production version of the Spiteful. He had taken off from High Post for a handling and longitudinal stability test at 30,000ft. Up to 28,000ft the climb was normal and he reduced boost and rpm to bring the aircraft to maximum cruising speed in level flight at 30,000ft. The indicated airspeed slowly increased to 240mph IAS when:

Suddenly there was a loud explosion and I saw something [in fact a piece of the engine] fly past the cockpit on the starboard side. At the same time the engine began to vibrate very violently, oil began to stream back over the windscreen and cockpit hood. The engine rpm counter was hard against the upper stop reading 4,000rpm – obviously the propeller had 'run away'.

The constant speed unit for the propeller had failed and put the blades into fully fine pitch, thus allowing the engine to overspeed far beyond its safe limits. The Griffon was in the process of shaking itself to pieces:

I took what action I could to deal with the situation. I brought the constant speed control lever back to positive course pitch, closed the throttle, pulled the engine cut-out, turned off the fuel and switched off the ignition. At the same time I pulled the nose of the aircraft up, reducing speed to 140mph IAS. I then opened the cockpit hood, released my safety harness and prepared to abandon the aircraft as I fully expected the engine either to disintegrate completely or to be torn from its mounting. The vibration and high rpm persisted, while oil and glycol streamed around and into the cockpit and I saw a crack develop in the starboard side of the cockpit immediately aft of the windscreen side panel.

It had been drummed into us at Boscombe Down that aircraft which went wrong during tests were valuable bits of evidence, and it was the test pilot's job to get them back on the ground in one piece if possible. So although I was ready to bale out, I decided to hang on and see if the aircraft could be saved. After about fifteen seconds the rpm fell rapidly, the airscrew came to a stop and the vibration ceased.

I called Boscombe Down on the radio and informed them that my engine had blown up and I was preparing for a forced landing. By this time I was over the Swindon area, which like Boscombe and High Post was covered in cloud.

To the east the skies were clear and as I did not feel like letting down through cloud with the engine out, and could see Farnborough clear and within gliding distance, I decided to land there and informed Boscombe. I had plenty of height and once the vibration ceased the Spiteful handled quite well as a glider. By the time I had descended to 5,000ft it was obvious that the aircraft wasn't likely to catch fire – if a fire was going to start it would have done so before then. So I re-fastened my harness and started to approach the long runway at Farnborough from the south-west. I knew this would bring me in for a downwind landing, but the surface wind was light and I preferred to approach the airfield over open country rather than over the town.

It was obvious that the hydraulic systems were no longer working fully and I had no idea what damage had been done to them. So, rather than risk finding that only one undercarriage leg would extend, I decided to land the aircraft with the wheels up. I selected flaps down and worked the hand pump until resistance ceased, at which point I had about ¼ flap.

I made my final approach and landed wheels-up on the grass alongside the main runway. Surprisingly, the touchdown was the least dramatic part of the whole business. The Spiteful had a large wide-span radiator under each wing and slid along the grass on these; it felt just like putting down a flying boat on water. As I touched down I saw the fire tenders and ambulance driving down the runway practically in formation with me.

On examination of the aircraft it was found that the first stage of the Griffon engine's supercharger had disintegrated completely. There had been considerable damage to the hydraulic, glycol and oil pipes at the rear of the engine, as well as to the cowling and fillets in the vicinity of the supercharger. On the starboard side, part of the crankcase had shattered and at least one of the connecting rods had broken. A few days later, Joe Smith, Supermarine's chief designer, sent Shea a copy of a letter the company had received from Sir Arthur Sidgreaves, the managing director of Rolls-Royce, in which he wrote:

The failure resulted in pieces of the engine being forced through the cowlings, and due to the inertia forces I understand the engine was nearly torn from the airframe.

There was also the possibility of fire, so that the pilot would have had every reason to abandon the aeroplane and descend by parachute. The fact that he held on and successfully landed the machine is of great value because it enabled the evidence to be retained and an examination made as to the cause of the trouble, whereas in so many of these instances of failure the evidence is lost.

Subsequently Shea received a more formal recognition of his feat, in the form of a King's Commendation. RB515 suffered surprisingly little damage as a result of the accident and, after repairs and the installation of a new engine, it later resumed flying.

In October 1945 Jeffrey Quill and Shea demonstrated the Spiteful during a display of the latest military aircraft at Farnborough. As the latter recalled, the newest Supermarine product was rather overshadowed:

Jeffrey flew the Spiteful on the first day and I flew it on the second. The occasion was a bit embarrassing for us, however, because Geoffrey de Havilland stole the show with his very impressive demonstration of the Vampire. It was clear that the writing was on the wall for the piston-engined fighter.

Due to the continuing Naval interest in the Seafang, and also because the Attacker jet under construction used essentially the same laminar flow wing, testing of the Spiteful continued.

From October 1945 most of my time on Spitefuls was spent mainly in NN664 doing high-speed dives – by that time she had been fitted with the larger tail. Much of this work was taken up exploring the aircraft's lateral control characteristics and measuring the stick forces required to apply various amounts of aileron. For this the aircraft was fitted with a stick force recorder and I had to note down the readings and rates of roll on my knee pad.

Supermarine wanted the figures to calculate the lateral reversal speed, because a similar wing was to be fitted to the Attacker jet fighter then being built. We established that with a generous safety margin the limiting diving speed of the Spiteful was 525mph IAS at 5,000ft. The aircraft handled well up to that speed and there were no difficulties about pulling it out of the dive. However, this was little better than the limiting speed of the late-model Spitfires or Seafires [the Seafire 47 fitted with folding wings had a safe limiting diving speed of 500mph]. In fact, it was confirmation that the Spitfire wing was a darn sight better and more efficient aerodynamically than had been supposed. And, at the same time, the supposed advantages of the laminar flow wing proved illusory.

Shea continued test flying the Spiteful until February 1946, when he left Supermarine after having amassed eighty-two hours flying on the type. Mike Lithgow took over from him as deputy chief test pilot and did much of the testing of the Seafang, before the production contract for the aircraft was also cancelled.

In my view two things killed the Spiteful as a service fighter: first of all, Boscombe Down took against it from the word go because of its low-speed handling characteristics. They were looking at it from the point of view of the average squadron pilot, and had to consider how he would cope with the aircraft. When I was at Boscombe we had to guess the capability of that mythical human being and there was a tendency to assume that he was more of a clot than he actually was. It was not that the Spiteful was really dangerous to fly at low speeds, it just did not feel very nice to anyone flying the aircraft for the first time and particularly so if one was comparing it with the Spitfire.

The other problem was that the laminar flow wing failed to produce any substantial increase in performance. Had the Spiteful been, say, 30 or 40mph faster than the Spitfire 22, I am sure there would have been far fewer complaints from Boscombe about the low-speed handling characteristics of the aircraft.

48

WHEN SPITFIRE FOUGHT SPITFIRE

By Wing Commander Gregory Middlebrook

It was all a ghastly mistake resulting from navigational errors, and afterwards there were apologies. The small battle fought over Ramat David deserves a place in this history because it was probably the first occasion when, quite deliberately, Spitfire fought Spitfire.

In the spring of 1948 I was a flying officer with No. 32 Squadron, which operated Spitfire XVIIIs from Ramat David in what was then Palestine. On 15 May the state of Israel came into being and as part of the general withdrawal of British forces from that area we were to depart for Cyprus the following week.

For a long time the situation in Palestine had been deteriorating, with a lot of killing on both sides. The Arabs and the Israelis were making obvious preparations for an all-out war, to begin as soon as the British troops were out of the way. For their part the Israelis were particularly keen to get hold of modern aircraft, especially Spitfires; they let it be known that they were prepared to pay £25,000 or its equivalent in other currencies, into a bank anywhere in the world, to the account of any pilot who would simulate an engine failure and belly-land on the beach at Tel-Aviv or elsewhere in their territory. But in spite of this tempting offer, I never did hear of any RAF aircraft disappearing in suspicious circumstances.

During the final week we completed our preparations for the move, sending out our heavier kit and cleaning out the bar stocks; we sold off the drinks at 1 Akker (about 1p) a shot, which gave rise to some pretty wild parties! On 21 May, the day before we were due to leave, three Dakotas arrived to take away the remainder of our kit and the ground crews the following morning. During the final evening we amused ourselves burning down the Mess and several of the other buildings; Ramat David was in the area to be taken over by the Israelis and because they had been giving us a hard time we resolved to leave them as little as possible.

At this time our main worry was sabotage. For some reason the Israelis thought we were about to turn the airfield over to the Arabs, while in their turn the local Arabs were convinced that we planned to present the Israelis with our aircraft together with the airfield; as a result, we seemed to have both sides against us. To meet the threat we had British troops in a defensive perimeter round us. Each night our Spitfires, and those of No. 208 Squadron which shared the airfield with us, were drawn up close together on the hard standing so that they could be more easily guarded.

On the morning of what should have been our final day, 22 May, I was up early. I was just pulling on my shorts when there were a couple of loud bangs, followed by the roar of low-flying aircraft. I dashed outside, but the aircraft – whatever they were – had already disappeared. Apparently there had been two of them, and each had dropped two bombs which had exploded near to the line of aircraft belonging to No. 32 Squadron. I grabbed a parachute and dashed across to one of the Spitfires and tried to start her up, but unknown to me, to prevent any possibility of one of our aircraft being stolen, the ground crew had removed the cartridges from the Koffman starter. After five attempts to get a non-existent cartridge to fire, I gave up.

As a result of the attack two of No. 32 Squadron's Spitfires and one of the Dakotas were set on fire. Our Spitfires had all been combat loaded with full magazines of 20mm and .5in ammunition and when the rounds in the burning aircraft began to cook off there were some unpleasant explosions with flying debris and the odd bullet. As a result, all but one of the Spitfires in that dispersal area suffered at least minor damage before being pushed clear.

Spitfire XVIII of No. 32
Squadron.

remind me. The airmen I had tried to warn were less fortunate, and we lost five killed and others injured in this new attack.

Almost immediately afterwards the other Spitfires made their bombing runs. It was all straight out of the textbook, just as though they were on a bombing range: they crossed the airfield at about 4,500ft, each did a 120-degree wing-over into a nice 45-degree dive, released the bombs and began to climb away. They managed to wreck a second Dakota, but by that time the Spitfires on the ground were all well dispersed and camouflaged, and thus escaped further damage.

It had all happened very quickly and, since we had no radar or other means of obtaining early warning, the attackers had been able to bomb before our Spitfires could interfere. One of the airmen did some accurate shooting with a Bren gun, however, and one of the raiders was seen flying away trailing glycol and losing height. But then the No. 208 Squadron people, who were mounting the airborne patrol at that time, got in amongst the others and the slaughter really began. We learned afterwards that the attackers were flying Spitfires Mk IXs – no match in a fight for our Mk XVIIIs – and in short order three were shot down. You could not really call it a dogfight: it was as though the raiders thought that they were the only aircraft in the sky, and made no attempt to fight back or even evade. The 208 Squadron pilots simply caught them up from behind and opened up from point blank range at sitting targets. Soon there was only one aircraft remaining out of the second wave – and still we did not know the identity of our tormentors. So the station commander ordered the pilot in hot pursuit of the remaining raider that before he did anything else he was to establish its nationality. Accordingly the pilot pulled up alongside, saw that the markings were Egyptian, then fell back and shot it down.

On 23 May we finally did depart for Cyprus, leaving the two sides to fight their war without our interference. The Ramat David incident was probably the first occasion when both sides in an action fought in Spitfires. After we withdrew the Israelis acquired some Spitfires of their own, and there would be other occasions when these aircraft battled with each other.

Still we did not know the identity of the attackers, but there seemed every likelihood that they would return, so the station commander had the squadrons mount a continuous standing patrol of four aircraft over the airfield. For the rest of the day there was considerable activity as relieving Spitfires took off and those airborne came in to refuel. Because many of the aircraft now needed minor repairs, our departure for Cyprus was delayed by twenty-four hours.

Then, later that morning, I remember glancing up and counting five Spitfires swinging round as though they were about to enter the circuit. I blinked, counted again and still there were five, and that meant more trouble because I knew that at that time we had only four airborne. I ran towards some airmen nearby who were busy working by a damaged aircraft and were oblivious to the threat and shouted at them to get down. Then I glanced up to see a Spitfire diving almost straight towards me – and a couple of 250-pounders just beginning to fall clear. I hurled myself down on the hard standing and the blast of the explosions went right over me, but the rough concrete took a lot of skin off my legs and I still have the scars to

49

SEAFIRES OVER KOREA: THE LAST OF THE FEW

By `Tommy' Handley

In January 1949 Seafire FR47 VR971 left the production line at South Marston, the last of more than 22,000 Spitfires and Seafires built. Only two frontline Royal Navy units were to receive the Seafire FR47: No. 804 Squadron, which operated with it between January 1948 and August 1949; and No. 800 Squadron which flew this version between April 1949 and November 1950. When the Korean War broke out, No. 800 Squadron happened to be in the Far East, and the unit took part in the initial stages of the conflict. Tommy Handley would be the last man to command a frontline Seafire squadron flying from a carrier, and in this account he describes the unit's operations during the period before and during the Korean War.

During the Second World War Tommy Handley flew Seafires and Hellcats with frontline units. After the war he remained in the Fleet Air Arm and in December 1949, with the rank of lieutenant, he was sent to Supermarine works at Chilbolton for a short conversion course on the Seafire FR47. He found the Mk 47 a great improvement over previous versions of Seafire:

> The Seafire 47 was a superb aeroplane in the air. It was a better fighter than previous marks, could carry a greater weapon load and had a better range and endurance. The Rolls-Royce Griffon fitted with the injector pump was a most reliable engine, and the squadron experienced no engine failures of any kind. The contra-rotating propellers were a big advance, and even at full throttle on take-off there was no tendency to swing. Also there was no change of rudder trim in a dive, which helped considerably when operating in the ground attack role.

On completion of the conversion course at Chilbolton, Handley went to Royal Navy Air Station Sembawang, Singapore, to take up his appointment as senior pilot (deputy commander) of No. 800 Squadron. The unit had disembarked from the light fleet carrier HMS *Triumph* and its Seafire 47s were conducting air strikes on areas of the Malayan jungle where guerrillas were thought to be operating.

> I flew only one of these sorties, on 20 January 1950, when I was briefed to shoot up a 1,000yd grid square reference in the jungle. I fired eight 60lb rockets and 400 rounds of 20mm into it. I saw no results and nobody appeared to fire back.

In February, No. 800 Squadron, together with 827 operating Fireflies, re-embarked in *Triumph*. During the next few months the carrier made a tour of the Far East, visiting Hong Kong and Japan. At each, the carrier's Air Group flew to a land base and carried on its training programme from there. There was a general reluctance by those in authority to fly the Seafire 47s from the carrier too often; the theory appeared to be that the less they flew the fewer would be written off through damage:

> Seafires were not easy to deck land. The Mk 47 was a much heavier aircraft than the previous marks, and heavy landings often resulted in damaged oleo legs. Also the fuselage aft of the cockpit was not sufficiently strengthened to withstand anything but a near-perfect deck landing. The long sting hook made catching a wire reasonably easy, but if the landing was much off-centre or made with any skid or slip on, then the wire would shake the aircraft rather like a terrier shakes a rat. The result could be a wrinkling of the after fuselage section.

During April, May and June 1950 Handley made only twenty-six deck landings, an average of about two per week. Most of his take-offs were unassisted runs off the deck. The catapult was

Seafire 47 of
No. 800 Squadron
wearing Korean War
identification stripes.

used when there was a light wind, or if the presence of other aircraft on deck left insufficient room for a full take-off run.

Triumph's peacetime cruise came to a sudden and unexpected end on the morning of 25 June 1950, when North Korean troops stormed over the 38th Parallel and advanced into South Korea. On the 26th the US Navy was ordered to support the South Korean forces, and on the 27th the Royal Navy placed its warships in Japanese waters under the operational control of the US Navy. Escorted by the cruiser *Belfast* and two destroyers, HMS *Triumph* left Japan and arrived off the west coast of Korea on 2 July. There she joined US Navy Task Force 77 which included the carrier *Valley Forge*.

On the following morning the two carriers launched a joint strike against airfields in the Pyongyang area. It was the Seafire 47's first operational mission from a carrier and, as Handley explained, some of them had to use RATOG (Rocket Assisted Take-Off Gear) to get airborne:

For the strike we had a big range of aircraft on deck. On a small carrier like *Triumph* that meant the aircraft at the head of the range did not get a full take-off run. So the four Seafires at the front were fitted with RATOG. RATOG was not popular – carrier operations were hazardous enough, without having to rely on cordite and more electric circuitry. The technique was to fire the rockets late in the take-off run, as the aircraft passed a mark on the deck. Firing the rockets gave quite a push, though not as much as going off the catapult. Once airborne, the pilot would jettison the rocket packs. With free take-offs or using RATOG we could launch at 15-second intervals (catapulting was a much slower business, with about one launch per minute). I did not use RATOG on that first mission, though I would on some of my later ones.

During that first action nine Seafires of 800 Squadron and twelve Fireflies of 827 Squadron attacked Haeju airfield. We found no enemy planes there so we attacked the hangars with rockets and cannon.

At Haeju the attackers encountered little return fire. One Seafire was hit by a rifle-calibre round, another suffered minor damage to a radiator when it flew through debris thrown up by the explosions of its rocket projectiles when they hit the ground.

On the next day, 4 July, *Triumph* launched seven Seafires and twelve Fireflies to attack targets along the rail line between Yonan and Haeju, and following these initial strikes Task Force 77 withdrew from the combat zone. During the lull in operations, US and Royal Navy carrier planes in the war zone had black and white identification bands painted on their wings and fuselage, similar to those carried by Allied aircraft at the time of the Normandy invasion in 1944.

When the carrier air strikes resumed on 18 July, it was agreed that *Triumph*'s planes would provide combat air patrols (CAPs) and anti-submarine patrols to cover the Task Force, while the heavier and more effective US Navy attack planes struck at targets ashore. The results of the new policy were immediately evident: Handley's log book shows that he flew a CAP on 18 July, two on the 19th, then there was a break in the flying as Typhoon Grace passed through the area and *Triumph* returned to Japan. Afterwards the carrier returned to the combat area and Handley flew two CAPs on the 25th, two on the 26th and two more on the 28th.

> Usually we carried a 50gal 'torpedo' tank under the fuselage. In addition we could carry a 22½gal combat tanker under each wing. The combat tanks were stressed for combat manoeuvres, but we did not like them because they reduced our maximum speed by about 20kt. They could be jettisoned, but as there were few spares we were ordered not to drop them except in a dire emergency. Shortage of range was never a problem for the Seafire 47s during the Korean conflict. All my flights were two hours or thereabouts and we always returned to the carrier with stacks of fuel.

What of the wrinkling of the Seafire 47 rear fuselages which would earlier have prevented these fighters from flying? As Tommy Handley recalled, that problem was solved by ignoring it:

> Soon after we began operations nearly all the Seafires had wrinkled rear fuselages. The wrinkling was not really visible to the human eye, but if you ran a hand over the skin you could detect the trouble spots. The worry was that the structure was less strong than it should have been. The engineer officer said they were outside the limits for peacetime flying – but he let them fly on operational sorties!

We found that we had far fewer deck-landing accidents once we started flying more. Flying on operations nearly every day, we became better at deck landings and aircraft were damaged less frequently.

Throughout this period no enemy aircraft were encountered, and the CAP missions became routine. The only excitement occurred on 28 July, when a pair of Seafires intercepted a B-29 and Commissioned Pilot White moved in too close to the bomber. The latter's gunners either did not see or did not heed the recognition bands, and opened fire. The Seafire burst into flames and White baled out. Suffering from burns he was picked up from the sea by a US destroyer, and returned to *Triumph*.

Following this brief spell of operations, *Triumph* put into Kure dockyard for ten days for essential maintenance. On 11 August the carrier went to sea again, this time to join the force mounting a blockade of the west coast of Korea, to prevent the enemy troops and supplies being carried south by sea. Again there were few targets to be found, however. On the 13th Handley took part in a rocket attack on oil storage tanks at Mokpo. On the 14th he flew a photo reconnaissance mission along the coast between Haishu and Chinnampo, his Seafire fitted with a single vertical camera. Later that afternoon he also flew a CAP. On the 15th he flew a visual reconnaissance of the coast between Kunsan and Mokpo, and on the 19th he flew another CAP. On the 20th he took part in an armed reconnaissance along the coast between Kunsan and Mokpo, during which he attacked a small naval craft with rockets and cannon. On the 21st he flew a reconnaissance mission and a CAP, did the same on the 26th and the same again on the 28th.

On 29 August Handley took part in another armed reconnaissance of the coast between Kunsan and Mokpo. This time the Seafires found two camouflaged motor junks and attacked them with rockets and cannon fire, leaving one on fire. Also on the 29th, No. 800 Squadron lost its commander, Lieutenant Commander Ian MacLachlan, in a tragic accident on the carrier:

> Ian was in the operations room in the island, watching the aircraft landing through an open scuttle, when a Firefly went into the crash barrier. The wooden propeller blades broke off and a large piece from one of them flew through

the scuttle and struck Ian on the head. He died a few hours later. It was a million-to-one-against accident.

Following this loss, Tommy Handley was promoted to lieutenant commander and assumed command of No. 800 Squadron.

By now the intensity of the operations was starting to tell on the Seafire force. On 1 September, No. 800 Squadron took delivery of the last of the replacement Seafire 47s held aboard the maintenance carrier HMS *Unicorn*. At the start of the conflict *Unicorn* had held fourteen replacement Seafires, which had been issued to the carrier in order of quality starting with the best. The final replacements were the least satisfactory of those available, and in some cases were little better than the machines they replaced. A shortage of spare parts compounded the problems of the maintenance teams, and it was a rare day when No. 800 Squadron had more than eight Seafires available for operations. Nevertheless, by dint of much hard work, the unit usually put up a daily effort of around twenty-five sorties.

During September HMS *Triumph* took part in operations against rail targets along the west coast of Korea. On the 4th Handley led an armed reconnaissance of Kunsan, and on the 6th he flew a CAP over the cruiser HMS *Jamaica* while she bombarded the railway terminus there. On the 8th he escorted a Firefly attack on Wonsan, and afterwards the Seafires strafed patrol boats in the harbour. On the 10th bad weather halted air operations. He flew a reconnaissance mission on the 15th and a CAP on the 17th. On 20 September Handley led an armed reconnaissance of the area around Chinnampo, which turned out to be the final operational mission by Seafires in Royal Navy service.

On 21 September HMS *Triumph* put in to Sasebo, Japan. The replacement carrier HMS *Theseus*, whose squadrons operated Sea Furies and Fireflies, was due to arrive in a few days. *Triumph* played no further part in the conflict and on 25 September she set sail for the United Kingdom. No. 800 Squadron had started the conflict with twelve Seafires, and during its course the unit received fourteen replacements for aircraft lost or damaged. The unit flew a total of 360 operational sorties, of which 115 were against shipping or ground targets. The Seafires never encountered hostile aircraft and they suffered no losses from enemy action, but non-combat attrition took a toll. As mentioned, one Seafire had been shot down in error by a 'friendly' B-29, and another was lost when its hook refused to lower; the pilot baled out and was picked up by a destroyer.

When *Triumph* left the operational area, No. 800 Squadron possessed nine serviceable aircraft, but once the pressures of war had been removed, the unit's engineer officer reasserted the peacetime rules and immediately declared six of the survivors unserviceable with wrinkled rear fuselages. At the end of eleven weeks of operations, of a total of twenty-six Seafires originally on strength or received as replacements, only three remained able to fly.

With the departure of HMS *Triumph* from the Far East, the Seafire's career as a frontline fighter in the Royal Navy came to an end. 'We were,' as Tommy Handley put it, 'the last of the few...'

50

SPITFIRES VERSUS GUERRILLAS

By John Nicholls

During the Malayan Emergency two squadrons of Spitfires took part in the initial air operations against the guerrillas.
However, their effectiveness in this role, as an aircraft designed fourteen years earlier as an interceptor, was questionable.

In June 1948, when the State of Emergency was declared in Malaya, I was a 21-year-old flying officer serving with No. 28 Fighter Reconnaissance Squadron which operated Spitfire XVIIIs from Sembawang on Singapore Island. With those of the similarly equipped No. 60 Squadron, there were a total of sixteen Spitfires in Malay and these, plus a few Beaufighters and Sunderlands, made up the Royal Air Force's entire offensive strength in the area.

Almost from the start we and the other squadrons began sending out strikes against the jungle hideouts used by the guerrillas. In the beginning it was a rather hit and miss affair, with one far more likely to miss than to hit. The maps we carried were almost devoid of detail except along the coast; they would show dominant features such as rivers, but after a short distance inland these would peter out into a dotted line with the helpful caption 'It is assumed that the river follows this line'! The reconnaissance Spitfires of No. 81 Squadron would take target photographs for us, but since their maps were the same as our own they had similar problems of navigation. In the jungle one tree-covered hill can look depressingly like a thousand others.

I vividly remember the first time I dropped a bomb in anger. On 2 July 1948 I went off with my squadron commander, Squadron Leader Bob Yule, to a target just across the causeway from Singapore, in South Johore. We took off at first light so that we could get in our dive attacks before the usual mid-morning layer of cumulus cloud developed. When we reached the target area we cruised round for more than half an hour looking for something resembling our briefed objective, before eventually we did attack. Diving from 12,000ft we dropped our 500-pounders, two from each aircraft, before we carried out a series of strafing runs with cannon and machine

guns. There was nobody firing back; it was really like being on the range – except that the target was far less distant.

During the months that followed we flew several similar strikes. Most of the targets were in deep jungle, and sometimes half a dozen of us would circle for up to an hour looking for the hut or whatever it was we were supposed to hit. Then the first pilot who reckoned he had found it would bomb, and the rest of us would follow and aim at his bursts; after that we would strafe the area until we had used up our ammunition. At that time our intelligence on the whereabouts of the enemy was poor. Moreover, only rarely could our troops go in to find out what the air strikes had achieved; sometimes a week or so after the attack we might hear a report that the target basha hut had been hit by cannon shells, but by the time the ground forces reached it there was rarely any sign of the actual terrorists.

It was all rather loose and inconclusive and the reasons were not difficult to understand. Guerrilla fighters make the maximum use of all available cover, they travel light, they move fast and they seldom concentrate; operating in dense jungle, they are extremely difficult to find. Broadly speaking, air attacks against them can be mounted in two distinct ways: precision attacks, or area attacks. Precision attacks, by definition, require the target to be visible or to be marked in some way. Area attacks demand a great weight of attack to saturate the area, and both depend upon up-to-date intelligence on the target for their success.

The ineffectiveness of the Spitfire in these operations illustrates the sort of problem we had, using an interceptor designed thirteen years earlier to bomb such difficult targets. Later, Lincoln heavy bombers equipped with radar took over the task of attacking the jungle hideouts, but even with their much greater bomb loads I am not convinced that they achieved much. Indeed, as Vietnam has shown, one needs a bomber the size of a B-52, laying down patterns of up to eighty-four 500-pounders, before one can make any real impression on the jungle; and even then, as I have said, one needs first-class intelligence if one is really to hit the enemy. The best way to go after men hiding in the jungle is to send trained troops after them; air strikes can drive the enemy out

John Nicholls pictured later in his career, when he held the rank of air vice marshal.

of areas one wishes to occupy and pacify, and into areas where they are faced by superior forces. The guerrilla can achieve his objective only if he can subvert the people he seeks to control; deny him that chance, and he will not succeed. It was when we got round to doing that, that we began to get the upper hand over the terrorists in Malaya.

I left No. 28 Squadron in mid-1949, before the Malayan operations were placed on a proper footing. I had had a lot of fun but had not, I think, done all that much to help defeat the terrorists.

Operating against the guerrillas in Malaya, we were really asking too much from the Spitfire. But I have no doubts regarding its value as an air fighter. It had that rare quality which comes from a perfect matching of control responsiveness and 'feel', which made the aircraft part of you once you were airborne. You strapped on, rather than got into, a Spitfire; your hand on the stick produced instant control reaction, and it would obey as accurately and almost as quickly as one's right arm obeys the commands from the brain. I have known a few other aircraft with this particular and highly personal characteristic: the Vampire and the Hunter, followed by the F-104A Starfighter which, despite its outstanding performance in terms of speed, retained that same unique quality as a perfect fighter pilot's aeroplane. However, for me the Spitfire was the first and so the one best loved.

51

STRONGER, SAFER, SWIFTER

By Eric Newton

After a five-year apprenticeship in mechanical engineering, and a brief spell in the Royal Air Force, I joined the Aeronautical Inspection Directorate of the Air Ministry in 1938. Gradually I became more and more involved with the investigation of aircraft accidents and in 1942 I was appointed an inspector of accidents; I have been involved with this aspect of aviation ever since.

During the early war years the business of accident investigation was largely unexplored ground and we in the Accidents Investigation Branch (which at that time came under the Air Ministry) learned many of its essentials from the Spitfire and her generation of aircraft. Of course, if there was an accident and the cause was fairly clear, obvious pilot error or a simple component defect or something like that, then we were not called in; but if an aircraft suffered a structural failure in the air or inexplicably caught fire on the ground, then the RAF would soon get on to us to try to find out why.

Out of a total of 121 serious or major accidents to Spitfires reported to us between the beginning of 1941 and the end of the war, sixty-eight involved structural failure in the air. Initially the most common reason for such failures, with twenty-three instances in 1941 and 1942, was aileron instability. The symptoms were not at all clear-cut: the aircraft were usually diving at high speed when they simply fell to pieces. Only after one of the pilots had survived this traumatic experience and parachuted successfully were we able to find out the cause. During his dive he saw both of his ailerons suddenly flip up, producing an extremely violent pitch-up which caused the wing to fail and the aircraft to break up. In collaboration with the Royal Aircraft Establishment at Farnborough we did a lot of tests and found that this aileron up-float was made possible by stretch in the control cables; in those days control tensioning was a hit-or-miss business, with no compensation for temperature. On our recommendation

the RAF introduced the tensometer, which ensured accurate tensioning of the controls; this, and the almost simultaneous introduction of the new metal ailerons, cured almost all the cases of aileron instability in the Spitfire.

The next most serious cause of structural failure in the Spitfire was pilots overstressing the airframe. She was extremely responsive on the controls and one must

Eric Newton of the Accidents Investigation Branch.

Spitfire Mark II after the wing failed due to excess of positive 'G'.

remember that in those days there was no accelerometer to tell the pilot how close he was to the limit. So it was not difficult to exceed the aircraft's 10G ultimate stress factor during combat or when pulling out of a high speed-dive; during the war we were able to put down forty-six major accidents to this cause, though undoubtedly there were many other occasions when it happened and we did not see the wreckage. Incidentally, if there was a structural failure in the Spitfire it was almost inevitably the wing that went; the fuselage was far less likely to fail first. I once asked a very senior RAF officer why the accelerometer, technically a simple instrument, was not introduced during the war. He replied that he was sure it would have had an adverse effect on the fighting spirit of the pilots. Whether that would have been so, I cannot say. But I do know that when they finally did introduce the accelerometer into service, in the

Hunter in 1954, and began educating the pilots on structural limitations and the dangers of overstressing, accidents to this cause virtually ceased.

By the way, I cannot remember a single case of metal fatigue failure in a Spitfire; but that was probably because in wartime they hardly ever survived long enough to fly the necessary number of hours for this to develop.

After structural failure, the next largest category of accidents proved, on investigation, to have followed loss of control by the pilot (thirty-six cases). Of these, twenty occurred in cloud and could be put down to pilot error; one must remember that early in the war, in the rush to turn out more pilots, instrument flying training was not up to the peacetime standards. A further thirteen accidents were shown to have been caused by oxygen starvation; on the early Spitfires it was easy to mishandle the oxygen system and

180

if this happened and the aircraft was flying at high altitude the pilot passed out. As a result of our investigations and recommendations, the oxygen system on the Spitfire was modified to make it easier to operate. The remaining three accidents in the loss-of-control category were initiated by the pilot pulling excessive 'G' and blacking himself out.

Engine failures and fires contributed a further seventeen accidents, and the remainder could be put down under the 'miscellaneous' heading. An example of the latter was the case at Hethel just after the war when, as the pilot was starting up an unarmed Spitfire XVL, it exploded and burst into flames. The singed and shaken pilot managed to clamber out, and stood helplessly by as the machine burnt itself out. Everyone was baffled by the incident, so we were called in to investigate. The first thing we noted was that the leading edge of the wing on the starboard side – there was no fuel tank in that position

Spitfire XVI which exploded on the ground at RAF Hethel due to an accumulation of fuel vapour in the starboard wing.

on the Mark XVI – was peeled right back. This was obviously the seat of the explosion and we were able to trace the smoke pattern, like a line of soot, from there to the engine exhaust stubs. Then the cause became clear: the fuel filler cap was just in front of the cockpit, and as a result of careless refuelling petrol had sloshed down the fuselage and on to the wing. Some of it was trapped in the leading edge. When the pilot climbed into the cockpit the explosive fuel-air mixture was waiting and when the engine fired – bang! Looking round, we found several other Spitfires with petrol lodged in the wing leading edge and this same accident just waiting to happen.

There were one or two accidents, and some very near misses, caused by the lightweight plastic seats fitted to some batches of Spitfires. The trouble was that they were not strong enough. If there was a heavy pilot who pulled a bit of 'G' they tended to collapse – on to the elevator control runs which ran underneath. We soon had that type of seat replaced.

As I have mentioned, we investigated a total of 121 Spitfire accidents during the war, and a further nine after it. The causes did not always fit simply into the neat categories mentioned above. For example, a pilot might lose control in a cloud and his aircraft then broke up in the ensuing dive due to aileron instability; in that case the accident would have been listed under two categories.

In the nature of my work I tend to concentrate on an aircraft's failings and ignore it if it is safe, but how safe was the Spitfire? I think the figures speak for themselves: a total of more than 22,000 of these aircraft were built, and we were called in on only 130 occasions – and in not all of these was the Spitfire found to be at fault. If one considers that she was not a simple trainer built for ease of handling, but a first-rate fighting machine the equal of any in the world during most of her service career, there can be no doubting that the Spitfire was a remarkably safe aircraft.

▲ ▲ ▲

In spite of the success of Eric Newton and others like him, in making the Spitfire a safe aircraft to fly, it remains a sad fact that the great majority of Spitfire crashes were not due to enemy action but to simple accidents which did not warrant deep investigation. All too often a hastily trained pilot's poor

airmanship placed him in a position from which he lacked the skill – or the luck – to extricate himself.

Typical of such accidents, and amusing rather than tragic since the only injuries were to the pilots' pride, is this one from the files of the Royal Canadian Navy. It illustrates clearly the dangers of pressing on in the face of deteriorating weather conditions, and it shows how imprecise communications can so easily lead to embarrassment.

A pair of Seafires were flying along the eastern coast of Canada when the weather began to deteriorate and soon the cloud base was down to 300ft in places. The estimated time of arrival for their planned refuelling stop at Presque Isle came and went, but they were unable to establish radio contact with the tower there. Nevertheless, the intrepid pair continued on, well beyond their ETA (and well beyond the extent of their maps!). At last they came to a town which they were able to identify, from the sign-board at the railway station, as Campbellton, New Brunswick – 110 miles beyond Presque Isle. With fuel running short they flew south along the coast of New Brunswick looking for a landing field and eventually found a group of hangars near Bathurst. A low-level reconnaissance revealed a runway covered with packed ice and snow and the only landing aid, a wind sock, wrapped firmly around its mast.

After they had inspected the runway, the No. 2 called, 'Will you have first go? Or will I?' The leader replied that he would 'have first crack at it'. The No. 2, however, understood this as 'have a crack at it'. The upshot was that both did, at the same time – from opposite directions! The No. 2 later described what followed:

I flew a normal approach from 400ft at 80kts over the end of the runway. I touched down on the very edge and when I felt I had the aircraft under control, I called the leader and said, 'I think I've made it' – but as I said it, we collided ... The left wings of both our aircraft were sheared off and we were spun around through 180 degrees.

The leader's account was similar:

I touched down in the middle of the runway and was rolling to a stop when I heard the No. 2 say 'I think I've got it made'. Then we collided...

52

TIME TO MOVE ON: SPITFIRE VERSUS VAMPIRE

As we observed in Chapter 37, for a piston-engined aircraft the Spitfire XIV was certainly no slouch. Yet when it was pitted in mock combat against the Vampire, this first generation jet fighter found there was no contest. To understand why, we need to go 'back to basics'.

During the late 1930s, aircraft designers came to realise that the laws of physics would impose a finite limit to the maximum speed that a propeller-driven plane could attain, and that lay somewhere around 500mph. The problem centred on the propeller's weakness as a means of converting the piston engine's rotational power into thrust. As a plane's speed neared 500mph, propeller efficiency fell sharply.

A few figures will serve to illustrate the point. In round terms, the Spitfire I attained a maximum speed of about

Left and overleaf:
The Vampire, with its relatively high power-to-weight ratio and its relatively low wing loading, established for itself as one of the most agile fighters in the world.

300mph at sea level with an engine developing about 1,000hp. At that speed, propeller efficiency was about 80 per cent, and the 1,000lb of thrust it produced equalled the drag from the fighter's airframe.

Now consider the engine power needed to propel the Spitfire I at twice that speed, 600mph. Drag rises with the square of the speed, thus if the speed doubled the drag is quadrupled. So 1,000lb of drag at 300mph becomes 4,000lb of drag at 600mph. To overcome that amount of drag, the aircraft needed 4,000lb of thrust, but at 600mph the efficiencyof the propeller fell to just over 50 per cent, so to drive the aircraft at that speed a piston engine would need to develop about 12,000hp. In 1945 the best piston engines produced a fraction over 1hp per 1lb of weight. Thus a piston engine developing the power to propel our notional fighter at 600mph would weigh about 11,000lb – nearly double the weight of a Spitfire I.

For high-speed flight the turbojet was a fundamentally more efficient type of power unit. It produced its output directly in the form of thrust, with no conversion losses from a propeller. The Goblin turbojet fitted to the de Havilland Vampire F1 developed 3,100lb of thrust for a weight of about 1,550lb, and gave the fighter a level speed of 540mph at 17,500ft. No piston engine and propeller combination offered a thrust-to-weight ratio to compare with that, and it was clear that for use in high-performance aircraft their days were numbered.

The Mark XIV was one of the fastest variants of the Spitfire, and at the end of the Second World War it was acknowledged to be among the most effective air superiority fighters in service anywhere. Yet in almost every significant aspect of air combat it was outclassed by the de Havilland Vampire. The comparative trial took place at the Central Fighter Establishment at West Raynham in the summer of 1946. The report on that trial, excerpts from which are reproduced below, illustrates the clear margin of superiority achieved by the first generation of jet fighters.

In making a comparison between the Vampire and Spitfire XIV, the properties of their engines must be realised. The piston engine maintains power throughout the speed range, while the jet engine produces maximum power only at the fighter's maximum speed. Thus the Spitfire had an inherent advantage over a jet aircraft when operating at the lower end of its speed range. The Spitfire XIV used in the trial was a fully operational aircraft fitted with a Griffon 65, giving 2,105hp at 7,500ft.

MAXIMUM LEVEL SPEEDS

The Vampire is greatly superior in speed to the Spitfire XIV at all heights, as shown below:

Altitude (ft)	Approx. speed advantage (mph) over Spitfire XIV
0	130
5,000	110
10,000	100
15,000	100
20,000	95
25,000	75
30,000	70
35,000	70
40,000	90

ACCELERATION AND DECELERATION

With both aircraft in line-abreast formation at a speed of 200mph (indicated), on the word 'Go' both engines were opened up to maximum power simultaneously. The Spitfire initially drew ahead, but after a period of approximately twenty-five seconds the Vampire gradually caught up and quickly accelerated past the Spitfire.

The rate of deceleration of the Spitfire is faster than the Vampire even when the Vampire uses its dive brakes. Once again this shows that the Vampire's dive brakes are not as effective as they should be.

DIVE

The two aircraft were put into a dive in line-abreast formation with set throttles at a speed of 250 mph (indicated). The Vampire rapidly drew ahead and kept gaining on the Spitfire.

ZOOM CLIMB

The Vampire and Spitfire XIV in line-abreast formation were put into a 45-degree dive. When a speed of 400mph (indicated) had been reached, a zoom climb at fixed throttle settings was carried out at approximately 50 degrees. The Vampire showed itself vastly superior and reached a height 1,000ft in excess of the altitude of the Spitfire in a few seconds and quickly increased its lead as the zoom climb continued. The same procedure was carried out at full-throttle settings and the Vampire's advantage was outstandingly marked.

CLIMB

The Spitfire XIV climbs approximately 1,000ft per minute faster than the Vampire up to 20,000ft.

TURNING CIRCLES

The Vampire is superior to the Spitfire XIV at all heights. The two aircraft were flown in line-astern formation. The Spitfire was positioned on the Vampire's tail. Both aircraft tightened up to the maximum turning circle with maximum power. It became apparent that the Vampire was just able to keep inside the Spitfire's turning circles. After four or five turns the Vampire' was able to position itself on the Spitfire's tail so that a deflection shot was possible. The wing loading of the Vampire is 33.1lb per sq ft compared with the Spitfire XIV's 35.1lb per sq ft.

RATES OF ROLL

The Spitfire XIV has a faster rate of roll at all speeds. The higher the speed the faster the Spitfire rolls in comparison with the Vampire. As previously mentioned at speeds of 500mph (indicated) there is a feeling of overbalance and aileron snatch when attempting to roll the Vampire.

COMBAT MANOEUVRABILITY

The Vampire will out-manoeuvre the Spitfire type of aircraft at all heights, except for initial acceleration at low speeds and in rolling. Due to the Vampire's much higher speed (i.e. 105mph faster at 20,000ft) and superior zoom climb, the Spitfire can gain no advantage by using its superior rate of climb in combat.

53

THE FINAL ACT

By John Nicholls

Eight years after the end of the Second World War, one of the few surviving airworthy Spitfires was flown in a battle trial against a Mach 2 Lightning Fighter. In this section we learn how this came about, and why.

In 1963 I was the wing commander in charge of the Air Fighting Development Squadron (the successor to the earlier Air Fighting Development Unit), which was part of the Central Fighter Establishment (CFE) at Binbrook. Earlier the CFE had taken on charge a Spitfire XIX originally intended for mounting on the station front gate; instead, she had been maintained in a flyable condition.

This was at the time of the Indonesian confrontation and, since the Indonesian Air Force operated a large number of P-51 Mustang fighters, we were interested in discovering how best a Lightning might engage such an aircraft. In the RAF we did not have any Mustangs, but at Binbrook we did have our Spitfire with a performance which was, in many respects, similar. Thus it came about that our Spitfire came to be involved in a short battle trial pitted against a fighter which was her successor by three generations.

Of course, from the start we knew that the Lightning could overtake the Spitfire by nearly 1,000mph – there was no need to run a trial to prove that. But we did find that the piston-engined fighter presented a very poor target to infrared homing missiles, especially from the rear aspect. And, since the Lightning would therefore very likely have to follow up its missile pass with a gun attack, a high overtaking speed would have made accurate firing very difficult. On the other hand, if the Lightning pilot slowed down too much he could end up playing the slower and more manoeuvrable fighter's dogfighting game – and lose. None of this was new; we had learned the same lessons during trials flown between the Lightning and the Hunter. Another problem was that if the Spitfire pilot had sufficient warning of the attack he could spin round to meet it head-on – and thus present the most difficult target of all.

In the end we evolved a type of attack which was the antithesis of all I had learned from my own operational experience of fighter-versus-fighter combat in Korea: instead of trying to get above the enemy and diving on him to attack, we found it best to use the Lightning's very high power-to-weight ratio to make a climbing attack from behind and below. From that angle the field of view from the Spitfire was poor, there was a good chance of achieving surprise and the infra-red source gave the best chance for missile acquisition. If the Lightning pilot did not acquire the target or bring his guns to bear on his first pass he could continue his steep climb – which the Spitfire could not possibly follow – and when out of range he could dive and repeat the process. Using such tactics, we felt that in the end a competent Lightning pilot could almost always get the better of an equally competent Spitfire (or Mustang) pilot.

Almost certainly that trial at Binbrook was the final operational act carried out in earnest in the Spitfire's long career.

An English Electric
Lightning fighter, an
aircraft more modern by a
couple of generations, was
tested against a Spitfire.

54

SPITFIRE SWANSONG

By M. Maffre

Now there are but few of them left. Only a few of those myriad Spitfires which once speckled the British sky from the Orkneys to the Isle of Wight, that droned singly or in sections, squadrons or wings across the Channel, that swept at treetop level or 30,000ft from the Pas de Calais to the southern reaches of the Elbe, that swallowed sand and harried the Afrika Korps from El Alamein to Tunisia, that duelled out of lonely Malta and chased the enemy from Sicily to the Gothic Line, that patrolled the aching sunlight in the Bay of Bengal, that teetered like tipsy seamen on flimsy undercarriages aboard aircraft carriers.

A babble of tongues chattered in them. Canucks and Yanks and Britons nattered over their radios; expatriate Frenchmen, Norwegians and Poles whooped into their microphones at the sign of black-crossed fighters. Aussies and South Africans drawled at each other at vast altitudes.

Grievous things were done to the Spitfire in the name of progress. Her wings were clipped and her supercharger blades cropped for better low-level work, and the outraged bird was dubbed the 'clipped and cropped Spitty'. They added blades to her propeller so that in the end she actually had two sets, one rotating against the other. Lumbering cannons poked out of wings designed to carry machine guns. They put a hook on her tail and called her a sea bird. Once, be it known, she slung beer kegs on her bomb racks and ferried cheer to the Normandy beach-head.

Today a vintage group of fighter pilots recall her peculiar whistling call as she arched across the sky. Nostalgia brings back the sound of her Merlin engine muttering in the misty half light of a hundred airfields, as crewmen warmed them up at dawn readiness. Some men who probably feel they live on borrowed time, still wonder how her stout iron heart achieved the mechanically impossible and brought them home alive. Those who did not know her may wonder how mortal man can cherish an undying affection for her gasoline-reeking camouflaged memory. And no one can tell them.

Appendix A

THE SPITFIRE FAMILY

From the time of its maiden flight, the Spitfire underwent a continual series of incremental improvements to improve its performance. By squeezing progressively more power out of the Merlin, and later the Griffon, series of engines, Rolls-Royce provided the impetus for many of these changes.

One rarely gets something for nothing in this life, however, and there was a downside to almost every step in the development process. With each increase in engine power there was an increase in engine weight and therefore an increase in fuel consumption. To restore the range of the aircraft, it required larger capacity (and therefore heavier) fuel tanks.

To convert that additional engine power into thrust, without increasing the diameter of the propeller, the Spitfire's propeller acquired additional blades. It progressed from a two-bladed propeller on the early production aircraft, to a three-blade, to a four-blade, and finally to a five-bladed propeller. The greater the number of blades on a propeller, the greater its weight and also the greater the twisting force it exerted on the airframe. To balance out these forces, there needed to be increases in the area of the tail surfaces. On production Spitfire Marks 22 and 24 the tail surfaces underwent a complete redesign, and became much larger.

The lessons acquired in air combat imposed other increases in weight, as various new items of equipment were added. The RAF demanded armour protection for the pilot and vulnerable parts of the structure. Also, as the war progressed, the Spitfire needed to carry a more powerful (and therefore heavier) armament.

In straight and level flight an aircraft could cope relatively easily with progressive increases in weight. But air-to-air combat was another matter. When the pilot needed to throw his fighter around, and pull 6G in a tight turn, every part of the structure weighed six times as much. If it had not been stressed to withstand the additional forces, the airframe might simply collapse. To cope with each major increase in weight, therefore, the internal structure had to be strengthened to restore the safe load factors, and, as night follows day, each bout of strengthening brought with it a further increase in weight.

In the history of aviation, no other aircraft design was so continuously, so aggressively, so thoroughly and so successfully developed as the Spitfire. The various changes produced a huge increase in its fighting ability. As a result the Spitfire retained its place at the forefront of fighter design from the biplane era, until the early years of the jet age.

In the course of that development the Spitfire's engine power almost doubled, from the 1,030hp of the Merlin II engine fitted to the Spitfire I, to the 2,035hp of the Griffon 61 engine fitted to Spitfire 21. Maximum speed increased by just over a quarter, from the 362mph of the Mark I to the 457mph attained by the Mark 21. The maximum rate of climb more than doubled, from the 2,195ft per minute of the Mark I to 4,900ft per minute of the Mark 21. Fire power was increased by a factor of five. A three-second burst from the eight rifle-calibre machine guns of the Mark I loosed off rounds weighing 8lb. A similar burst from the Spitfire 21's four 20mm cannon loosed off rounds weighing 40lb. At the same time, the normal maximum take-off weight rose by more than two-thirds, from 5,280lb for the Mark I to 9,124lb for the Mark 21.

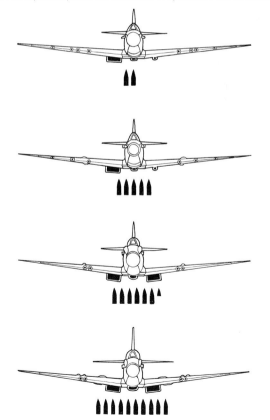

During the course of her development life there was a five-fold increase in the fire power of the Spitfire, as her armament progressed from the initial eight rifle-calibre machine guns to the ultimate four rapid-firing cannon. The diagrams show the approximate weight of bullets and/or shells which could be loosed off during a three-second burst (in action it was rare for a pilot to be able to hold his aim for longer). Figures are approximate because the rate of fire of weapons of the same type coud vary by as much as 10 per cent. Each 'shell' represents 4lb fired.
1) Mark I (1937): eight .303in machine guns; 3-second burst, 8lb.
2) Mark VB (1941): two 20mm cannon and four .303in machine guns; 3-second burst, 20lb.
3) Mark XVIII (1945): two 20mm cannon and two .5in machine guns; 3-second burst, 26lb.
4) Mark 24 (1946): four 20mm cannon, 3-second burst, 40lb.

THE DEVELOPMENT OF THE SPITFIRE

Mark I: First production fighter version, powered by the Rolls-Royce Merlin III engine. Made its maiden flight in May 1938 and entered service in September.

Mark PR I: These were reconnaissance aircraft designated from 1A to 1G, depending on the configuration of the cameras and the additional internal fuel tankage. Designated as follows:

PR IA: Modified Mark I fighter, with the armament removed and a 5in focal length camera mounted vertically in each wing. Two aircraft delivered and began operations in November 1939.

PR IB: As PR IA, but with additional fuel tank for 29gal fitted behind cockpit.

PR IC: As PR 1B, but with 30gal blister tank under the port wing and two vertically mounted cameras in a blister under the starboard wing.

PR ID: Much modified Mark I, with 61gal integral tank in the leading edge of each wing and a 29gal tank in the rear fuselage. Two vertically mounted cameras behind the cockpit. It became the most numerous Spitfire PR variant in the early war years, and was later redesignated as the Spitfire PR Mark IV.

PR IE: Unarmed variant optimised for low-altitude oblique photography, with a bulge under each wing to accommodate a camera pointing outwards and a small angle downwards. Only one aircraft, N3117, was modified in this way.

PR IF: Unarmed variant with a 30gal tank under each wing. One 29gal fuel tank and two vertically mounted cameras in the fuselage.

PR IG: Armed variant, optimised for low-level oblique photography. It retained the eight .303in guns for self defence. One 29gal fuel tank, and one oblique and two vertical cameras behind the cockpit.

Mark II: Fighter variant similar to the Mark I, but it was fitted with the slightly Merlin XII engine. Entered service in September 1940.

Mark V: Fighter version developed from the Mark I, but fitted with the Merlin 45 series engine. This version entered service in February 1941 and it was built in very large numbers. During the mid-war period it was the first variant fitted with bomb racks, to allow it to operate in the fighter-bomber role.

Mark VI: High-altitude interceptor developed from the Mark V, but fitted with a pressurised cabin and longer-span wing. Power was from a Merlin 47 engine, which included an additional blower for cabin pressurisation. Built in small numbers, it entered service in April 1942.

Mark VII: High-altitude interceptor developed from the Mark VI, but powered by the Merlin 61 series engine fitted with a two-stage supercharger. Built in moderate numbers, the first squadron became operational in April 1943.

Mark VIII: General-purpose fighter developed from the Mark VII, but without the pressurised cabin of the latter. Entered service in the summer of 1943. Built in large numbers, all of which served outside the United Kingdom. This variant also saw widespread use in the fighter-bomber role.

Mark IX: General-purpose fighter version developed from the Mark V, but fitted with the Merlin 61 series engine. Entered service in June 1942. Intended as a stop-gap, pending large scale production of the Mark VIII. In the event, however, the Mark IX remained in production until the end of the war, and it was built in greater numbers than any other variant. It also operated in the fighter-bomber and fighter-reconnaissance roles. Late production aircraft fitted with cut-back rear fuselages and bubble canopies.

Mark X: Photographic reconnaissance variant with the enlarged internal fuel tankage of the PR 1D, but fitted with the Merlin 61-series engine and a pressurised cabin. Entering service in May 1944, it was built in small numbers.

Mark XI: Photographic reconnaissance variant similar to the Mark X but without the latter's pressurised cabin. Despite the later mark number, the Mark XI entered service in December 1942, some time ahead of the Mark X. The Mark XI became the most-used photographic reconnaissance variant during the mid-war period.

Mark XII: Fighter version developed from the Mark V, but fitted with the Griffon II engine with a single-stage supercharger. Built in moderate numbers as a low-altitude fighter, production aircraft had clipped wings. Entered service in February 1943.

Mark XIII: Fighter reconnaissance version carrying vertical and oblique cameras, and also carrying an armament of four .303in machine guns. Only a few were built, which entered service in 1943.

Mark XIV: Fighter version developed from the Mark VIII but fitted with the Griffon 61 series engine with two-stage supercharger. This variant entered service in February 1944. The final production aircraft featured a cut-back rear fuselage and bubble canopy. A fighter-reconnaissance version went into service in small numbers, fitted with vertical and oblique cameras in the rear fuselage.

Mark XVI: General-purpose fighter similar to the Mark IX, but powered by the Merlin 266 engine produced under licence in the USA by the Packard Company. The Mark XVI entered service in September 1944 and late production aircraft were fitted with a cut-back rear fuselage and a bubble canopy. Variant also operated in the fighter-bomber role.

Mark XVIII: Fighter-bomber version developed from the Mark XIV and powered by a Griffon 61 series engine and fitted with a bubble canopy. This variant featured a redesigned and strengthened wing and carried additional fuel tanks in the rear fuselage. It entered service in 1945, just too late to see action in Second World War. A fighter-reconnaissance version of the aircraft also appeared.

Mark XIX: The definitive photographic reconnaissance variant, it combined the Griffon 61 series engine and the pressurised cabin, with the wing leading edge tanks of the Mark XI. It entered service in the summer of 1944 and became the most-used reconnaissance variant during the final year of the war.

Mark 21: Note: by now the unwieldy Roman numbers for variants had given way to Arabic numbers. This fighter version had a redesigned and strengthened wing and fuselage, fitted with the Griffon 61 series engine. The Mark 21 entered service in April 1945 and saw some action before the war ended.

Mark 22: Fighter version similar to the Mark 21, but with a cut-back rear fuselage and bubble canopy. Production aircraft fitted with an enlarged tailplane, fin and rudder. Entered service in November 1947 and became the main post-war production variant. Remained in service with Royal Auxiliary Air Force squadrons until 1951.

Mark 24: Fighter version based on the Mark 22, but fitted with two additional fuel tanks in the rear fuselage and wing fittings to carry six 60lb rockets. Only one squadron operated this variant, which remained in frontline RAF service until January 1952.

Basic Specifications of the Main Production Fighter Variants of the Spitfire

Mark I
Span: 36ft 10in
Length: 29ft 11in
Max. T/o Wt: 5,819lb
Power: Merlin II/1,030hp
Max Speed: 362mph
Service Ceiling: 31,900ft
Gun Armament: 8 x .303in

This information relates to the first production Spitfire, K 9787, during its service trials in May 1938.

Mark V
36ft 10in
29ft 11in
6,525lb
Merlin 45/1,470hp
371mph
37,500ft
2 x 20mm, 4 x .303in

Information relates to an early production aircraft, W 3134, during its trials in May 1941.

Mark IX
36ft 10in
30ft 0in
7,400lb
Merlin 61/1,560hp
409mph
38,000ft
2 x 20mm, 4 x .303in

Information relates to the converted Mark V, AB 505, during its trials in April 1942.

Mark XII
36ft 10in
30ft 9in
7,415lb
Griffon IIB/1,700hp
397mph
32,800ft
2 x 20mm, 4 x .303in

Information relates to the Mark XII prototype, DP 845, during its trials in September 1942 when it had full-span wings. Production Mark XIIs had clipped wings.

Mark XIV
36ft 10in
32ft 8in
8,400lb
Griffon 61/2,035hp
446mph
44,000ft
2 x 20mm, 4 x .303in

Information relates to JF 319, a converted Mark VIII, during its trials in September 1943.

Mark 21
40ft 4in
32ft 8in
9,124lb
Griffon 61/2,035hp
457mph
43,000ft
4 x 20mm

Information relates to the prototype Mark 21, PP 139, during trials in 1943 when it was fitted with extended-span wings. Production Mark 21s had rounded wing tips, span 36ft 11in.

Visit our website and discover thousands of other History Press books.
www.thehistorypress.co.uk

The History Press